Money CLIPS

365 tips that will pay one day at a time

Spurge ink!
Making Business Accessible

Encino, Californ

➤ Make Money ➤ Save Money ➤ Invest Money

Money CLIPS

Lorraine Spurge

Spurge Ink!
16350 Ventura Boulevard, Suite 362
Encino, California 91436
Tel: 800-854-6239 or 818-705-3740
Fax: 818-708-8764 or 818-705-0692

Library of Congress Card Catalog No: 98–061064

First printing August 1998
Printed in the United States of America.
Published simultaneously in Canada.

ISBN 1-888232-44-7 (softcover)

Text Illustrations
Retro Photographs: PhotoDisc, Inc. Volume 11 ©1994, Volume 37 ©1996, Volume 47 ©1997
Spot Art: Art Parts: Half the Parts ©1992, 1993, 1994; Art Parts: The Other Half ©1994, 1995; Adobe Systems Inc./Everyday Woman ©1997.
Newspaper Excerpts: Reprinted by permission of the *Wall Street Journal.* ©1998 Dow Jones & Company, Inc. All rights reserved worldwide; Reprinted by permission of the *New York Times.* ©1998 The New York Times.

Spurge Ink! books are available wherever books are sold.
Distributed in the United States and Canada by National Book Network.

For retail sales in U.S. and Canada contact National Book Network at 301-459-3366 or www.nbnbooks.com.

For export sales and foreign language translations contact Business Books Network at 603-749-6155 or bizbooks@aol.com.

For information about special discounts for bulk purchases by corporations, institutions, and other organizations, subsidiary rights, premiums, scholastic and classroom use, related seminars, author appearances and interviews, contact Spurge Ink!, at 818-705-3740 or info@spurgeink.com.

To my children, Nicole & Renee,

who have made my life worthwhile…

Credits

Managing Editor & Creative Director
Debra Valencia

Research Consultant
Pamela Nelson, CFA

Copy Editors
Mari Florence/Backbone Books
Janis Hunt Johnson

Research Assistants
Tamera Rogers
Kristen Sekora
Elizabeth Zelnick

Proofreading
Ask Janis Editorial & Rewrite Services

Indexer
Linda Purrington

Photo Captions
Susan Sabel Advertising

Graphic Production Support
Vannika Bell
Brad Frost
Mark Heliger
Sean P. Riley

Legal Counsel
Homer, Kirsch & Mitchell

Important Caution to Our Readers

Please keep the following important cautions in mind when reading and using this book.

Because of differences in the laws of various states and countries, the constant changes in tax law, the unique circumstances that may apply to the individual reader, as well as other factors, the publisher and author cannot guarantee that the information and advice discussed in this book are appropriate and accurate for every reader. For that reason, readers are strongly cautioned to consult an accountant, attorney or other professional advisor before making financial decisions, and this book is not intended to replace such professional advice.

Accordingly, this book and its contents are sold without warranties or guarantees of any kind, express or implied, and the publisher and the author disclaim any liability, loss or damage caused by the contents of this book or its use by readers.

About Lorraine Spurge

As the Brooklyn-born single mother of two small daughters, Lorraine Spurge began her career as a secretary and broke through the glass ceiling to reach the highest ranks of the investment banking world. There she raised more money for American businesses than any other woman on Wall Street—more than $200 billion in growth-producing capital, for companies such as MCI Communications, Time-Warner, Turner Broadcasting, Revlon, Hasbro, Mattel, Chrysler and United Airlines to name a few.

In 1989, Lorraine took that same dynamic spirit and created her own business, Spurge Ink! a business communications company. Her concept is simple: The More You Know, The More You're Worth.

Because Lorraine was trained on-the-job, she is capable of making complicated business issues sound simple. In her Los Angeles appearances as CBS 2 News' money expert, she "projects an image over the air that is warm and relaxed. She takes a subject that could be cold and off-putting and makes it entertaining and personal," says Tony Henkins, floor director for CBS 2 News. On her East Coast radio talk show, "Working with Lorraine"—which reaches 3 million listeners—Lorraine and her guests frankly answer callers' questions on all the issues facing working women today.

In 1997 alone, Lorraine has been featured on more than 100 TV and radio stations across the country, including national spots on MSNBC, CNBC, CNN's "Business Unusual," "It's Only Money" and Fox News' "O'Reilly Report." "One of Lorraine's best features is that she can provide smart, understandable, up-to-the-minute commentary on any breaking business news event, from an industry-wide layoff to a stock market crisis. We'd love to have her back on a regular basis," said Don Johnson of KTVI Fox 2 in St. Louis, Missouri.

As an author, Lorraine is the editor of the award-winning *Knowledge Exchange Business Encyclopedia* and *MCI: Failure Is Not an Option*, a compelling story of how MCI single-handedly overthrew and revolutionized the communications industry. She writes "Ask Lorraine," a bi-weekly column for the *Los Angeles Business Journal* answering everyday questions that entrepreneurs have about successfully managing their businesses.

As a public speaker, Lorraine was invited recently to more than 25 U.S. cities, including appearances at The Houston Forum, the National Association of Corporate Treasurers, Town Hall Los Angeles, the Women's Global Business Alliance and the California Governor's Conference on Women. She is also a guest lecturer at business training programs including the University of Southern California's Entrepreneur Program and The Learning Annex. Lorraine serves on the Boards of George Washington University and CaP CURE, the Association for the Cure of Cancer of the Prostate.

Table of Contents

Introduction

Introduction: One Day at a Time

There is nothing quite so intimidating as organizing your finances. I know countless successful, accomplished people who shrink at the mere mention of money management. And it's no wonder! The financial experts—whether it's the talking heads on TV, or the portfolio managers who manage your mutual fund—seem to go out of their way to make the world of finance completely inaccessible. Talk of "triple witching hours," "Ginnie Mae's" and "annuity streams" could scare off the bravest soul.

Don't be intimidated! Once these foreign phrases are deciphered, you'll be amazed at how easily you'll grasp these concepts. With just a small amount of time and concentration, concepts like investing, family budgeting, and tax planning can make sense to the most financially challenged of individuals.

Many people I know say they simply don't have the

time—that they'd rather hire someone to handle their finances. I think this is akin to hiring a nanny to raise your kids. Because how you handle your money is an incredibly personal part of your life—only *you* know what your goals are for you and your family. Only *you* know what kind of life you'd like to lead when you're older, and where you want your kids to go to college. That means that *you* should be in charge of the big decisions in your financial planning.

That doesn't mean that you have to get bogged down in the details. It's fine to hire an accountant to set up your tax-free retirement plan, but *you* have to make the decision to have one in the first place. Similarly, you can let someone else choose your individual stocks for you (through a mutual fund) but you're the only one who really understands what kind of return you want, and what kind of risk you're willing to take. You should make the decision to be in stocks (versus, say, bonds) in the first place.

Estate taxes?—sure it seems complicated at first glance. But once you understand a few simple basics, you'll be able to tackle this subject, and probably save your family plenty of money and trouble in the long run. Same goes for pension plans, long-term disability insurance, and even tax planning. These are all areas that you should at least understand on a fundamental level to be a responsible adult.

"But where do I start ?" I can hear you say. "There seems to be so much to absorb and so little time." First of all, don't become overwhelmed by the idea that you have to understand every detail. In Section 5, for example, I point out that if you understand the difference between stocks and bonds, you'll be way ahead of most people I know. And you'll have a good idea how to make a reasonable decision about your long-term investments.

Secondly, trust your instincts. You'll be surprised at how much of this "expert advice" is really based on common sense. Well *of course* you should pay down your credit card debt first if it has the highest interest rate. You didn't need me to tell you that—right? But because many people simply don't take the time to focus on such simple points, they make mistakes that seem silly in hindsight.

These are all valuable lessons, and believe me—I learned many of them the hard way. In fact, I realized while working on *Money Clips* that this is the book I wish I'd had twenty years ago. If someone would have given me these tips, I could have avoided plenty of angst, and saved even more money and time. I hope *Money Clips* will save you the trouble.

Section 1

Making Money

If you don't have enough money to begin with, you certainly can't save or invest. So it only makes sense that this book begins with how to get where you want to be. Maybe you're in a job you really don't like, but it pays the bills. Or you've made a career change and have had to take a cut in salary. Perhaps you're thinking of leaving the workforce and starting your own business from home. If one of these sounds like your dilemma, it's time to reevaluate your life's work—or at least the way in which you're pursuing it.

A good first step is to honestly assess your work situation and determine what kind of a financial foundation you are building for your future. How can can you turn what you love into a paying occupation? Where do your skills lie? Why is your industry performing well this year when it almost bottomed out the year before?

While you can—and should—do your research on the market, your successful career lies in thorough self-evaluation. You'll face some pretty tough questions that only you can answer, but the payoff is truly great: living the life you love, with money to save!

Choosing the Career of Your Dreams

1 **Do you want a job or a career?**

If you need to clock in from 9 to 5, if your mantra is TGIF, if you give just enough of yourself to get by while expecting to get the most—then you're looking for a *job*. A *career* is a life-long experience. It's giving as well as getting. Having a career is about getting excited about going to work in the morning and not looking at your watch to check if your day is over. It's about wanting to share your day's events with friends and family long after your work day is done. *Simply put, you should love what you do for a living.*

Loving what you do not only improves the quality of your life and enhances your own well-being, but also the lives of those around you. It's an extremely rewarding process. Many people base their career ambitions on what they think is monetarily rewarding and overlook the obvious: what will drive them to get up and go to work, excited, every day.

JUST THE FACTS

The New Career Landscape

- The face of the American workplace has changed dramatically in the last decade. The days of working for one employer for your entire career are over for the majority of the workforce. In fact, 1 out of every 3 Americans will likely change careers in the next three years.
- Downsizing and reengineering are here to stay. Today, layoffs don't happen just during slow periods, they are a constant part of corporate life as old jobs are eliminated and different ones created.
- Business can no longer be your second language. No matter where you are in your career—just starting out, at your peak, or starting over—you must understand business terms and concepts, and use them.
- Success comes from being passionate about your work. Choose a job that you love to do, not one that you merely have to do.

2 Start by appraising yourself.

A career choice should be made with careful consideration. So before selecting a potential career, ask yourself some critical questions:

- What skills do I have? Does my desired career choice require any of these skills?
- What am I really, uniquely good at? What makes me stand out from the next job candidate?
- What job activity makes me happiest?
- What job activity makes me both happy and proud—because I do an outstanding job?
- What gets me turned on about a job? Does my current job exhaust or energize me?
- How can I transfer my hobbies, interests, or unrelated skills into a career?
- Without thinking about money, what would I most like to spend my time doing?
- What contribution do I want to make to my community?

If you are determined to do what you love, and to share your gifts with others through your work, the money will come as a natural result.

Wake up to a fabulous dream job.

Did You Know?

Ever Heard of the Herd Theory?

Ninety percent of American workers are employed in only 300 job fields, and 50 percent of those are employed in only about 50 job fields. Knowing this gives you a tremendous opportunity. Dare to be different. Follow the road less traveled, as poet Robert Frost suggested, and you're likely to find a rewarding career that will challenge you as well as compensate you for your efforts!

Worksheet: Assessing Yourself

Use this simple worksheet to take stock of your abilities and favorite pastimes. Don't limit yourself to "job-related" answers.

Learned Skills (i.e., computer programs, degrees)

Personal Skills (i.e., "good with people," or "natural organizer")

What has been your favorite part of past or current jobs?

What particular task or job has given you the greatest satisfaction? (i.e., a summer camp you organized, or a database you built)

What are your hobbies and interests? (Imagine the way you'd most like to spend your day.)

What are your community interests? (i.e., helping the school, or raising money for the local homeless shelter)

Now carefully consider your own answers—especially the ones that seem to make you happy. If the happiest, most productive experience you've had is organizing a theater troupe, but you make a living as a bookeeper, you might ask yourself why. Are there ways to turn what you love into your dream job?

3 A good attitude will take you anywhere.

Your attitude is so important—not just for getting a good job, but for your mental health and overall well-being. Face it, the workplace is full of stresses. Learn to view them as obstacles to be hurdled, not walls you've come up against. When frustrated, try this imagery technique: just close your eyes and say to yourself, "I'm going to switch to a different attitude about this thing (or person) that's bothering me," and view yourself successfully managing the situation. Sometimes that's all it takes to begin to relieve some of the pressure and stress. Try it and see how your attitude changes.

Tip

Dare to be different. Consider the economics of supply and demand. Try to identify a career path that might be out of the mainstream.

You have more skills than you think. Make a list!

Personal Perspective

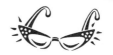

"When I graduated from high school in Brooklyn in 1969, my lifelong goal was to be a secretary. I loved answering phones, typing letters, photocopying, and organizing files. Most of all I loved being needed and helping others. I couldn't have articulated this ambition at age 18, but it eventually manifested itself to me in many different ways. I enjoyed working so much I would get to the office two hours early. And if I was sick and we needed to get a project done, I was there anyway. I can remember once coming in with a 102° fever because we had a big presentation to make. My boss ran around getting me tea, bringing me a heater to warm me up—he couldn't thank me enough—the best thanks came at Christmas when I got a big bonus and raise. But it's funny, looking back now, I wasn't even thinking about the money. I just wanted to do the best job I could possibly do.

"I take that work ethic with me in everything I do. Today I am CEO of my own business. But if we're up against a deadline you won't find me sitting behind an executive desk. I'm there, assembling marketing packages, photocopying, and collating—whatever it takes to get the job done."

4 **Go on a fact-finding adventure.**

Research skills will not only help you manage your career, the skills you'll develop will help you manage your money, and ultimately, your life. Find out about careers and opportunities and how they might suit your skills and background. Even if you're unemployed and looking for a job, or still in school, it will give you a chance to call prospective employers and interview them for your own research purposes, while you don't have the anxiety about getting a particular job. Remember, you're on an adventure.

When you're looking for a long-term career, this strategy will open doors or paths that you never dreamed of, and may not even have considered.

5 **Network your way to success.**

Every meeting, phone call, or acquaintance has the potential to bring you closer to your dream career. This is a building process—a foundation of information that you will inventory for current and future use. It will help you build a database of contacts that can become your network to success.

6 **Conduct information interviews.**

They could be with people you think you'd like to work for or with people who are doing what you'd like to be doing. This gives you a tremendous opportunity to talk with other professionals at a particular company or in a specific industry. Don't even bother with Human Resources departments. Go straight to the person who has the job that interests you. People love to talk about themselves—and you can often find out more about the company and industry than you could ever learn through its promotional materials.

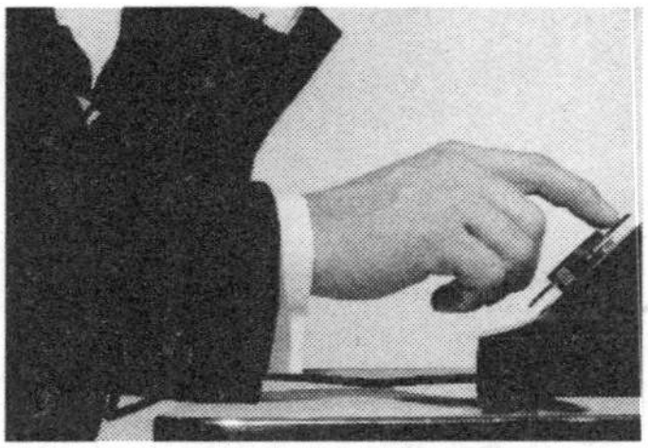

Network! Network! Network!
Follow up! Follow up! Follow up!

Worksheet: Networking to Success

Networking is unstructured by definition, but that doesn't mean you can't impose some discipline on the process to make sure you're doing everything you can. Try writing down—every day—people you've contacted and spoken with about a possible job. You'll be amazed at how many leads can come from a bit of determined legwork (and phonework).

Friends

Name ____________________ Talked about ____________________

Leads ____________________

Family

Name ____________________ Talked about ____________________

Leads ____________________

Current Coworkers

Name ____________________ Talked about ____________________

Leads ____________________

Name ____________________ Talked about ____________________

Leads ____________________

Past Coworkers

Name ____________________ Talked about ____________________

Leads ____________________

Name ____________________ Talked about ____________________

Leads ____________________

Questions to ask when networking:

- Why did you pick this job in this particular industry?
- What do you like most about your line of work?
- What do you dislike most about it?
- What is your vision for the future of this industry?
- Besides your company, who are your competitors?
- Whom would you recommend I speak with for additional information?

Trap Don't forget to follow up, follow up, follow up. One of the mistakes many people make is neglecting to follow up with a phone call, card, or letter. Many people give up after one attempt at contact. Don't. Be persistent. Always follow up a telephone or face-to-face interview with a thank-you note, and make a note on your calendar to call or meet again.

Tip Try to get a sense of the buzzwords used in the industry you are seeking. This will give you a bit of an inside look at what's going on.

Tip If your research reveals that a company you're interested in is weak financially, it doesn't mean the company might not appreciate and reward talented people like yourself. Young and growing companies might offer the greatest future rewards, even though they might not be able to offer huge starting salaries. And remember, not all rewards are monetary.

U.S. Employment

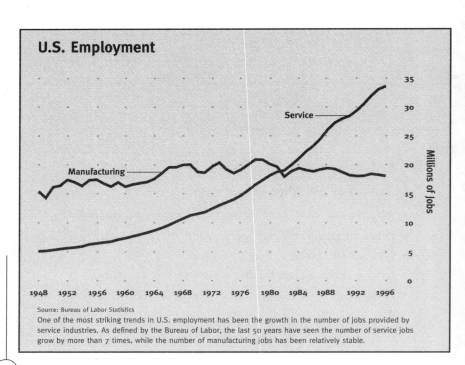

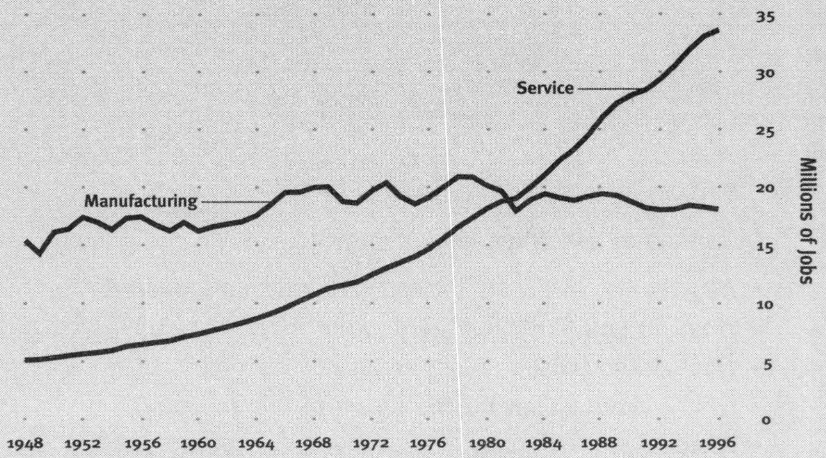

Source: Bureau of Labor Statistics

One of the most striking trends in U.S. employment has been the growth in the number of jobs provided by service industries. As defined by the Bureau of Labor, the last 50 years have seen the number of service jobs grow by more than 7 times, while the number of manufacturing jobs has been relatively stable.

Hitting the Pavement: Looking for Work

There are 2 basic truths about the job market:

1 **There will always be jobs available.**

2 **How you get one depends upon what method of job search you use.**

7 Create a picture of your ideal job.

Unite your transferable skills (those you already have), with your knowledge base (things you have learned), and your interests (things that energize or fascinate you).

This will help you draw a visual image of what your ideal job or career might look like.

THINGS TO THINK ABOUT

Where Do Jobs Come From?

For many years the prevailing opinion has been that small companies create the majority of jobs—a notion that gained wide acceptance in the 1980s after a well-known study by MIT researcher David Birch. His assertion that 88 percent of all jobs were from companies with fewer than 20 employees has been used repeatedly to emphasize the importance of small businesses to the U.S. economy.

Today Birch backs away from the small-versus-big issue, instead putting companies into 3 categories:

1 **Mice:** companies that start and stay small,

2 **Gazelles:** firms that start small but grow quickly, and

3 **Elephants:** big companies likely to stay that way. He points to gazelles (examples: Intel, Microsoft, and Wal-Mart) as the real source of job growth in the 1980s and 1990s.

What you can do, but should avoid

- **Mass mailing resumes.**
- **Answering ads in trade publications, and in local and national newspapers.**
- **Engaging a private employment agency.**

What you should do

- **Seek job leads from family, friends, and neighbors.**
- **Research companies that you might want to work for.**
- **Call or visit contacts at companies.**

THINGS TO THINK ABOUT

Increasing Your Odds on the Job Hunt

Your chances of getting hired decrease dramatically as you move down this scale of job-hunting techniques.

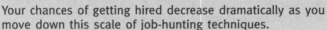

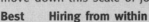

Best

Hiring from within
Easily your best bet, and the reason why getting in at a lower level job is the best way to move up in a company.

Personal recommendation
The second most popular route for most potential employers, which is why networking is so critical.

Search firm recruiting
Potentially productive, since it does involve the company searching for you. But if you use a headhunter to help you find a job, never let them blanket the job market with your resumes.

Human resources
Usually a useless exercise, although not counterproductive. The best outcome of this strategy is usually that they keep your resume on file, and call you much later—usually when you already have another job.

Newspaper advertisement
Almost never worth the paper your resume is printed on. Even if you're the perfect candidate, with exactly the right skills, your submission will be lost among hundreds of other responses.

Worst

Unsolicited resumes
Equally as futile. If you really want a job at a specific company, go the networking route!

8 Customize your resume.

This advice is obviously common sense, but I am amazed at how many people don't follow it. It's so simple to do: determine the attributes that a company is looking for, and highlight them in your resume and cover letter. That doesn't mean that you should be dishonest—that never pays off in the end—but it does mean that you should point out exactly why your skills and experience make you perfect for the job. Does the job call for someone to design a new catalog? Then don't just give them a standard list of brochures, annual reports, and books that you've designed—highlight the sales products you've designed which have been most like a catalog. In your cover letter, tell them why it was such a successful piece and how happy your client was. That's the kind of tailor-made approach which will land you the job.

Tip **Put yourself in your interviewer's shoes. What would you be looking for if you wanted to build the perfect marketing team or find the right person to edit your science magazine? Imagine what you'd like to see in a resume or cover letter if you were on the other side of the desk.**

9 After you get the job, keep the promise.

Your abilities themselves matter—not just how artfully you presented them in your resume. In other words, your resume shows only what you know how to do so far, but what are you willing to do, learn, and be—now? That's what really counts.

ailor your resume to a career that suits you well!

"Attempt the impossible in order to improve your work."

—Bette Davis

THINGS TO THINK ABOUT

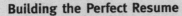

Building the Perfect Resume

Here are the effective elements of a resume that ought to be included:

- **Objective**
  This is an important line that can be most easily tailored to the specific job. If you're applying for a job as a marketing manager at a design firm, try "To build a successful marketing design department," rather than "to obtain a job in marketing."
- **Employment or experience**
  Give a clear description of what you've accomplished in each of your jobs. Use action verbs like "built," "designed," and avoid passive terms like "performed" or "duties included"—that makes it sound as if you just showed up to perform the bare minimum.
- **Skills summary**
  Again, tell them what you have that they can use. If they're looking for a COBOL programmer, guess which skill you should list first? Make it strong: "COBOL Programming, Extensive Experience designing systems, 10 years."
- **Education**
  If you've got a degree, major, or minor that specifically applies to the job, then highlight it here.
- **Interests**
  Many people don't realize that this is one of the best ways to become friendly with your interviewer. It can be even more useful if you know something about your interviewer: if she's an equestrian, then you definitely want to list your riding experience. (But never, never make it up! That's the best way to get into a conversation that will make you look foolish.)
- **Related experience**
  If you're just graduating from college, or re-entering the work force after a long period, and don't have a lot of employment experience, consider adding related experience. For instance, if the job you're applying for requires research and writing, and you wrote for the school paper, that is certainly related experience; you can also add a section called *Aims and Assets*—which can include some selling points about yourself that would make you uniquely attractive to the employer.

Personal Perspective

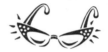

"When I review a potential employee's resume, the first thing I look for is the type of experience and companies the individual has worked for, not what their degree is in or what school they graduated from. Next, I look at what they like to do in their spare time, because I think that gives you a lot of insight into their personality.

"Even though we are a business communications firm, I am always intrigued by people who have majored in history, or other subjects that require a lot of research and writing. I believe that sort of training and discipline are very important in today's modern organization.

"Remember, a resume is really just a key to get in the door—so make it stand out. I'm never impressed solely by a written resume—I want to visit with the person face-to-face. But they have to get through the door first."

"Avoiding danger is no safer in the long run than outright exposure. The fearful are caught as often as the bold."

—HELEN KELLER

The road less traveled made all the difference in my career.

Things to Think About

Lorraine's Road Signs to the Top

Stuck at your rung on the ladder? Stumped at how to impress your stubborn boss? Keep these reminders in a desk drawer—if they don't move you ahead, it's time to find a new job.

1 **Become an asset to your company.**
Put yourself in the shoes of your boss. What is it that would help her most? Is there a task that she dreads every month that you can make easier? Or is there a weakness she has that you could compensate for? Address those questions and you can become the most valuable employee in the office.

2 **Be passionate about what you do.**
Of course, the best way to become passionate about your work is to pick the job you love in the first place. But even if you're still making your way to your dream career, you can find elements of your job that you love. Concentrate on those tasks, and you're bound to be happier and more successful.

3 **Don't box yourself in.**
Remember—the only person who can truly limit your horizons is YOU. Your boss might tell you that you're not ready for a promotion, but you should know better. If you're an administrative assistant, that doesn't mean you can't be a CEO or sales manager or accountant. Sure, you may have to get some training or on-the-job experience, but you can find a way to get where you want.

4 **Don't take *no* for an answer.**
There's an old saying many sales people live by: A *no* means *maybe*; and a *maybe* means *yes*. If your boss tuned you out the last time you brought up a promotion, give her some time, then ask again. Try asking in a different way, but keep asking. Politely, respectfully, but persistently.

5 **Take initiative.**
If there's an opportunity to go beyond your job description—take it. Take your skill sets for a spin and see what you can do. It will give your boss the opportunity to observe your other talents, and you the chance to test out other jobs.

6 **Find a mentor.**
Don't be shy about asking for advice or help from someone you respect. They'll often be flattered to be asked, and you'll gain the benefit of their experience and influence.

7 **Be accountable.**
Passing the buck is a dangerous (and tempting) practice. Nobody likes to take the heat when things go wrong. The secret is learning to take responsibility while suggesting a solution (i.e., instead of

"Steve shipped out the orders on Tuesday, when I told him they should go by Monday," try: "Our department shipped out the orders late, but I know who to call to get an extension"). You'll gain the respect of your boss, believe me, for being the responsible voice in a crisis.

8 **Don't refuse menial tasks.**
If copies need to be made in a hurry, the phone needs to be answered, or a package needs to be sent: jump to it. Too many people (usually those who are defensive about their status) ignore such simple assignments, and end up missing out on making new contacts and building relationships.

9 **Stay ahead of your boss or your client.**
Always do your homework before a meeting. If you're an administrative assistant or junior associate, read incoming mail and know what your boss is working on. Stay on top of the current list of clients, know them by name, affiliation, and project.

10 **Speak up.**
Don't be intimidated about making suggestions or recommendations. If you've been paying attention, your input has value, no matter what your position. (In fact, I often think that the people on the front lines—the administrative assistant handling the mail, or the receptionist who visits with clients on the phone—have some of the most valuable insights.)

11 **Use your instincts.**
In the corporate world, we often forget about this very important judgement tool—maybe the most important. (I happen to think this is an area in which women have an advantage.) If you have an uneasy feeling about a new business partner, or a great one about a new product, learn to take it into account. You'll often find that a little more research can validate your gut reaction.

12 **Grow a thick skin.**
The business world can be a ruthless place, so you'd better get used to being criticized. A productive business environment means that opinions—good and bad—will be freely exchanged. Learn not to take every critique of your work as a personal insult.

13 **Think outside of the box.**
Think about your job in new contexts, not just within your job framework. I think an excellent exercise is learning to read the newspaper for ideas. How do the stories relate to your job? Are kids spending more money?—maybe your department could develop a product to sell into the trend. A new trade agreement with China?—does your company have an export office there? You'll be amazed at the ideas it can spark, and the interest it can add to your job.

Personal Perspective

"When I transferred from the New York office at Drexel Burnham Lambert in 1980, I not only took a cut in pay but a lower position—going from Executive Secretary to the President to Sales Assistant.

"As the new kid on the trading desk, one of my responsibilities was answering the phones. Now, if you've never been on a trading floor, visualize a large bank of phone lines—about 100 flashing lights. And from the time the market bell rang—around 6:00 a.m. Pacific Standard Time — until the market closed, around 1:00 p.m.—those lights were ringing all day long. It was like monitoring a switchboard. You might think that this could be a bit demeaning, coming from the executive floor of the home office.

"But I appreciated the opportunity to work in Mike Milken's High Yield & Convertible Department so I took to my task with enthusiasm. I made answering the phones a challenge—I tried to recognize the caller when they said "hello"—sort of a "Name that Tune" telephone strategy! I actually got quite good, if I say so myself.

"So one day when a young man called and asked 'for Mike Milken,' I responded by saying, 'Hello, Steve.' To which Steve Wynn, CEO of Mirage Resorts said curtly, 'Who's this?' I simply answered, 'Lorraine.' 'What do you do?' he asked. 'I'm a sales assistant.' 'Can you tell me where my stock's trading?' So I did. "Where'd the market close? And what was the volume?' I gave him all the answers.

"So, not only did I impress him by recognizing his voice on 'hello,' but now he knew I could actually think and give him quotes, rather than just put him on terminal hold. I was providing a service to a very good client. And this turned into a long-term relationship. The first time Steve came into the office after our chat, he asked Mike if he could meet me. So now my abilities were being brought to my boss' attention by a client!

"Later, when I became syndicate manager, I helped raise more than $2 billion for Steve Wynn's companies.

"So next time you think a task is too menial for your expertise, remember this story. You're the one who can make things happen!"

"It was the best of times, it was the worst of times..."
—Charles Dickens, *A Tale of Two Cities*

10 Change with the times.

It sure has been the best of times lately—as far the economy is concerned. In 1997, the U.S. federal deficit was reduced to its lowest level in more than twenty years, with unemployment down to its lowest level in decades. The stock market broke records by hitting the $8 trillion mark, with the interest rate low and stable.

But it has also been the worst of times—for workers who have seen job security as we previously knew it shattered. Life-long jobs are now a thing of the past, and changing careers is the wave of the future. Don't let yourself become obsolete by neglecting to update your job skills and knowledge. Keep on the cutting edge in your industry and there will always be a job for you.

11 Gauge your job security.

You don't need a crystal ball to predict a potential layoff. There are many obvious signs, if you keep your eyes open. For instance, if you stayed home for several days and no one missed you—that's a good indicator that if things get tough, you just might be one of the first ones cut. Or if a computer can do your job quicker and more efficiently than you can, that's another good indicator of imminent danger.

It's time for a career change!

It is anticipated that during your lifetime you can expect eight different career changes. Your sole protection must remain: be prepared. Stay alert to sudden changes in your company or industry, and constantly upgrade your skills so that you can transfer them from one career to another.

The New American Way: Changing Careers

12 The best time to find a new job is when you don't need one.

While this advice may seem obvious, few people actually follow it. The reasons for doing so are clear—you have more time and less financial pressure to look for work when you've already got it.

If you're stuck scrambling for employment now, let's figure out how to turn a negative into a golden opportunity. First, let's evaluate your skill sets, what you like to do, what type of people you enjoy working with, where you want to live (and work), etc. Now that you are "a free agent," you do have some choices.

13 Look for new directions.

Nowadays there are interesting opportunities that might not even have existed when you entered the work place, such as working as a consultant, or working part-time for several different companies, or working from home. If you think entrepreneurially, you might even want to consider starting your own business.

THINGS TO THINK ABOUT

Career Change Pointers

- Change jobs when you're not desperate.
- Look for new directions either within your industry or in a related one.
- Identify your skills. If necessary, update.
- Consider relocating.

JUST THE FACTS

Transferable Skills: An Economy in Transition

No economic region has provided a more positive illustration of transferable skills than Southern California (my home) during the last decade. Our state lost millions of jobs in the defense and aerospace industries, which are now being replaced two-to-one by jobs in entertainment. How can a steel worker find work in the movie business? Easy—movie sets, television shows, and independent productions all need heavy construction work, and small contractors sprang up to fill the gap. The entertainment industry here employs millions of lawyers, accountants, caterers, and construction workers—all people who realized that their skills could easily be applied to a growing new industry.

THINGS TO THINK ABOUT

Could Your Job Skills Apply to Another Career?

OK—so maybe your public relations work won't translate to being a neurosurgeon. But you'd be surprised at how many overlapping skills there are between seemingly disparate careers. Consider some of these examples:

- **Reporter to Stock Analyst:** An analyst needs to be able to collect, synthesize, and communicate breaking news about the stock market quickly and on deadline. The move could be a natural one to a financial reporter.
- **Engineer to Marketing Manager:** An engineer must understand the needs of the end user, communicate the plan to build the product, and organize the steps to the market place: many of the skills any good marketing manager would need.
- **Accountant to Producer:** A good line producer will need to know plenty about numbers, reports, and organization. Someone with accounting experience could be perfect for a transition.

If you want to really understand your transferable skills, create your job description in a way that avoids titles and standard phrases, like "performed stock analysis." Instead think about the basics: "interviewed company employees, gathered and interpreted company numbers, wrote reports, responded to questions from investors."

14 Identify your transferable skills.

Ask yourself: what skills have I developed throughout my life that are transferable to completely different professions or industries? Be creative!

This is a very interesting exercise, for several reasons: It helps you look at yourself as an asset to a company, and it helps open your mind to new jobs and industries you might never have considered in your wildest dreams.

Personal Perspective

"At the end of a presentation I delivered in White Plains, New York, a gentleman in the audience approached me for advice. He was probably in his mid- to late-40s. This was his first day in White Plains. He and his family had just moved there from Cincinnati, because his wife had accepted a promotion with her company (this is definitely a 90s story!).
What surprised me was the fact that he was a preacher. You'd think that a man (or woman) of the cloth would keep that profession for life. But he found himself without a congregation. So he wanted some advice on how to transfer his skills to a new vocation.

"My first thoughts were that he could offer his counseling services, since some of the largest corporations in the country are based right there around White Plains—IBM, Xerox, GE, etc.—I assured him they would very likely require outside consultants to help their employees with personal problems (drug/alcohol abuse, divorce, problems with parenthood, etc.) and that his experience working with a congregation might be of help to them.

"Next, I asked him about what he most enjoyed about being a preacher. His response was even more unusual than his profession: He said he loved putting on events! So my next suggestion was to go to those same large corporations, and offer to coordinate events for them, emphasizing on his resume that his unique experience and background would be perfectly relevant.

"The moral of this story is—when you begin to analyze your transferable skills, combined with what you like to do, along with an existing need, you'll be happily surprised at how many different areas you are qualified to work in."

15 Be willing to relocate.

Maybe it's time for a complete change—not only of a career or job, but also of locale. Once again, keep your mind open to new ideas and suggestions.

There might be more potential in a different city or region for the type of career you want. It's possible the pay is better and the cost of living lower. If you're flexible, you may find yourself fielding some very interesting offers. When you're considering your options in other parts of the country, consider these 10 states with the lowest unemployment rates:

Nebraska	2.39%
South Dakota	2.82%
North Dakota	3.14%
Iowa	3.28%
Utah	3.36%
Minnesota	3.45%
Wisconsin	3.67%
Colorado	3.85%
New Hampshire	3.89%
Delaware	4.11%

Source: U. S. Bureau of Labor Statistics

THINGS TO THINK ABOUT

Relocating?

Questions to ask yourself when considering a move to a new area:

- Would I like the climate?
- Does the area have abundant opportunities?
- How would I fit in?
- Does it feel right for me?
- Will my family be more comfortable?
- Can my spouse find adequate work as well?
- Will the activities of the community meet with my satisfaction?

JUST THE FACTS

Making a Smart Move

Let's take another adventure and look at the best places to live and work. *Places Rated Almanac* is a good reference source. Read surveys in magazines, and check out the information available from U.S. cities and towns at your local federal or state employment office and at Chambers of Commerce. Pertinent information you'll want to gather:

- Cost of living
- Types of employment
- Housing
- Transportation
- Education
- Health care
- Crime rate
- Culture
- Recreation
- Climate
- Food
- Population diversity

Once you have this information, you may find that certain cities or regions appeal to you. If so, expand your job search to include these areas.

Personal Perspective

"I've known many young people who have grown up in Los Angeles and wouldn't move to the East Coast regardless of the opportunities. Or New Yorkers who love the excitement of their urban lifestyle, and couldn't possibly move to Des Moines. Then there are others who have given up the country for the big city, or the city for the suburbs, and have become quite content, even happy. So it's all a matter of opinion.

"When I moved my family to L.A. from New York City back in 1980, we were in total culture shock. Not only that, I was suddenly making less money in L.A. than I had made in New York, and the cost of living was actually higher overall. A car became a necessity, my kids now went to private school, and my rent was more than my mortgage had been (plus I didn't get the tax write-off), and so on. So I got a second job. But eventually, it all paid off and I find myself happier and more successful.

"Today, I would be hard pressed to live anywhere else (even with the riots, fires, floods, earthquakes, mud slides, and other natural—and unnatural—disasters)."

THINGS TO THINK ABOUT

The Joys of Small Town Living?

In *Money* magazine's 1997 "Top 10 Cities" survey, the big winners were all relatively small towns (with population sizes less than 250,000). The survey factored in a cross-section of criteria, including the economy, housing, health, crime, education, weather, transit, and leisure, and came up with these winners.

1. Nashua, New Hampshire
2. Rochester, Minnesota
3. Monmouth/Ocean counties, New Jersey
4. Punta Gorda, Florida
5. Portsmouth, New Hampshire
6. Manchester, New Hampshire
7. Madison, Wisconsin
8. San Jose, California
9. Jacksonville, Florida
10. Fort Walton Beach, Florida

Money also ranked the 5 worst places based on the same judging criteria. They are:

1. Sioux City, Iowa
2. Lima, Ohio
3. Anniston, Alabama
4. Rockford, Illinois
5. Davenport, Iowa

Trap

Don't be caught by surprise. Maybe the passions you had when you were straight out of school have changed. Maybe your company went through a merger and your job was cut. Whatever your circumstances, now is always the right time to start thinking about a new job or career. When you do have to make a change, which direction will you choose?

Getting Paid What You're Worth

Just as important as landing a job is being fairly compensated. Many job hunters are nervous about being too aggressive during salary negotiations, for fear that they'll blow their job offer. But it's important to remember that the easiest time to get an increase in your compensation is before you start that job. That's when your employer is most determined to get you, and will be willing to push through an increase on your behalf. (Of course, you should stay in the same ballpark—being aggressive might mean a 20% increase from their initial offer, not double.) Here are some tips to help you through the critical compensation phase, both before you get the job and after.

16 Determine your value to the company.

- Check the open market by calling personnel agencies to see what the going rate is for people with your experience and expertise.
- Ask peers you trust—inside your company and elsewhere—how much they earn.
- Review trade publications with classified ads for the going salaries.

17 A successful salary negotiation means both parties walk away winners.

Neither you nor your employer should feel taken advantage of after a good salary negotiation. If you feel underpaid from the start, then imagine how you'll feel six months down the line. And good employers want you to be happy—they don't want someone who's resentful and potentially unproductive. Don't be a martyr or think that you can fix it later—ask for what you're worth from the start.

But what if you've already got the job, but you're long overdue for an increase?

18 Learn to take an impersonal approach to discussing a raise.

Everyone knows that asking for a raise can be a harrowing experience. These are the points you'll want to review before going in for the talk:

- **Your quantifiable contribution:** Improving your company's bottom line by at least 10 percent can justify a request for a 25 to 30 percent salary increase.
- **Where you work:** Remember, location, location, location, if you want to make the most at your current job. New York City salaries, for instance, are 10 to 35 percent higher than anywhere else in the country. (Keep in mind, of course that the cost of living is high as well, but you might consider sacrificing a little convenience by living in the suburbs).
- **Taking a risk:** Whether you go to work for a company in financial distress, or a young, growing business just starting out, you might be compensated for that risk with a 5 percent positive increase in pay.
- **Your industry:** For example, the public utilities have some of the lowest-paid executives, while software execs are bringing in lots more. Trends and mergers will also affect the industry.
- **Years of service:** Tenure doesn't necessarily mean higher pay, but often it can—particularly if your company is one that prides itself on employee loyalty. If not, you might be better off changing jobs to increase your income than asking for more money where you are.

Keep in mind that, even if you deserve it, there's the possibility that your company just might not be able to give you what you want, due to circumstances beyond their immediate control. In that case, you may want to ask for some form of nonmonetary compensation. Be creative!

Did You Know?

Not All Raises Are Created Equal

Typically a CEO or other top manager will average an annual raise of 30 percent. At the other end of the spectrum is the production worker, whose average annual increase is about 5 percent.

19 Practice stating your case.

It will help to write down the reasons you deserve a raise:

- Explain how you go above and beyond your responsibilities.
- Explain how you are constantly improving your skills.
- Explain how you are self-motivated and driven.
- Explain how your job is and will continue to be an asset for the company in the future.

"I've been rich and I've been poor. Rich is better."

—Sophie Tucker

Things to Think About

Learning to Talk About That Raise

- Request a quiet setting so that you can get your boss's undivided attention.
- Use a positive approach, and keep your voice calm and relaxed.
- Avoid confrontation. Discuss only the future of your job related to the company's business and how it will benefit from your work. Keep the discussion lively and relevant.
- Don't fear silence: take a moment to think before you respond to each question.

Weighing the Options: Money, Perks, & Benefits

Of course, your salary is just the first part of your compensation package. Don't forget to consider the other aspects of the company's offer. You need to weigh carefully the pros and cons of different types of benefit packages. Your family's needs will determine which type of benefits offered will prove to be the most rewarding.

20 Look carefully at the health care package.

This is particularly true if you or your family has any special health care needs.

- Basic coverage takes care of about 80 percent of all your health care costs, including hospitalization and visits to the doctor.
- Look at deductibles, co-payments, and lifetime caps on benefits.
- Some of the best plans will include dental care, eye exams, alternative health care coverage (for treatment such as chiropractic), and mental health benefits.
- Some of the premium plans will include chemical dependency treatment and orthodontic visits as well.
- Today, many companies offer "cafeteria plans" to reduce your costs. These plans allow you to pick only the benefits you need.

21 Factor in your family responsibilities.

If you are newly married and considering having a family, check out the maternity- and paternity-leave policy.

If you're a working parent with young children, you might be interested to know whether the benefits include a child care program, or if the company contributes toward your child care payments. (Since this is a significant cost if you have young children, this benefit could be very helpful to your net worth).

22 Find out about professional education opportunities.

Tuition reimbursement can be of interest. If you want to improve your skills, the company may pay for you to do so. That is not only a savings now, but an added value to your future earning power—whether you stay with this particular company or eventually move on.

23 Be sure you understand the pension plan.

In today's business environment, most companies have abandoned the traditional pension plan and offer 401k plans. Check out whether or not your company matches funds in a 401k. In other words, if you put in $1,000 a year into your 401k plan, the company might add $500 (matching 50 percent of your contribution) into the fund.

24 Don't forget about the perks.

Instead of a raise, your company might offer other perks instead. These options should be considered carefully for their value in the long run.

- **Interest-free loans:** Your company might be able to lend you the money to buy your home without charging you interest. That's an enormous savings to you.
- **Free financial planning:** This can be very helpful to you and your family. The advice could both save you money and make you money.
- **A "golden parachute":** In the event of a future layoff, a promise of a generous severance package.
- **Higher commissions or bonuses:** Better payout for better performance.
- **A company car:** This could save you a bundle (and don't forget the expense account).
- **Additional paid vacation:** You could also ask about other payment for time off, such as jury duty, sick days, and holidays.

- **Other employee services:** Consider perks like a health club membership, a low-cost cafeteria, discounts at a company store, or free work clothes.
- **Stock options and bonuses** (see Things to Think About below).

THINGS TO THINK ABOUT

Stock Options and Bonuses

Questions to ask yourself:

- Are they linked to the company's performance?
- Do you have a set amount or percentage guaranteed?
- If you receive the maximum bonus, what will you keep after taxes?
- With stock options, what is the vesting period—i.e., how long do you have to be with the company before you earn any stock options?
- After you're vested and receive your stock options, what is the strike price—i.e., at what price do you have to pay to buy the stock?
- When can you sell the stock after you exercise your options?
- What are the tax consequences after such a sale?

Translate your dreams into career opportunities.

Work for Hire: The Consultant's Life

"Find a job you love and you'll never have to work a day in your life."

—JIM FOX

25 Become a "permanent" temporary.

Previously, temp work and part-time work were for entry-level or administrative positions. Today, that has changed. From accountants to electricians to lawyers, and everything in between, specialized temporary agencies for seasoned professionals and freelancers have sprouted up everywhere.

Temporary work is an opportunity for workers and employers, giving *both* increased options. Being a temporary gives you the chance to embark on an adventure as you seek a new career. You can try out different types of positions in different companies and industries, and leave if you're dissatisfied. Think of it as sort of a test run. The employers take advantage of the fact that they don't have to pay benefits, and they can let you go without repercussions.

Tip **At temp jobs, you'll make lots of valuable contacts. Temporary positions often open doors to other avenues for work, and can even get you a permanent job with your temporary employer. Your database of contacts will continue to grow. All sorts of options are available these days when you keep your eyes and ears open.**

Trap **There are some pitfalls to temp work. As you consider temporary, part-time and freelance work, remember you will probably have to cover your own taxes. Before you begin, find out how to get set up properly: discuss any IRS questions with a tax accountant you trust.**

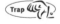

26 It might pay to go independent.

Business owners are usually willing to pay more to independent contractors—often 20 to 40 percent more than they would pay a regular employee. The reason: in today's marketplace, many companies are increasing their number of independent contractors to avoid the huge costs of fixed salaries, benefits, labor laws, workers' compensation costs, and unemployment taxes. They also save on space and equipment, since many independent contractors work out of their own homes. (Often, to avoid complicated labor laws, they can't and won't have you work on-site.)

27 If you go independent, be sure you're safe from the auditors.

How can independent contractors and small businesses mutually protect themselves against IRS audits? Strategies in the following points can help avoid (or withstand) an IRS audit.

Trap

Don't take the step without doing your homework! Find out what the rules and regulations are pertaining to freelancers and independent contractors. If the IRS audits either you or a business you've worked for, if you haven't cooperated ahead of time to establish your working relationship properly, you'll both lose:

For the business, it can mean retroactive payments of Social Security, Medicare, taxes, penalties, and interest. Recently it has been calculated that the IRS has reclassified about 440,000 past workers, collecting about $670 million from business owners.

If you're an independent contractor who gets reclassified as an employee, it can mean you'll owe pension plan and other business deductions, plus possibly losing your home office status. Not only that, but you could forfeit potential work by not getting hired again as a freelancer because of the expense and aggravation to a company.

28 Find out the rules for being classified as an independent.

The IRS has "reasonable basis" as to what is standard for how workers are classified as independents in a particular industry—conform to that standard. It also wouldn't be a bad idea to rely upon the formal opinion of a lawyer or accountant who is an expert in this area.

29 Define the relationship.

As an independent contractor, you are really in control. When you are hired as a freelancer for a specific job, the employer won't spend hours teaching you how to get something done or constantly ask you to report back, as that would be treating you as a regular employee. Make sure this sort of trusting relationship is established up front. Know that the employer has delegated the work to you with an implicit trust that you'll be responsible for getting the job done.

30 Agree on proper compensation.

Just like a small business owner, an independent contractor bears the risk of profit or loss. That's why you may be better off if you charge by the job rather than by the hour. Weigh your options carefully. As a rule of thumb, freelancers do not receive benefits or get reimbursed for expenses. Cover your costs in your invoice to the company (and remember to keep track of every tax write-off). The employer will report your compensation on IRS Form 1099 at the end of the year. The IRS will look upon you with favor if you have incorporated, licensed yourself with a business license and/or a D.B.A. ("doing business as" a fictitious business name), and it is better for you to be paid as a business, rather than as an individual.

31 Establish your independence according to the rules.

According to rules and regulations, as an independent contractor, you need to be self-sufficient. You should have your own office and equipment, pay your own taxes, have your own insurance, and be employed by more than one client. You should be doing your own advertising and marketing, and not be integrated in any way, shape or form into a business's operations. Before hiring you, the employer should be able to check your references and credentials.

32 Be sure you have a written contract.

The contract should consist of the terms and conditions of the working relationship, including many of the points mentioned above. It should state the fact that neither party has the right to terminate the transaction without written notice of a given period of time, or some failure to complete the project as defined. If it is a "work for hire" project that includes intellectual property rights, it will probably have a clause protecting ownership of copyrights and/or confidentiality regarding trade secrets. Take these provisions seriously.

"To love what you do and feel that it matters—how could anything be more fun?"

—Katharine Graham, Chairman, *Washington Post*

I got the contract!

Things to Think About

The Upside of Working for Yourself

Being an independent contractor will help you:

- Set your own hours. (Work when you want to, instead of from 9 to 5.)
- Determine your own income. (The amount you'll earn will be up to you!)
- Be your own boss. (Exercise more control over your career and your lifestyle.)

Home Is Where the Office Is

So wouldn't it be nice not to have to commute? Think of all the money you'll save, not to mention the time! Maybe you won't be late picking up the kids from school, and no more missing the first act of a child's performance! Wouldn't that be wonderful? It can be. But before you hang up that business suit for pajamas, take a look at the big picture.

First, stop counting all that commute money you think you're going to save—because you probably won't have it. Those who work at home often make up to 30 percent less than their colleagues working at the office.

I still prefer working in flannel.

Did You Know?

The Workforce At Home

Approximately ⅓ of the American workforce, 39 million people to be exact, do some sort of work from home. Included in that number are 23.8 million who own their own businesses, 8.5 million who take work home, and 6.5 million who are labeled telecommuter-employees who sometimes work from home during regular business hours.

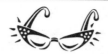

Personal Perspective

"In 1997, I made the decision to shut down my traditional office and set up my business from home. It was such a liberating concept. My employees and partners—who were all women—were in favor of the idea.

"Don't get me wrong—it was totally traumatic at first. Having the phone ring twenty-four hours a day in my house—receiving orders from around the world—was no picnic. And having my assistants come to work in the morning around 8:00 a.m. while I was still trying to get dressed—was off-putting at first and felt a little bit like an invasion of privacy. But we got into a routine, and now it is working like a charm.

"That's not to say that some day I might not open up an office again. I'm still not totally convinced that I wouldn't do better working in the midst of a flurry of activity (remnants of my trading desk days)."

Tip

Install at least one more phone line in the house (more if necessary). You'll find out very quickly that to keep your sanity and your family intact, you must keep your personal and business calls separate. You'll probably discover that you want a separate line for a fax and/or for on-line time too. And, as your business and flexibility grow, you may need additional phone numbers, voice mail, an answering service, a pager, etc.

33 Consider how you'll manage your time.

It's often easier to cope with family matters when you're not there. Consider how you're going to juggle the family and still have time to do your business.

As much as possible, maintain regular "office hours." Make sure your customers know you're not available around the clock just because you work at home (in fact, they don't even have to know).

Tell your spouse, family, friends, and neighbors what your work hours are—that you're not available during those times even though they see that "you're home."

THINGS TO THINK ABOUT

Questions to Ask Yourself When Deciding to Work From Home

- Do you have enough room for a work space? You must create some privacy and space to work where there won't be a lot of interruptions—so the kitchen table is not going to be your best spot. A separate office, with a door you can close, is ideal.
- Are you disciplined enough to work out a schedule, get all of your work done, and still have time for yourself and your family? Many people are surprised by the intrusion that an at-home office presents to their family time.
- Do you have the motivation it takes to constantly find new business? The biggest obstacle for every newcomer is finding new customers. It's like constantly being on a job hunt! You can never stop, since selling your services and products is now your livelihood, and your responsibility!
- Can you tolerate working independently, and possibly feeling isolated? When you work from home you're all alone. You can't take that 15-minute coffee break to relax and brainstorm with your colleagues, getting some fresh ideas and input (unless you can telephone other sympathetic home business owners). There's no one to chat with but the dog.
- Do the laws in your state and in your neighborhood allow you to conduct business from home? (Some places, for example, have laws regulating the number of clients who can come to your door, or rules against signage.) Find out what the laws are before you begin. Consider meeting clients only at their offices (or at a local restaurant) rather than allowing strangers to traipse through your house.
- Have you talked to your tax consultant about the possibilities (or lack thereof) for deductions? Be sure you understand all of the implications before you make the leap.

All these things are much more difficult to do than they may appear to the envious outsider, so make sure you're honest with yourself before you give up your day job!

Careers for the 21st Century

You really don't need a crystal ball to predict the future. There are things we know now that give us some pretty good clues as to what's in store for the next few decades.

34 Americans are getting older.

An increasing sector of the U.S. population is elderly. The fastest growing population in this country is the octogenarian crowd; the second fastest are in their 70s; the third fastest are over 50. Get the picture?

It makes sense that a significant area for the creation of new jobs will be in affordable and accessible health care. Taking care of our senior citizens will require a hands-on approach. So there is definitely a growing need for all sorts of skilled professionals in geriatrics and related fields.

Not only that, but the industries serving retired folks—travel and leisure—will be expanding. With baby boomers turning 50, there will be a growing need for specialized semi-retirement leisure homes, facilities, and communities. The baby-boom generation is likely to desire innovative and stimulating ways of living that haven't even been invented yet. Research into figuring out new ways to help this generation spend their leisure time would certainly lead you to a rewarding career.

35 The world is getting smaller.

The world is getting smaller and smaller, with new forms of communication coming into play at lightning speed. The world has fewer and fewer boundaries, and diminishing borders.

Don't be surprised that those who are sensitive to the nuances of other cultures and countries (including immigrant populations) will be the more desirable employees.

Those who speak and write in foreign languages—especially Chinese, Japanese, Russian, and Spanish—will definitely hold the advantage in our global marketplace.

The development of products, and selling them to world markets, will be another burgeoning area where you would be wise to focus your attention.

36 Computerization is here to stay.

You cannot consider any career or business strategy without becoming computer literate. Period. So whether you begin taking courses yourself to get with the program, or you choose to make a living teaching others how to use computers and software—there are going to be countless opportunities here for everyone. Plus, there is a growing need to help people learn how to use computers or software programs.

37 Our population's ethnic mix is changing dramatically.

By 2010, the minority in this country will become the majority. For the first time in a century, no longer will American ancestors be primarily European; they will be from Latin America, Africa, and Asia.

Developing products and services to help immigrant populations assimilate and blend into American culture will create rewarding and challenging careers. Whether it's selling multicultural restaurant supplies or developing educational courses, training programs, new on-line technologies, and affordable ways for people to communicate with or travel to their homelands, and so on—this will be an extremely lucrative business opportunity for the next few decades.

This changing population is also a factor in the overall global marketplace (see Tip 35).

38 Increase your education, increase your pay.

After you've done all the right research, networking, and soul-searching, remember, too, that gaining the education you need, if you don't yet have it, will help ensure a higher salary, and increase your attractiveness and value to prospective employers. Consider these statistics from the Census Bureau:

1995 Median Education Income

9th–12th grade	$ 8,057
High School Graduate	$ 12,046
Bachelor's degree	$ 24,065
Master's degree	$ 33,509
Professional degree	$ 38,588
Doctorate degree	$ 39,821

As you can see, it pays to go back to school!

Look to the future for new career opportunities.

Ask Lorraine

Q&A

Q. *I'm so uncomfortable bringing up the subject of a raise with my boss—how can I make it easier?*

A. First of all, establish to yourself the reasons that you deserve a raise. See Tip 18—appraise your own work. Write down what you've contributed to the department or company (new business brought in, more efficient systems, etc.) that specifically justifies a higher salary. Once you've done that, set up a specific time with your boss to discuss your raise, rather than casually bringing it up. That will give you a chance to be prepared, and get the message across that you're serious.

Q. *I hate my job. I'm looking for another one, but hate grinding through every day in the meantime. Should I quit?*

A. No! Find something you like about the job you have now. If you can, try to take on new tasks that you might find more satisfying. That way, you might be happier while you search for another job and will turn in a better performance. Remember—they're the ones who'll be called for references someday.

Q. *I've been looking for a job for weeks, and I'm beginning to get discouraged. What can I do to keep my enthusiasm up?*

A. I always tell people to set goals that lead up to a job. For example, set a goal of a certain number of job leads to follow up every week. If you have ten good leads every week, you're doing great. (And that doesn't mean a blind resume with no follow-up.) Count every positive development—a good contact, another lead—as a success. Most of all, I remind job seekers that it takes time to find the right job. But if you continue to follow the right steps diligently, you'll find a job within 3 to 6 months. That realistic goal should keep you from feeling down about not getting a job in a couple of weeks.

Q. *I'm beginning to feel uneasy about my job security, but I don't want to overreact. What can I do?*

A. Start looking now. That's not an overreaction as long as you do it discreetly. As a matter of fact, I encourage people to go through this process anyway—even if they're happy and secure with their job—every 2 years or so. I think it's a great way to keep perspective about your worth on the job market, especially when salary negotiations roll around. But most importantly, finding a job is much easier when you already have one. Don't wait until you've been let go to hit the job market.

Resource Guide

Don't Know Where to Start?

- Check out *The Dictionary of Occupational Titles* (D.O.T.)—published by the U.S. Department of Labor's Bureau of Labor Statistics—for a comprehensive list of occupations.
- America's Job Bank is another helpful resource at: *www.ajb.dni.us*

If You're Considering Moving

- The *Places Rated Almanac* (Macmillan General) is a great source for information on different places to live.
- Contact the National Occupational Information Coordinating Committee (NOICC) for information on state labor market. The national Web site is: *www.state.nh.us/soiccnh/noicchom.htm*

If You're Looking to Update Your Skills

- The *Buyer's Guide and Consultant Directory* (published by the American Society for Training and Development) can give you a list of companies that provide a bevy of training options. Call: 703-683-8100

For Family-Friendly Jobs

- Contact the Families and Work Institute for more information on companies that are considered "family-friendly." Call: 212-465-2044
- *Working Mother* magazine also publishes an annual list of the best companies to work for if you're a working mom. It's posted at: *www.womenswire.com/work/work.html*

Looking for an Internship?

- Contact the NSEE (National Society for Experiential Education) for information on both hiring and becoming an intern. Call: 919-787-3263

Section 2

Managing your household finances takes plenty of skill!

Managing Your Household

There is no greater set of skills than being able to successfully manage your household finances. Yet while this seems like something that any reasonably responsible person should be able to accomplish, the reality is that most of us just stumble by. The reason is simply that the many things we regularly need to do—creating a budget, finding reliable child care, choosing to rent or buy a house, or making a car purchase—can be incredibly complex and confusing.

Don't be discouraged, you have the skills. You're just lacking the information to make better, more informed decisions. And you'll be surprised to find that once you understand a few simple concepts, these once-confounding issues will seem relatively uncomplicated.

There's a reason that household duties carry such a large burden: their impact upon you and your family is significant. Your choice of a type of mortgage can impact your life for years—as can the way you manage your bills. But once you understand the "mystery" behind these essential tasks, you'll be better equipped to make the decisions that will continue to build your financial picture. From the number-phobic to the math wizards: everyone has the tools to build an efficient household system.

Learning to Live Within Your Means

39 Create a snapshot of your financial picture.

Here's an easy way to determine your net worth:

- Calculate the value of your assets.
- Deduct the value of your liabilities.
- The total equals your net worth.

Here's a breakdown:

Assets (what you own)

- **Cash (or cash reserve assets):** All the excess cash or equivalents, i.e., investments or savings, that can be turned into cash quickly (in less than one year), such as money in your savings account, money market accounts, checking account, CDs, Treasury bills, or the cash value of your life insurance policy.
- **Investments (or investment assets):** Stocks, bonds, mutual funds, 401k's, IRAs, annuities, and anything else that might be considered a long-term investment (more than one year).
- **Personal property (or personal assets):** Possessions that you own outright (less any money owed to a bank). Some of these possessions, such as antiques, stamp collections, and art, might appreciate (increase) in value. Others, such as cars, boats, and electronic equipment often depreciate (decrease) in value.
- **Real estate:** Your home, which usually represents your largest asset (you can use it yourself, rent it out to others, or even sell it for a profit). This can also include raw land or other real estate you might own, e.g., a time-share condo in Florida or a second home in the mountains.

Liabilities (what you owe)

- **Short-term debt:** Current bills that you owe, i.e., credit card charges, vacation loans, installment loans, income and real estate taxes, and insurance payments (usually loans made for under seven years).
- **Long-term debt:** Your mortgage and other installment loans that must be repaid over a period of seven years or more.

Tip

Thinking of applying for a loan? Lenders like to see a history of solid credit. Most lenders also want to know about your ability to save money, as evidenced by how much money you have accumulated through investments in IRAs or other retirement accounts, and in other long-term investments. From their viewpoint, this would give you the resources to pay off your new loan in an emergency.

40 Your net worth statement is the first step to getting financially fit.

It's a starting point, like when you get a check-up and your doctor tells you how much weight you need to trim off (or add) during the coming year, or how to get your cholesterol down, etc. In the case of your net worth, you'll want to boost your assets up and bring your liabilities down—like a balancing act—but you'll want to end up with more assets than liabilities—that's your overall objective.

Determine the health of your financial condition.

Worksheet: Your Net Worth

Assets

Cash Reserve Assets
(savings, checking, short-term investments like money market accounts)

Investment Assets
(investments for more than 1 year: stocks, bonds, mutual funds, 401k's)

Personal Assets
(things you own outright—cars, boats, art—less money owed to a bank).

Real Estate
(your home, and other real estate)

Liabilities

Short-term Debt
(current bills that you owe, i.e., credit card charges, loans, taxes)

Long-term Debt
(mortgage and other installment loans with payback periods of seven years or more)

41 Here's the bottom line: what your net worth means.

If your net worth is half or less your annual income, or even a negative number:

- Unfortunately, you're like the majority of Americans.
- If you're in your 20s, this isn't so bad. But if you're older, it's much more disturbing. You should start now to get these numbers in a better balance. Start by paying off some of your debts and cutting back on spending, and begin to build a safety net for yourself equal to three to six months of living expenses.

If your net worth is more than half your annual income, but less than a few years' annual income:

- If you're under 40 and own a home you are in pretty good shape.
- If you're older and are still renting, you need to cut back on your spending and your debt and increase your savings as soon as possible. You might even want to consider buying a home before you reach retirement age.

If your net worth is more than a few years' annual income:

- If you're under 40, you're in excellent shape.
- If you're over 40, you're probably right on track and should continue with the strategy that got you here in the first place.

THINGS TO THINK ABOUT

How Your Credit Can Work Against You

When you apply for a loan, the bank may take into consideration your entire available credit card line—assuming fairly that at any given time you can charge up to that amount. While this might affect how they calculate your net worth, understand that your credit line also reflects potential liabilities.

42 Why it's important to understand your net worth.

Calculating your net worth means more than just measuring yourself against the average statistic. It should set your overall guidelines—spending, saving, and cutting back on your debts. Consider it a barometer that should be checked every three months (quarterly), similar to the way companies report to their shareholders. Understanding your own financial condition will also help you understand business; the same set of guidelines are used in business, just with more zeros at the end of the numbers!

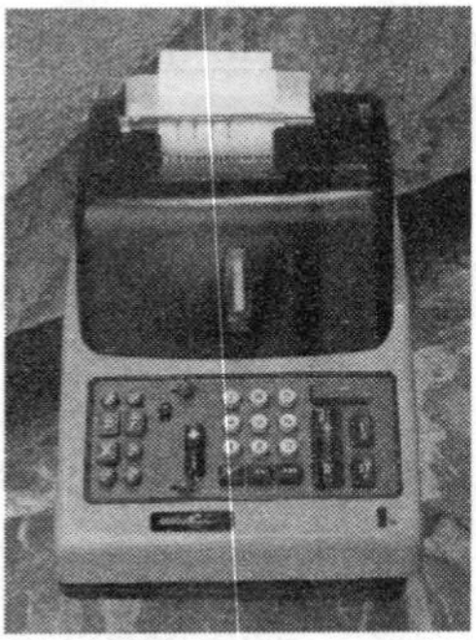

Calculate your net worth every quarter.

"Money is better than poverty, if only for financial reasons."

—Woody Allen

Taming the Family Budget

"Why is there so much month left at the end of the money?"

—John Barrymore

43 Pretend you're the chief financial officer of a company —the person who manages the company's money.
Now imagine that company is your family. And what do you want most for your family? To become financially fit.

44 Pay yourself first.
If you're like most people, what's left over is what you put into savings. To force yourself to save, try paying yourself first: write a check to your savings account before you pay your bills. Make a habit of this, and watch your savings grow. The key to sticking to your budget is making it simple and realistic. Try it! It's easier than you think.

45 Create a family budget.
Look at your family budget the way a CEO would prepare a zero-based budget. Let's start with a blank sheet of paper and begin to fill it in. (See next page.)

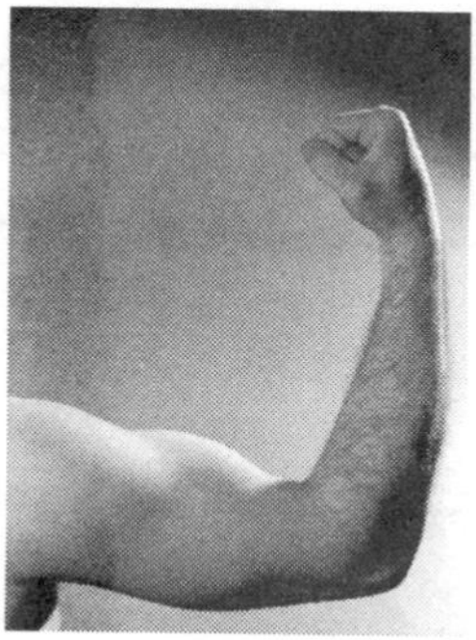

Keep your family financially fit.

Worksheet: Organizing the Family Budget

1 First, let's start by listing your inflow of money.

Take-Home Pay (after-tax salary)	$
Investment Income (from stocks or bonds, real estate)	$
Scholarships, etc.	$
Other forms of Income	$
	$
	$

This is your working capital—the money you have to cover all of your expenses.

2 Next, let's list your family's essentials.

Rent or mortgage	$
Utilities (gas, electric, telephone)	$
Food	$
Clothing	$
Transportation (car payments, public transportation)	$
Insurance (car, life, medical)	$
Childcare	$

3 Finally, list the extras.

Eating Out	$
Entertainment (movies, sports events, hobbies)	$
Vacations	$
Gifts	$
Membership Fees	$
Other	$
	$
	$
	$
	$

Here are a couple of tables that should give you an idea of where your monthly savings will put you in a few years. The top table assumes that you're getting a 5 percent annual return, and the bottom assumes 10 percent. (Notice the difference: $100 per month after 20 years is $41,103 at 5 percent, versus $75,937 at 10 percent.)

Present Value Table—5 Percent Annual Return

	Years to Retirement			
Monthly Savings	5	10	20	30
$100	$6,801	$15,528	$41,103	$83,226
$200	$13,601	$31,056	$82,207	$166,452
$500	$34,003	$77,641	$205,517	$416,129
$1,000	$68,006	$155,282	$411,034	$832,259
$3,000	$204,018	465,847	$1,233,101	$2,496,776
$5,000	$340,030	$776,411	$2,055,168	$4,161,293

Present Value Table—10 Percent Annual Return

	Years to Retirement			
Monthly Savings	5	10	20	30
$100	$7,744	$20,484	$75,937	$226,049
$200	$15,487	$40,969	$151,874	$452,098
$500	$38,719	$102,422	$379,684	$1,130,244
$1,000	$77,437	$204,845	$759,369	$2,260,488
$3,000	$232,311	$614,535	$2,278,107	$6,781,464
$5,000	$387,185	$1,024,225	$3,796,844	$11,302,440

JUST THE FACTS

The Math: Future and Present Values

The **future value** of an amount is calculated like this:

$FV = \text{Present Value } (1+r)^n$

Example: Future Value of $1,000 put away for 10 years at 5% interest rate is:

$\$1{,}000\ (1.05)^{10} = \$1{,}628.89$

The **present value** of a future payment is calculated like this:

$PV = \text{Future Payment} \div (1+r)$

Example: You'll receive a $1,000 in a year, and the interest rate you think is fair is 7%.

The Present Value of that future payment is :

$\$1{,}000 \div (1.07) = \$934.58$

46 Don't spend more than 30 percent of your take-home pay per month on your rent or mortgage.

Depending on where you live, this gets easier or more complicated. If you live in Cincinnati or Oklahoma City this is very attainable. But if you live in Los Angeles or New York City, it gets much harder to find a nice place to live in a decent neighborhood. You might need to consider living in a suburb for a while—a bit of an inconvenience, but it could save you money. Or you could consider exploring unique housing options that may be more affordable. Be creative.

47 Follow the debt guideline: the total amount of money you owe each month (not including your mortgage) should not exceed 20 percent of your take-home pay.

If it's more, you need to start cutting back as soon as possible. If you're at the 20 percent level, you're in pretty good shape, but you should always strive for less.

48 Also follow the savings guideline: you should try and save at least 10 percent of your take-home pay each month.

While this isn't a hard and fast principle, it is one that you should start as soon as possible to get yourself financially fit for the long-term.

Don't try to save money and then overlook paying off your high-interest credit cards. You need to pay off your debts first, and then start saving as much as you can, as soon as you can.

49 Set up a financial filing system.

Have you cleaned out your garage lately? Wondered why you kept every bill or piece of paper sent to you? Maybe it's time to get organized and sort through your paperwork! You don't need to keep every bill or receipt. In general, you should hold on to receipts related to tax-deductible expenses or papers dealing with warranties.

Here's what you can throw out now:

- Old phone bills
- Old utility bills
- Supermarket receipts

What you should keep for at least 1 year:

- Canceled checks (except those you need for tax returns)
- Store receipts and credit card statements (in case you need to return an item, for taxes, or if an item gets lost or stolen for insurance purposes)

Here are some items you may want to keep for at least 3 years or longer:

- Credit card agreements (at least for as long as you have the card)
- Loan agreements
- Warranties
- Home improvement receipts

- Insurance policies
- Tax returns (keep them for at least 7 years—that's how long the IRS has to do an audit)
- Year-end transaction statements from mutual funds or brokerage firms

50 Store the really important stuff separately.

Of course there are certain documents you'll need to keep indefinitely:

- Birth certificate
- Passport
- Marriage license
- Divorce decree and settlement agreement
- College transcripts

51 Get computerized!

Once you get accustomed to using a computer, there is no faster way to organize your storage. It's a great way to save space: memos and documents saved on your computer (properly backed up, of course) can save storage and paper. Use a computer program to organize your record-keeping. That way you'll have a clearer picture of your financial life at your fingertips.

"Money is a terrible master but an excellent servant."

—P. T. BARNUM

Keep the records you need, get rid of the rest.

Taking Care of the Kids: The Child Care Puzzle

52 Explore your child care choices.

Many families today are reverting back to extended family situations, such as teaming up with a sister, friend, or mother-in-law to find reliable, reasonably priced child care. However, this trend isn't realistic for those of us who have to rely on outside individuals to help care for our children. Here are a few choices:

- **Child care at home: nanny or au pair?**

  A **nanny,** aged 18 to 80, can live in or away from your home, and has experience working with children from infants to teenagers. A nanny works 50 to 60 hours per week, and will perform general housekeeping duties. Average pay: $200-$600 per week.

  An **au pair,** age 18 to 25, lives in your home like an exchange student from another country. An au pair usually works up to 45 hours per week, does not care for infants under 3 months old, and only helps with child-related tasks. Salary averages about $115 per week.

  Both can be hired through an agency, but the fee for an au pair is often significantly higher than for a nanny, and often the restrictions for an au pair can be limiting. Make sure you understand the parameters of any contract before you enter into it.

- **Day care centers**

  Day care centers are usually open five days per week from around 6:00 a.m. to 6:30 p.m. For children in diapers, the cost is about $200–$500 per week. Older children cost approximately $150–$400 weekly, including meals and snacks. If you have 2 children, you can probably get a 10 percent discount off tuition, so for 2 children, a low-end day care center might cost $17,290 annually, while a high-end day care center could cost $39,520.

JUST THE FACTS

The Working Parents' Dilemma

- One of the toughest decisions facing parents who work is not only where to look for quality child care, but how to pay for it. Since more than 36 percent of today's workforce has children under the age of twelve, there is a growing need for high-quality, affordable child care for millions of working Americans.
- Only 2 percent of the available space at state-licensed day care centers is open for infants.
- According to the Census Bureau, the average U.S. household income spends nearly $320 per month, or $3,840 per year on child care.

53 Face up to the downside of child care.

So here's the bad news. If you're in America's median salary range, and pay 28 percent in taxes, your take-home pay would be about $32,000. After you factor in child care costs, even at the low end of approximately $10,500, you would be left with $21,500; at the high end, you would land at a negative $800.

A single parent moving off welfare—probably getting a job at minimum wage—may spend 50 percent of income on child care and up to 90 percent of income for infant care. Similarly, a parent re-entering the workforce may spend most—if not all—of one's salary on child care.

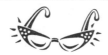

Personal Perspective

"When my kids were 2 and 4, I worked full-time. But I was only earning about $15,000 a year pre-tax. So finding affordable child care was definitely an issue. But I have always been creative, so I came up with several interesting strategies.

"My best friend, who lived next door, also had two children. She didn't work, so we cut a deal. She watched my kids 2 or 3 days a week for free and I took all the kids on the weekend so she could relax or get some of her errands done in peace.

"This worked out really well for both of us. On the off days, I convinced my mother to come and watch the kids. This was even better, because not only did she care for them, she made dinner, washed clothes, and took care of the house as well.

"Later on, I found an older woman who lived next door who was like their grandma. She needed some extra money, and it was really convenient, because she could stay in my house or take the kids to hers and the kids could still play with their friends.

"So remember that if you're having problems with childcare, there are plenty of other moms in the same predicament. Why not try to coordinate in a way that helps you all? And don't be shy about asking for help from family and friends—you might be able to trade services or time with them, or even pay them for their help."

54 Check out your company's child care plans.

Many companies offer programs to help parents with their childcare options. Plans can range from on-site daycare (at the most progressive companies) to helpful programs like flextime and job-sharing. Be sure you know everything your company offers before you set up something on your own.

Your child care solution might be right next door.

55 Team up with other parents at your company.

Coordinating with co-workers who have similar child care issues can be truly constructive. You might find that you can coordinate on carpools or babysitters, or join forces to create a new child care-friendly plan at your company.

"The only thing money gives you is the freedom of not worrying about money."

—JOHNNY CARSON

THINGS TO THINK ABOUT

Help from Washington

Child care is finally becoming a major economic and political issue. President Clinton acknowledged the strain on working families of taking care of their kids by announcing a major child care initiative in January 1998. He committed a total of $20 billion over 5 years for various child care programs—some of which could trickle down to you:

- More subsidies for lower-income families. (Ask about the Child Care and Development Block Grant connection in your community.)
- Tax credits for other working families (ask about the Child and Dependent Tax Credit).
- Tax credits for businesses that offer child care services. (Talk to your employer!)
- After-school care through the 21st Century Community Learning Center program. (Ask about the partnership in your area.)
- Working parents should cheer this help from Washington! Make sure that your support is heartily registered where it counts. Write or call your senator(s) and let her or him know what you think.

Home Sweet Home

56 Know the advantages of renting your home.

There are many advantages to both renting and buying a home, as well as some disadvantages. Your choice should be made my weighing all your needs, both financial and personal.

- You don't have to drain your savings to make a large down payment. (Your money might appreciate faster through investment in mutual funds than in a home.)
- There are no costs related to repairs and maintenance.
- Some of your utilities bills might be covered as part of your monthly rent.
- You'll have more flexibility when you want to move, because you won't be responsible for finding a new tenant (or buyer).
- You don't have any of the risks associated with home prices dropping in value.
- You don't have to pay property taxes.
- You might be able to get a rent-controlled apartment, which will hold your fixed costs down.

Did You Know?

Rent-controlled Apartments

If you can, find a neighborhood that offers rent-controlled apartments. Then, if you're lucky enough to find one, check to make sure that the law is still in place and not being repealed. Rent control gives you the advantage of securing a place to live for a low rate that is guaranteed not to rise significantly; this will help you save money, since you'll be reasonably certain what your rent will be for the next few years. Be sure to read your lease very carefully, since many of these apartments have very strict regulations.

Did You Know?

How Much Do You Spend On Your Home?

According to the Bureau of the Census, about 18 percent of an American household's total expenditures goes to housing expenses (i.e., the rent or the mortgage). Of course, in areas like Los Angeles and New York, the average is closer to 24 percent.

57 Know the advantages of owning your home.

- As it appreciates in value, your property will build equity, which you can borrow against in the future or sell at a profit.
- You can deduct mortgage interest and property taxes on your tax return.
- You might be able to defer paying taxes on the profit of your home if you buy another home within two years.
- If you buy a home wisely, you might get more living space for less money.

58 Land your dream home without breaking your budget.

With today's strong economy, low mortgage rates, and a runaway stock market, housing prices have been climbing an average of 5 percent a year for the last two years. Home buyers, beware: home-bidding wars are back in a big way for the first time since the booming 1980s.

59 Make sure the neighborhood is really hot, not just hyped.

Don't take the word of your real estate agent. Ask for listings of homes in the area. If homes are selling around 5 percent of the asking price within the first month, that's an indication of a strong market.

60 Don't pay more for a house than it's worth.

Check out comparable homes—the selling prices of similar houses in the area. Then, avoid paying more than 3 percent above the average price. If you overpay for your home, your bank may not give you the mortgage you need.

61 Show them the money.

In a hot market, you must act quickly. You might want to get your mortgage pre-approved by the bank for a certain amount of money. Sometimes a seller even accepts a lower bid from a buyer who has a pre-approved mortgage.

62 Make your first bid count.

In a hot market, you may get one shot at nailing the deal. If your first bid is too low, you could be shut out of the game. When a deal is hot, you may be asked to waive the financing contingency in your contract. If you agree to this, and cannot get a mortgage, you could lose your 10 percent deposit, based on the price of the house.

63 Be careful that you don't overspend.

Sometimes people get so caught up in the bidding process, they become obsessed with getting a house at all costs. You may end up winning, but with a house you can't afford.

64 Understand the tradeoff for buying versus renting.

It's your personal preference whether to buy a home or rent. The best luxury, however, is having enough money to be able to make that choice. More than 65 percent of all Americans do decide to buy. There are several types of properties you can own: a house, a condo, or a co-op. The differences are as follows:

- **House:** It's all yours, but there are plenty of costs (aside from the mortgage) that go along with that benefit. Primarily taxes (based on assessed value), maintenance, and repair costs, as well as insurance.
- **Condo:** Again, this should be yours free and clear (meaning you can use or rent it however you please.) You'll still be paying taxes (based on assessed value), as well as a monthly maintence charge and insurance.

- **Co-op:** In this case, you'll be subject to board approvals for things like selling and renting your property. You won't have individual taxes, but you will pay a maintenance charge which includes real estate taxes, along with other costs for the building.

65 Determine whether or not you can afford to buy your own home.

The Rule of Thumb: lenders usually require that you spend less than 28 percent of your gross income on your mortgage payments, property taxes, and home insurance.

Personal Perspective

"My first 'home' purchase was a townhouse in Tarzana, California, affectionately termed 'The Valley.' It was a duplex with 3 bedrooms, a large kitchen, living room, dining room and a den. It had a very small backyard, but enough to have a place for our dog during the day. The unit was part of a planned community with all of the amenities one might find in Southern California: a shared pool, gym, party room, garage, etc. I thought I had died and gone to heaven—it seemed perfect for a working single mother. I didn't have to worry about maintenance, the lawn, etc.

"But not for long. After 6 months, I decided we had made a mistake. I really wanted my own home, with some privacy. My town house started to feel more like a glorified apartment.

"Now's the tricky part, trying to sell. I found out the hard way that townhouses don't appreciate in value the same way a house does (or at least that's what my broker told me!). And since I only owned it for 6 months, I was going to get hit with commissions coming and going! So I lost some money on the sale, but I did find my dream home with my own pool, large yard, and lots of privacy.

"The lesson here is to pay attention to values for different types of homes and ask questions. Request answers with statistics (i.e., prices of similar homes bought and sold in a particular area, etc.). Also, make sure you buy the type of home you really want…and not one you're simply settling for."

THINGS TO THINK ABOUT

The Hidden Costs

Most of us just calculate the mortgage payments. But there are so many other related expenses which we can easily overlook:

- **Insurance:** Your lender will stipulate that you must have enough coverage for the complete replacement value of your home.
- **Property Taxes:** Local and state taxes will vary enormously—check before you buy in a particular area.
- **Maintenance:** Inspection of your new home will help determine how much work the house will need. But you will also need to have some emergency money socked away for surprises. Co-ops and condos have monthly maintenance charges that tend to escalate, so check to see how this will affect your monthly budget.
- **Office Commutes:** If you move to the suburbs and work in the city, your monthly commute expenses will increase. So calculate how much this will cost you per month and try and find some alternatives, like car pooling.
- **Schools:** Buying a home in an area with excellent public schools may cost more (and these neighborhoods are usually in high demand), but you should measure this against choosing to send your kids to private schools.

Sock away extra for those unexpected home improvement expenses.

66 How much home can you buy?

Use this table to get a ballpark idea of what kind of loan amount you'll be able to handle. (Keep in mind that insurance and fees will add to the total cost.)

Loan Amount (based on a 30-year loan length)

	6.00%	7.00%	8.00%	9.00%	10.00%	11.00%	12.00%
$80,000	$480	$532	$587	$644	$702	$762	$823
$100,000	$600	$665	$734	$805	$878	$952	$1,029
$120,000	$720	$798	$881	$966	$1,053	$1,143	$1,234
$150,000	$900	$998	$1,101	$1,207	$1,316	$1,428	$1,543
$200,000	$1,200	$1,331	$1,468	$1,609	$1,755	$1,905	$2,057
$250,000	$1,500	$1,663	$1,834	$2,012	$2,194	$2,381	$2,572

67 Shop smart for a mortgage.

Consider all of your options including banks, savings & loans, and thrifts. Usually they offer the best interest rates, particularly if you have an account with them or are investing in CDs. Here are a few other sources you might consider.

- **Developers:** They may be motivated to work with lenders (banks and others whom they have done business with in the past) and might be able to get you attractive rates and fewer points, particularly if they are anxious to unload their property. They might even be willing to make the loan themselves.
- **Mortgage brokers:** For a fee, they will act as intermediaries between you and the lender. If you're having a hard time getting a good deal, they might prove worthwhile.
- **Mortgage companies or mortgage bankers:** They may offer lower rates, and the application process may be easier than at a bank, since this is their primary business.
- **The seller:** A seller might be willing to lend you the money you need, or give you a second or a third mortgage, if you can't get a mortgage to cover the entire amount of the home.

68 Get help from the government.

If you can't afford a big down payment and expensive closing costs, but you can qualify for a mortgage, there are other options available to you.

- **Federal Housing Administration (FHA) loans:** Under several different mortgage programs, the federal government does not actually lend you the money for your home, but it will insure or guarantee the amount of the loan for the lender. Your down payment may be reduced to only 3 or 4 percent (instead of 20 percent) and the fixed rate will be lower than what you'd pay on a traditional 30-year mortgage. The disadvantage of this program is that the credit limit given might not be enough to cover the entire cost of the home. The maximum amount is roughly $151,000 in most areas. Add in the median cost of homes in the U.S. minus 3 to 4 percent and see how it works out for the majority of country today.
- **Veterans Administration (VA) loans:** These are partially guaranteed by the VA (part of the federal government). To qualify, you must have some current or previous military service. While no down payment is required by the VA, the lender might require one. You will get lower fixed rate interest payments. You will pay a one-time charge (a funding fee) to cover mortgage insurance, ranging between 0.5 percent and 3 percent of the mortgage, depending upon the terms of the loan.

69 Check out the Community Home Buyer's Program.

This could be your cheapest way to go. The down payment is only 5 percent, and 2 percent of that can be gifts from family or friends. The 2 percent gift portion doesn't show up on your credit report, so it doesn't prevent you from borrowing additional money. You also don't need to cover two months' worth of mortgage payments, which is the norm for other low-income loans.

Trap **Little or no down payment may sound good—but remember, the amount you'll owe will be more, and that increases your monthly payments.**

70 Find the right mortgage for you.

The average mortgage usually lasts about seven years, at which time it will be paid off primarily due to the sale of the home.

There are basically two types of mortgages:

- Fixed rate mortgages
- Adjustable rate mortgages

The choice is usually yours. The primary difference between a fixed rate and an adjustable rate mortgage is simply this: With a fixed rate, the rate of interest you will pay for the life of the mortgage will remain the same from the time of the mortgage-closing (say, for example, 7 percent); but with an adjustable rate mortgage, the interest rate will fluctuate depending upon current market borrowing costs. (See Resources Guide at the end of this section for information on finding lenders.)

71 Know the truth about ARMs (adjustable rate mortgages).

With an ARM, your interest rate will change at certain points in time—say once a year. It will be readjusted up or down, depending upon the current market cost of borrowing. You will not be able to calculate the total cost of your mortgage, since it will change from time to time.

Lenders use 2 basic types of measurements to determine the current market rate of interest:

- **The Index:** This is the basis from which your rate will be determined. It is often a number published in the newspaper, like 3-month Treasury bills, LIBOR (London Interbank Offered Rate), or prime rate.
- **The Margin:** This is usually the spread of basis points, which will be added to the index figure to determine what current interest rate you'll pay on your mortgage payments for a particular period of time, e.g., this year's interest.

Here's an example: Your index is based on the prime rate, which is currently 5 percent; your margin is 200 "basis points" over prime—that means your interest rate will be 7 percent.

Most ARMs have caps, or limits on how much you'll have topay on your mortgage. An annual cap will limit how high your interest rate will be allowed to go in a single year; a lifetime cap will limit the amount for the entire term of your mortgage.

Did You Know?

The Math: Adjustable Rate Mortgages

The formula for an ARM is generally:

ARM = INDEX + MARGIN

Example: If the index is 7% treasury rate, and the margin is 2% (or 200 basis points), then the ARM = 7% + 2% = 9%

72 Make sure you understand your ARM cap.

Lifetime caps on ARMs are usually 5 to 6 points—but they are not over your "teaser" rate, which might be lower for the first few months of your mortgage. In our example, your initial rate might be 5 percent, but the actual rate is 7 percent. That means if you have a lifetime cap of 6 points, for example, you could pay as much as 13 percent for your mortgage if your index happens to go up to 11 percent—a rate that was not uncommon during the 1970s and early to mid-1980s.

Trap **Negative Amortization. This means that you may continue to owe money after your mortgage has matured. Here's how: if your index rises 4 percent in one year, and your annual cap is 1 percent (or point) you would owe the 3 percent difference. The interest would be added onto your mortgage's principal amount, thus extending the term of your mortgage payments so you can pay the additional money you owe.**

Tip **Not all ARMs permit negative amortization. Make sure you ask the question and evaluate the answer before agreeing to your mortgage. If your ARM does allow negative amortization, it is limited to 125 percent of the original mortgage, and some sort of arrangement must be made on how to make repayment—either in a lump sum at the end or through a loan extension.**

JUST THE FACTS

The Basics About ARMs

- Adjusted according to a published index, like the 1-year Treasury rate, or the cost-of-funds index (Office of Thrift Supervision)
- Adjusted once a year by the lender, according to current interest rates.
- Capped to a 2-percentage-point increase in any given year
- Capped to a 6-percentage-point increase over the life of the loan.

Trap

ARMs seem to work well for first-time home buyers trying to qualify for a loan. The teaser rate keeps your initial costs down, and your variable rate will drop if interest rates go down. So your interest payments could drop. The problem stems from the fact that because the interest rate varies, you'll have a hard time budgeting for your mortgage payment—one more uncertainty, and a big one. You are exposed to paying much higher rates if interest rates go up, and this could cause you some financial difficulty.

73 Beware of teaser rates.

Just like the name sounds, these are used by the lender to tease you into your mortgage. This isn't necessarily a bad thing, but let's be sure to call it what it is: it's simply an introductory rate, lower than the actual cost you would incur at the time of closing. This gives you lower closing costs and a few initial months of payments at a discount—so it helps make mortgages more accessible to more people. For lenders, this offering makes them more competitive. After a few short months, the rate is back up to what it would have been in the first place.

Tip

If ARMs appeal to you because of the teaser rates, you might want to think about refinancing your house with a fixed rate mortgage as soon as you can. This way you'll get the most out of the lower up-front rates, then take advantage of the security of fixed rate payments each month.

74 Look into fixed rate mortgages.

With a fixed rate, the mortgage's total monthly payment—principal and interest—is at a fixed rate each month. You usually repay principal and interest in monthly installments over the life of a 15-, 20-, or 30-year mortgage.

Tip **In the future, if market interest rates go down, you can still negotiate the loan again to get the benefit of lower interest rates on the balance of your mortgage.**

75 Also explore hybrid mortgages.

Also called multiyear mortgages—offering the best of both worlds—hybrid mortgages may offer an initial fixed rate for about 5 to 10 years (just like a traditional fixed rate mortgage), and then at that time, the rate adjusts at some margin over a specified index (just like a traditional ARM). Since the traditional mortgage only lasts about seven years anyway, this might be a viable option, because the fixed rate is set for that period of time. Before it comes time for the adjustment, you can either refinance your mortgage at a lower rate; pay off the mortgage at closing (if you intend to sell your home); or take your chances and wait to see what happens to interest rates when the fixed rate option expires. (Don't wait too long, however, because if interest rates are moving up, you'll be forced into paying a lot more in interest on your mortgage when your payments start to vary with an escalating index).

Trap **The problem with a hybrid is that at the end of the fixed rate period, if interest rates are low, your choices are either to refinance at a long-term fixed rate, or to have the mortgage payments adjusted to a low index, which might be appear equally attractive. But if interest rates are high, you will be left in a very precarious position: a fixed rate mortgage might be extremely expensive, and the variable rate of an ARM might cause you the same type of financial difficulties it would have had you taken it in the first place.**

76 Calculate the tradeoff between interest rate and points.

The two most important factors involving the cost of your mortgage are interest rate and points. The interest rate is the fee you are charged by the bank for loaning you the money, represented by a percentage. Points are another fee a bank gets for lending you money. Points are different from interest (which you pay regularly for the entire term of the mortgage) because they're paid only once, at the time of closing.

Therefore, points are part of your closing costs. One point equals 1 percent of the loan amount. So 1 point on a $100,000 loan would cost you $1,000, 2 points or 2 percent would be $2,000, and so on.

Did You Know?

The Math: Loan Points

1 "point" equals 1 percent of the loan amount:
1 point on a $100,000 loan = $1,000

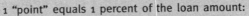

77 Negotiate with your lender on interest rate and points.

Just about everything in life is negotiable. The more points you pay, the lower the interest rate you may get, and vice versa. How should you best position yourself between points and interest rates? That depends on how long you plan to live in your home.

If you plan on living in this home for a brief period of time, you may want to pay less in points with a higher interest rate.

Example:

Here's an illustration of the tradeoff. Let's assume a $100,000, 30-year mortgage. The bank gives you an option: either an 8 percent interest rate 2 points up front, or an 8.25 percent mortgage with only a 1-point payment.

	Upfront Payment	Monthly Payment	Cumulative Payments Year 1	Year 2	Year 5	Year 10	Year 30
8.00%, 2 points	$2,000	$734	$10,808	$19,616	$46,040	$90,080	$266,240
8.25%, 1 point	$1,000	$751	$10,012	$19,024	$46,060	91,120	$271,360

Clearly, the 8 percent loan with the higher up-front payments is more expensive in the early years. But after about year 5, it becomes cheaper than the loan with lower up-front costs. If you're considering this type of tradeoff, ask your lender to show you a table like this so that you understand the cost differences over time between the 2 loans.

Tip

There are places you can go for help—including HSH Associates, which surveys more than 2,000 lenders in 125 major cities. They also publish a weekly list of the best current deals. To get your own copy, call 1-800-UPDATES. You will get a list of about 25 lenders in your area for the nominal cost of $20. You should also consult with your local newspapers to check the banks' advertisements—they'll publish the APRs currently being offered.

JUST THE FACTS

What's an APR, Anyway?

The total cost of a loan, which includes interest rates and points, is called your APR (annual percentage rate). The federal government obligates lenders to tell you what your APR amounts to depending on the variables between points and interest rates.

78 Think carefully about the term of your mortgage.

How long you take to pay your mortgage is another cost factor. The most common term for a mortgage is 30 years. But you can also get 15- and 20-year fixed rate terms as well. The shorter the term of your mortgage, of course, the faster you'll pay it off. And you'll build equity more quickly as well. The disadvantage to a shorter mortgage is that it is more difficult to obtain, and your monthly payments will be higher.

Should you consider a shorter mortgage? Let's consider the same $100,000, 30-year, 8.25 percent mortgage from the previous page. What happens if you want to pay it off in 20 years?

	Up-front Payment	Monthly Payment	Total Outlay	Total Interest
20 Years	$1,000	$852	$204,480	$104,496
30 Years	$1,000	$751	$270,360	$170,456

That's a huge savings if you go with the shorter 20-year loan—nearly $65,000, to be exact—that you'd save in interest. So that's the easy choice—right? Maybe not. Remember, rather than putting that extra $100 a month into your home for 20 years, you could be putting it into an investment: possibly one that pays even more than the 8.25% more you're paying here.

	Mortgage Outlay	Investment Savings	Net
20 years	($204,480)	$174,528*	$29,952
	*$852/month, 10 years, 10% annual return		
30 years	($170,456)	$226,049*	$55,593
	*$100/month, 30 years, 10% annual return		

Over the long run, if you can get a better investment return than your mortgage rate, you're better off taking the longer loan.

79 Avoid prepayment penalties.

If you do opt for a 30-year mortgage, if at all possible, try to get one that does not have prepayment penalties. This will allow you to refinance or repay your mortgage sooner without penalty—should you get that opportunity—giving you a possible future alternative to trying to meet the expensive and restrictive terms of a 15- to 20-year mortgage right now.

Trap

Two types of mortgages you might want to avoid are graduated payment loans and balloon mortgages. Both seem attractive at first blush, but as you investigate further they have very negative terms.

80 Watch out for the downside of graduated payment loans.

This means you do not pay all the interest owed each month. Instead, the unpaid interest accumulates, and is added to the balance of your mortgage. This strategy keeps your monthly mortgage payments low, but that's because the interest is being tacked on to your balance. Should you have to sell your house prematurely, you'll be in deep trouble, unless your house has appreciated in value at the same rate that the interest accumulated to the back end of your mortgage.

Know the advantages of owning your own home.

81 Be careful of the balloon mortgage.

In this scenario, you make small monthly payments for a fixed number of years (between 1 and 7 years), and then you're obligated to repay the remainder of the mortgage in a lump sum. You might want to take this type of loan if you are expecting a large chunk of money to come your way during that period of time—perhaps due to an inheritance—because you can benefit from the lower up-front payments if you know you'll be able to make the balloon payment at the maturity of the loan. Should something go wrong, however, you could lose your home if you can't come up with the balance due or refinance the loan.

Tip

The cost of a loan—Time is money!

What your loan will cost you depends on these factors:

- **the finance charge**
- **fees**
- **the term (or length) of the loan**

You have little control over the rate or fees—but you can borrow money for a shorter period of time. Sometimes, the cheapest loan actually isn't the one with the lowest payments, or even the lowest interest rates. You must calculate your fees with interest rates to figure out your total cost.

82 Don't forget about home ownership perks: the home equity loan.

Sometimes known as a second mortgage, the interest rate on a home equity loan can be either variable or fixed. You can borrow up to 80 percent of your home's market value minus the balance on your mortgage. You'll get all the money in one lump sum, and repay it over 5 to 15 years.

83 Your home equity can be used like a line of credit.

This is a revolving credit arrangement, similar to a credit card. Your credit line is at a fixed amount, and you can write a check for any amount up to that limit. NOTE: Don't use home equity loans or lines of credit to pay off your day-to-day expenses.

Tip

The advantages of a home equity loan or line of credit:

- **They're easy to get.**
- **Rates are usually lower than for personal loans.**
- **Interest can be tax-deductible. (Always check with a tax expert first.)**

Trap

The disadvantages of a home equity loan or line of credit:

- **They can be expensive, if you look at total overall cost.**
- **Even if the value of your home decreases, the loan stays the same.**
- **If you fall behind in your payments, you risk foreclosure.**

"The best way to save money is not to lose it."

—Les Williams

Living within your means pays big dividends.

Buying Your Wheels: Don't Get Taken for a Ride

84 Fallen in love with a car? Before buying, find out if it has a twin.

Before you dash off to spend your hard-earned money, check to see if the car of your dreams has a twin. A twin is a clone of a higher priced car that looks and feels like the same car. (For instance, the Geo Prism is basically a Toyota Corolla in the U.S.) *Consumer Reports* annual issues will give you the inside scoop on twins.

Tip

***The Complete Car Cost Guide* costs about $45, and can be obtained by contacting Intellichoice Inc.: 1-800-227-2665. This invaluable consumer guide evaluates gas consumption, cost of insurance, repair frequency and depreciation, so that you can easily determine average cost. Particularly helpful are the statistics on the cost to operate and maintain each car over a 5-year period of ownership.**

85 Be sure of the mileage.

When looking at pre-owned vehicles, as they are now so cleverly called, remember that the mileage on an average car is 12,000 to 15,000 miles per year. So if you see a 5-year-old car with only 5,000 miles on it you should ask why. There might have been some tampering done to the odometer.

86 Time your purchase if you can.

The best time to buy a car is when the dealer is anxious to sell one to you. One good time is in winter, when salespeople are starved for sales and most potential customers have already spent their savings on Christmas presents.

87 The best deal might be the one you're willing to leave on the table.

One of your greatest powers as a consumer is the option to walk away from a deal. Trust me, the salesperson wants you to own this car more than you do! Until that moment when the salesperson realizes that you'll walk away from the car and the deal, you won't get the best terms available.

88 Read the fine print.

It's easy to get caught up in your desire to own a new car, and to be swept away by the attractive advertisements of clever car dealerships.

For instance, the ad says "only $299 a month," and you can own the car of your dreams! But will these payments become part of your nightmares? So, you see the unbelievable amount of $299 per month for a car you thought would cost you tens of thousands of dollars. You walk into a friendly dealership with an extremely willing salesperson there to immediately wait on you. There's a quick credit report-and voilà! The papers are drawn up and you are the lucky owner of a spanking new car!

It's just not that simple. When the dealer wants you to think in terms of monthly payments, make sure there are not additional amounts tacked on to that $299. What about a down payment?

Ask yourself:

- What is the total cost of the car when all is said and one?
- How does that $299 payment per month stack up against your yearly take-home pay, i.e., what percentage does it represent?

"Whatever you have spend less."

—Samuel Johnson

89 When you make your final payment, what will your new car have cost you?

Let's really look at this dreaded question. Remember to add in taxes, registration, insurance, and maintenance over the 7 or so years it will take you to pay off the loan.

Before you get too emotionally attached to a car, it might be wise to check with a consumer guide before you buy: look at whether or not this particular dream car is expected to be in good shape by the time you would own it free and clear—and what the book value of the car might be when you are ready to trade it in for your next new dream car.

2-Year Loan

Amount	7.00%	8.00%	9.00%	10.00%	11.00%	12.00%
$10,000	$448	$452	$457	$461	$466	$471
$12,000	$537	$543	$548	$554	$559	$565
$15,000	$672	$678	$685	$692	$699	$706
$20,000	$895	$905	$914	$923	$932	$941
$25,000	$1,119	$1,131	$1,142	$1,154	$1,165	$1,177

Total layout for a $10,000, 10% loan: $461 x 24 months = $11,064

3-Year Loan

Amount	7.00%	8.00%	9.00%	10.00%	11.00%	12.00%
$10,000	$309	$313	$318	$323	$327	$332
$12,000	$371	$376	$382	$387	$393	$399
$15,000	$463	$470	$477	$484	$491	$498
$20,000	$618	$627	$636	$645	$655	$664
$25,000	$772	$783	$795	$807	$818	$830

Total layout for a $10,000, 10% loan: $323 x 36 = $11,628

"Having money is rather like being a blond. It is more fun but not vital."

—Mary Quant

5-Year Loan

Amount	7.00%	8.00%	9.00%	10.00%	11.00%	12.00%
$10,000	$198	$203	$208	$212	$217	$222
$12,000	$238	$243	$249	$255	$261	$267
$15,000	$297	$304	$311	$319	$326	$334
$20,000	$396	$406	$415	$425	$435	$445
$25,000	$495	$507	$519	$531	$544	$556

Total layout for a $10,000, 10% loan: $212 x 60 months = $12,720

As you can see, by stretching out your loan period, you can lower your monthly payment significantly. But keep in mind that you'll be paying more in interest over time by doing so. If you choose to pay off a $10,000 car over 5 years rather than 2, your monthly payment will drop from $461 to $212, but you'll be paying $1,656 more over time. To get an idea of what your total payout will be, just multiply your monthly payments by the total number of months in the loan term.

THINGS TO THINK ABOUT

Time Is Money

Let's look at 3 different terms on the same $13,500 car loan at 12 percent:

- After the third year, it would cost you a total of about $16,200
- After 4 years, about $17,200
- At the end of 5 years, that same $13,500 car would cost you $18,200—an additional $1,000 for each year of the loan.

When you consider that any car depreciates in value as soon as you drive it off the lot—you are getting a double whammy!

90 Do your homework before you hit the dealership.

Check out deals for a car loan at several different financial institutions, including your bank (which wants to keep your business), several competitive banks, and a credit union. A credit union will probably offer you the lowest initial interest rate, but your personal bank, where you keep your savings and checking accounts, might be willing to match that rate, so at least give them the opportunity. Sometimes you can negotiate a lower rate if you are willing to have the bank withdraw the payments directly from your savings or checking account.

Shop around: in some cities, the interest rate spread between one bank and another can be as much as 4 percentage points. In the end, a difference of even half of 1 percentage point can save you $1,000 to $5,000, depending on the bank.

91 Cut a deal on the exact price of your car before negotiating terms.

This will give you much more leverage on the cost of the car itself. If you let the salesperson start to get into the financing of the loan before the price of the car has been established, it could end up costing you much more in the long run.

92 Never, ever pay sticker price.

Most dealerships jack up the price of a car by 10 to 20 percent. Check with *Money* and *Consumer Reports*, which estimate dealers' costs—then aim to buy your car at just 5 percent over those costs.

93 Always be skeptical of deals offering no money down.

Remember, no one gives away anything totally for free. Find out how much more it will cost you in the end if you don't have to pay any up-front money.

94 When it comes to car loans, the shorter the loan the better.

The average length of a car loan is about 4 years. If you can afford it, try to get a loan under 4 years. Since a car loan is probably going to be one of the highest debts you'll carry, try to keep it to the fewest number of years you possibly can.

95 Master the leasing-versus-buying tradeoff.

Choosing a car also means choosing how to pay for it. Everyone would love to buy that dream car. But is buying always the best deal? First you have to borrow the money. But maybe you should just borrow the car! Either way, you must apply for credit.

With a car loan, the bank lends you the money and you repay the principal plus interest in monthly installments for a period of 3 to 5 years. You can pay off the loan at any time. You can put as many miles on the car as you wish, and maintain the services of the car. Insurance is your responsibility, and if the car gets stolen, your insurance company will settle with you.

If you lease a car—or "borrow" it, if you will—you must pay a full lease amount. There are mileage limits, often 12,000 to 15,000 miles per year, so you'd have to pay a mileage charge of 10 to 15 cents for any miles over that limit. Maintenance is your responsibility, but some leases specify that the dealer will make any repairs. You arrange for insurance, but if the car gets stolen or totaled in an accident, you must still pay the leasing company its cash value plus any past due payments.

Tip **If you can pay cash for a car, or have enough for a down payment, buy a car outright. But if you have no cash, leasing a car might be your answer. You are paying only part of the car's actual costs, and you don't have to worry about depreciation or loss of value.**

"Money is always there but pockets change."
—Gertrude Stein

Tip

The greatest financial appeal of leasing is the low up-front costs: You pay a leasing fee of only $500 or less, depending on the car, plus one month's payment and 1 additional month as a security deposit. And if you're swapping an old lease for a new one, you might even be able to avoid these charges altogether.

Did You Know?

The Leasing Trend

Twenty-seven out of every 100 new car deals are leased rather than bought outright. Why the growth? Because with car prices escalating, it might turn out to be cheaper to lease than to buy. And the concept of turning your car in every 2 years for a new one is extremely attractive.

96 Know the difference between a closed-end and open-end lease.

In a closed-end lease, both the lease period and the monthly payments are fixed. You also have a fixed price for the car if you wish to purchase it at the end of the lease period. With an open-end lease, both the lease period and the price you'd have to pay if you decided to buy the car vary with the market value and the car's condition at the end of the lease period.

Additional factors to consider before leasing a car:

97 Look at the lease rate.

While there isn't an interest rate charge on your lease, there is a comparable charge called the lease rate, or the money factor. Ask your leasing agent to give you that figure so you can calculate what the comparable interest rate is that you'd be paying for a lease.

"It's just as easy to be happy with a lot of money as with a little."

—Marvin Traub

*"From birth to age 18, a girl needs good parents,
from 18 to 35 she needs good looks,
from 35 to 55 she needs a good personality,
and from 55 on she needs cash."*

—Sophie Tucker

98 Find out the actual price of the car on which the terms of your lease are based.

In leasing jargon, this figure is called your net capitalized cost. You should be aware of this figure, since it is comparable to the price you would pay if you were going to buy the car at the time of the signing your lease agreement.

99 Determine the probable value of the car at the end of your lease.

You should consult the *Automotive Leaser Guide*'s Residual Percentage Guide. This costs about $12.50, and you can order it by calling 1-800-418-8450. A high residual value might be better for you (and automobile manufacturers are often motivated to assign a higher residual value in order to close a leasing deal), because your monthly payments are based on how much the car will depreciate during the lease period. A higher residual value means lower depreciation, and therefore lower monthly payments. NOTE: This could backfire on you, however, if you plan to buy the car outright at the end of your lease period. Of course, at that time you'd once again have the ability to haggle over the residual value with the leasing company.

Tip **There is a computer program called Expert Lease that costs about $50 ($100 for the deluxe version) that will help you do an analysis of whether or not to lease or buy a car. For details, call 1-800-418-8450.**

"Nothing buys happiness, but money can certainly hire it for short periods in expensive restaurants or careless weeks on Austrian skis."

— Irma Kurtz, Writer

Saving Big on the Little Stuff

100 Shop smart. Discipline yourself, and you'll save money.

- Take only cash with you, and leave most (or all) of your credit cards at home.
- Be careful not to fall for items just because they're "on sale." A bargain isn't necessarily a bargain until it's been reduced by at least 40 percent.
- Keep your credit card balance as low as possible. (Zero is best.) Don't buy something if you can't afford to pay back the full balance when the bill comes, unless you absolutely need it.

THINGS TO THINK ABOUT

Stretching Your Entertainment Dollars

Does your new budget leave next to nothing for the fun stuff? Try a few of these tips for stretching your entertainment dollar.

- Cook at home as often as possible. Make it fun—have a barbeque, turn it into a picnic with the family—have everyone pitch in and make their own special dishes.
- Rent a movie instead of going to the theatre.
- Be creative about your vacation plans. Drive to your next vacation or use bonuses—like frequent flyer miles (which you should be trying to collect, by the way, through your credit cards, telephone bills, etc.)
- Plan ahead on your gift-giving. You will have the time to give something thoughtful (even handmade), and will probably save money, too. (We all know what it's like to rush out and overspend on a gift because we've waited until the last minute.) Consider drawing names during big gift-giving holidays to cut back on everyone's spending.

101 Develop discipline at the grocery store.

When buying an item, make sure to check the shelves thoroughly. Grocery stores often place the most expensive items in clear view, while the generic and cheaper brands are on the bottom shelf.

Comparison shop. Often you can buy the same items at another grocery store for a lot less. Get in the habit of noticing which stores carry the items you normally buy and compare prices. If it's worth it—in time, money, and convenience—split your grocery bill between a couple of different places and you'll save money.

102 Consider the truth behind buying in bulk.

Buying in bulk doesn't always mean you're saving money. Although you can sometimes save 30 to 50 percent this way, let the buyer beware. Usually, the price listing on the shelf includes the price per ounce in small print next to the price of the item; this will tell you what the savings are, if any.

Don't get carried away when shopping at a warehouse supermarket.

Ask yourself:

- Do I really need it?
- Will I really be able to make use of these quantities? Or will the items just go to waste?

Trap

In your enthusiasm to save money, don't underestimate the value of your time. I've been guilty of this "do-it-yourself" mistake a few times—spending hours trying to install a computer program, or painting a room myself. I might have saved a little money, but I lost valuable time that I could have used to earn money too. Know when to call the experts and get back to your job.

103 Find out the truth about your long-distance phone bill.

If you're confused about which long-distance phone company is offering the best deal, you're not alone. With hundreds of long-distance carriers offering dozens of calling plans, there's no simple solution to finding the best deal.

If you're still paying standard rates, it's like paying the sticker price on a new car. Yet a majority of consumers are paying basic rates for long-distance phone calls. If you're one of those people, there are some things you can do right now to save money:

Do your homework. Let's check out some of the discount plans at the Big Three—AT&T, MCI, and Sprint—which are constantly changing:

- AT&T offers a flat rate of 15 cents a minute 24 hours a day.
- MCI has one plan that offers 12 cents a minute 24 hours a day, when you spend $15 or more per month.
- Sprint offers 10 cents a minute for calls between 7 p.m. and 7 a.m., undercutting both AT&T and MCI by a few pennies.

Then there are the lesser-known companies—Allnet, LDDS WorldCom, and LCI, which might offer you a better price than the Big Three, but the quality and service may not be as good. (And they may charge a monthly minimum rate, which could get costly, if you don't make very many calls.)

104 Get the best airline deals.

We all know how expensive airlines have become. Especially during holidays and other peak seasons, when many of us want to travel to visit our loved ones, it is difficult to find a low price. Airline ticket prices have become as volatile as the stock market, changing daily, sometimes hourly—so it's hard to keep up with the cheapest fares. The good news is, if you look long enough, fares are still cheap, even during peak travel times.

Here are a few other tips to help keep your airfares down:

- Some airlines offer lower fares if you can depart on a Saturday and return on a Tuesday.
- Always ask the airline for your options. Sometimes just leaving at a different time of day (e.g., taking the "red-eye" late-night flight), flying through a particular city on your way to your destination, or simply choosing a different airport at your destination, can all make a tremendous difference in price.

Ask Lorraine

Q. *I feel uncomfortable going through friends and family to find a job. Won't they think I'm using them?*

A. This part of networking makes a lot of people uneasy. Many people also let their pride get in the way—they don't like to ask for help from a friend. My approach has also been a direct one—I tell the person I'm calling that I'm looking for a job, right from the start. That way you don't appear to be misleading or insincere.

Q. *I'm happy in my job, but I get lots of calls from headhunters asking me to consider other positions. I admit I'm curious, but I'm afraid that it would get back to my office here. Should I go?*

A. Yes! If it makes it easier, think of it as a fact-finding mission. It's always smart to know what other options you have. For example, if you find out that another job would pay you 20% more, you'll certainly have more leverage the next time you talk money with your boss.

Q. *Can I borrow money for my down payment?*

A. You probably can, with a motivated seller. The seller might take back paper as a second or even a third mortgage. You also might be able to do a trade—a boat, a mobile home, a car, stocks or bonds—in lieu of a cash down payment. It's worth a try. If you don't ask, you'll never know!

Q. *How does leasing a home with an option to buy work?*

A. Some lenders refer to this as an equity-release method of financing. Under this method, part of your monthly payment is credited toward your eventual purchase price.

Q. *How can I get the money I need?*

A. Brokerage accounts. Borrow against stocks, bonds, or mutual funds, using them as collateral. This is also called borrowing on margin. (See Section 5).

- Life insurance policies. Borrow against the cash value of your insurance policy.
- Real estate, cars, jewelry. Borrow against the value of high-value assets.
- Credit card balance. Borrow against the line of credit you have on your credit cards. Use only as a last resort, if this is a short-term fix and you are very confident you can pay off this high interest rate fast.

Q. *Can we use the money we've put away in our retirement accounts for a down payment on a home?*

A. Yes. Many companies with 401k plans allow their employees to borrow against their account balances at a low interest rate to buy a home. The limit is most often 50 percent of your balance—check with your company for their restrictions.

Q. *What kinds of information will we need to give a lender when applying for a home loan?*

A. If you use a real estate agent, they will walk you through this exercise. But as a general rule, a lender will want to see the following:

- Your financials: W-2s, etc. to document what you earned last year before taxes. This also includes a list of your assets—what you own: stocks, bonds, homes, boats, cars, cash value of life insurance policies, savings and checking accounts, etc., as well as a list of your liabilities—what you owe: credit card balances (including limits), and other loans (for car, vacation, college, etc.). NOTE: If you're self-employed, the lender will want to see your last two federal tax returns and a financial statement. You might also be required to provide a profit and loss statement for your business.
- Your social security number.
- Your previous address if you haven't lived at the current address for two years or more.

Q. *No matter how hard I try to enforce some discipline over our household finances, we seem to go overboard on the extras here and there. What system might work for us?*

A. For many families, the simple envelope system can work miracles. Once a month, place the amount of money you'd like to spend on specific items into designated envelopes (like "eating out," "gasoline," etc.). This system seems to work well, because it's so basic—when the money's gone, it's gone—and may teach your family to plan better the next month.

Q. *No matter how well prepared I am before I go to a car dealership, I always seem to come away confused. How can I force the salesperson to keep it simple?*

A. The key thing to remember with a salesperson is to be firm. If a salesperson wants to sell you a car, he or she should be able to explain the details in your language. Be sure that you understand how much the TOTAL PRICE will be of the car, with interest, extras, and tax included. You should also know exactly what your payments will be every month for your car loan and for your insurance. Even further, they should be able to pinpoint those three numbers for different models, so you have a fair comparison.

Resource Guide

Finding the Lender for You

- Contact the National Council of State Housing Agencies for the phone number of your state housing agency—they'll provide you with a list of lenders.

  NCSHA
  444 North Capitol Street NW, Suite 438
  Washington, DC 20001
  Call: 202-624-7710
  Web site: *www.ncsha.org*

- HSH Associates compiles an excellent survey of the best current deals.
  1-800-UPDATES

Credit Issues

- Get your credit report quick and easy through *TRW*
  Call: 1-800-682-7654
- Start with Debtors Anonymous, at
  314 W. 53rd Street
  New York, NY 10019
  212-969-0710

Car-Buying Resources

- *The Complete Car Cost Guide* is an excellent resource.
  Call: 1-800-227-2665
- Edmund's Consumer Information Experts have an excellent Web site with lots of tips and pricing guidelines, both new and used cars at
  www.edmunds.com
- *Kelly Blue Book* is probably the most accepted new and used car pricing guide. Pick up the most recent copy at your bookstore or magazine stand, or see the Web site at
  www.kbb.com

Leasing versus Buying

- Get the Automotive Lease Guide's *Residual Percentage Guide*:
  1-800-418-8450

Travel Information

- Web sites worth visiting include The SABRE Group's travel site at *www.travelocity.com.*

Section 3

Shop for the bank that offers more for your money.
BANK
Passbook

Banking Basics

It's hard to imagine how our economy could function without credit. Yet it wasn't until 1916 when Arthur Morris originated the installment loan that credit became accessible to everyone. The Morris Plan was launched despite conventional wisdom that lending money to working people was a plan doomed to fail.

Banks have made their living on the credit needs of consumers, and for most, it's a win-win relationship. Face it, we need the myriad services banks offer, from credit cards and checking accounts to cashier's checks and ATM cards. It seems, however, that many people are dissatisfied with their banking relationships.

Well, if you're one of those people, do something about it. Like any industry, banking is competitive and needs customers like you to stay alive. Comparison shop and be brutally honest about what you absolutely need and what you think you need.

Chances are that once you really see what you're spending on the "little things" like ATM visits, you'll reevaluate your banking decisions. That means either changing banks or changing your habits. Either way you'll find simple ways to save money, not to mention angst.

Credit: How to Get It, How to Keep It

105 Buy now and pay later?

Every time you borrow money or use your credit card to make a purchase, you're using credit. Credit is more available today than in any other time in history; it's become the American Way. Credit can be a good thing, but it can also easily get out of control. It serves us well to recall times not so long ago, when workers owed their very lives to the company store, and farmers lost their homesteads to banks.

On the positive side, credit has given all of us the ability to live better, by letting us buy the things we want now and paying them off through regular monthly bills—rather than having to wait. It's not impossible to use credit wisely. But you must be very careful that you don't get overextended.

106 Get a handle on your debt.

If your total debt is more than 20 percent of your annual take-home pay (excluding mortgage payments), you need to start cutting back, now.

107 Find out the truth about credit.

Finance companies usually charge a higher interest rate than banks, which usually charge more than credit unions.

A loan that is secured by assets—car, home, stocks—costs less than an unsecured loan, which is backed only by your word. Some assets are viewed as better collateral than others, e.g., a new car is better than a used one, etc.

The longer the term of a loan, the lower the monthly payments. However, the longer you take to pay, the more the loan will cost you in the end, because of the interest.

Worksheet: Adding Up Your Debt

First, list all of your types of debt.

Credit cards	$
Car loan	$
Student loans	$
Bank lines of credit	$
Other	$
	$
	$
Total	$ (a)

Now, multiply your after-tax earnings for the year by 20%:

Annual earnings (after-tax)	$
x 20%	$ (b)

Is line (a) larger than line (b)? If not, you've probably got a reasonable debt load. But if it is, then you should start paying if off, and soon.

108 Restructure your personal balance sheet.

Prevention is still the best cure: don't get into too much debt in the first place. While credit cards can sometimes help you through tough financial times, if not used carefully, they can keep you at a permanent deficit, and even threaten your good credit standing.

Consider getting rid of most of your credit cards if you have a hard time controlling your spending. Just have one or two, and only choose accounts that charge the lowest interest rate possible.

"A bank is a place that will lend you money if you can prove that you don't need it."

—Bob Hope

109 Start a system to repay your debts.

There are two things you can do right now to get yourself in financial shape:

- If you have any savings, use them to pay off your high-rate debt. Often, the best use of your money is not to earn 2 percent interest in a savings account, but instead to pay off that 15 percent credit card debt.

  In other words, you'll earn $20 on that $1000 sitting in your 2 percent savings account, while that $1000 balance on your 15 percent credit card will cost you $150. It's clearly wiser to use that savings to pay off your credit card.

  In finance, this is called cost of carry—the rate at which it costs you to borrow money versus the amount you're earning on your invested money.
- Transfer your debt from high rates to lower rates by refinancing your existing loans and switching credit card balances to those with lower interest rates.

110 Pay off high-interest debt first.

Identify the debts with the highest interest rates: they're costing you the most, so pay those off first. Then work your way through your lower-rate debts, such as student loans, and pay them off last.

111 Find low-cost ways to pay off high-interest debts.

Be creative:

- Borrow against the cash value of your life insurance policy.
- Borrow against your employer's retirement account.
- Sell investments held outside of retirement accounts.
- Sell something of value you don't really need.
- Borrow against the equity of your home.
- Borrow from family and friends at a lower interest rate (or interest-free).

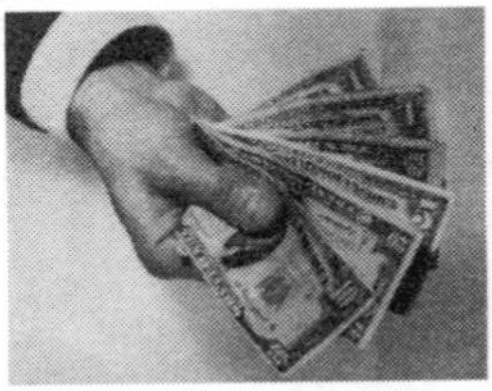

Save money by paying off debt first.

Paying Off Your Debt: How Long Will it Take?

Use this table to get an idea of how much time it will take to pay off your debt. At the top of the columns, find your total balance, and then your interest rate along the left. We've given you a few scenarios ($20, $50, $100, and $200 per month) to provide a ballpark estimate of how many months it will take to pay off your balance.

If you can pay $20 per month...

	$1,000	$2,000	$5,000	$7,500	$10,000
8%	61	165	never!	never!	never!
10%	65	216	never!	never!	never!
12%	70	never!	never!	never!	never!
14%	75	never!	never!	never!	never!
16%	83	never!	never!	never!	never!
20%	108	never!	never!	never!	never!

If you can pay $50 per month...

8%	21	47	165	never!	never!
10%	22	49	216	never!	never!
12%	22	51	never!	never!	never!
14%	23	54	never!	never!	never!
16%	23	58	never!	never!	never!
20%	24	66	never!	never!	never!

If you can pay $100 per month...

8%	10	22	61	104	165
10%	10	22	65	118	216
12%	11	22	70	139	never!
14%	11	23	75	179	never!
16%	11	23	83	never!	never!
20%	11	25	108	never!	never!

If you can pay $200 per month...

8%	5	10	27	43	61
10%	5	10	28	45	65
12%	5	11	29	47	70
14%	5	11	30	50	75
16%	5	11	21	52	83
20%	5	11	33	59	108

112 Resist temptation.

Here are some good ways to get yourself back on the right track:

- Ask to have your credit card limits reduced. This will slow down your spending.
- Better yet, get rid of your extra credit cards, and only keep one. Don't even carry it with you. Use it only as a last resort in an emergency.
- The best choice of all is to cut up all of your credit cards. Just a few decades ago, people didn't even have credit cards. We paid with cash or check—that's it. Why not try that again today?
- A good alternative to credit cards is a charge card—such as American Express. With a charge card, you pay no interest, but you are forced to pay off the full balance each month. This very good discipline will keep you on your financial toes.

113 Make responsible credit card buys.

Try to limit your credit card spending to purchases that last, e.g., furniture, appliances, dishes, or clothing. These are items that might be necessary for your household, and they'll be around for a few years or more. Stay away from using credit cards for meals, movies, and entertainment: they're here today, gone tomorrow.

Tip

Whenever you go window shopping, go with only a little bit of cash in your pocket, and leave the plastic at home. This will prevent you from buying on a whim. If you really like or need an item, you'll make the effort to return to the store at some other time to make your purchase.

114 What about bankruptcy?

An alarming 1 million Americans file for bankruptcy protection every year. That's about 1 out of every 100 households.

In some cases, filing for bankruptcy can allow you a little peace of mind, give you some breathing room, and remove the overwhelming stress of being in debt. The types of debt you can walk away from are: credit cards, medical bills, utilities and back rent. Debts that cannot be discharged are: child care, alimony, and court-ordered damages, such as drunk driving settlements. What you get to keep when you file for bankruptcy varies by state, city, and region.

Here are the pros and cons of filing for personal bankruptcy:

Pros

- You get legal protection from your creditors.
- You can resolve your debts working within a time frame you set.
- You won't lose your home.
- The IRS can't seize your property for lack of payment on back taxes.
- You'll have a chance to start over.

Cons

- Loss of privacy: The filing of bankruptcy opens up your financial records to the court, and to the public. The court will have control over disbursing assets and working with creditors to pay off your debts.
- Damaged credit: Bankruptcy remains on your record for about 10 years.
- Some debts may still be outstanding.
- You will lose some assets.
- Filing fees and court costs add up: Ironically, it costs money to file for bankruptcy—from about $200 if you do it yourself to $1,000 or more if you pay a lawyer to do all the paperwork for you.

115 Think about borrowing from family and friends.

Borrowing money from those you love may be your only way out of debt. But it can also complicate your relationship, unless you carefully follow borrowing etiquette.

Sometimes the best intentions—people you love deciding to lend you money—can end up backfiring. I've seen many families torn apart due to conflicts about money. So when your parents generously offer to lend you the money to pay off that $3,000 balance on your credit card compounding away at 18 percent, here are some steps you can take to ensure a pleasant transaction:

116 Borrowing from family: make sure the deal is good for both parties.

Pay back the money with interest at a rate you both agree is fair: say 5 to 8 percent. That's a good deal for you since it's much less than the 18 percent you're currently paying; and it's a good deal for your parents, because they're probably only getting (at the most right now) about 4 percent interest from their savings account.

117 Treat it as a business transaction.

Put everything in writing. Draft an agreement that includes the terms of the loan, like the dates each payment is due, the interest rate and how it will be calculated, whether you have to pay a fee for a late payment, and when you are expected to finish paying the loan. This sounds pretty formal, but it helps avoid any confusion or family strife.

118 Make sure there aren't any negative tax consequences.

This may sound strange, but the IRS sets a minimum interest rate—called the applicable federal rate or AFR—that family members and friends are required to charge on loans. So even if your parents want to lend you money without charging you any interest, they might have to pay taxes on the interest you should have paid but didn't. The rules are complicated, so check out the current tax guides for more details. Look in the index under "loans." For the current AFR, check with your bank or local IRS office.

The Perfect Match: Finding the Right Credit Card for You

119 Find the credit card for your spending habits.

If you're going to use a credit card, you might as well look into getting one that charges the lowest interest rate. There are two ways to handle your balance: you can carry a balance from month to month, or you can pay in full every 30 days. If you always pay in full each month, you won't have to worry about a charge. But if you carry a monthly balance, you'll want to get the best deal you can. Interest rates vary wildly, so do your homework. The current standard rate is about 17 percent, and some (especially department store cards) can go as high as 21 percent.

According to RAM Research's Web site (www.ramresearch.com), the credit cards with some of the lowest rates in the country as of May 1998 are:

- Next Card, 2.90%, No Annual Fee (CA)
- First USA Bank, 5.9%, No Annual Fee (DE)
- People's Bank, 5.9%, No Annual Fee (CT)
- Commerce Bank, 6.9%, No Annual Fee (NE)

Even if these are out-of-town banks, you can still call them to obtain a credit card.

Tip

Looking for the credit card with the lowest interest rate? Check out an organization called Bankcard Holders of America for more details on how to get and keep a credit card. They can also give you a list of institutions that offer secured credit cards. Bankcard Holders of America, 524 Branch Drive, Salem, VA 24153.

Trap **Watch out for those sneaky credit card hikes! There have been cases where credit card companies have raised their introductory rates from 6 percent to 13 percent, even before the promised expiration date. The only way to protect yourself against being overcharged by your credit card company is to check your statement carefully every month. Watch for notices of new rates or fees that the issuer may slip into your bill. To find out who oversees your credit card company, call Consumers Action, a nonprofit group, at 415-777-9635.**

120 Get a credit card that fits your lifestyle.

Finding the right credit card is like finding the perfect outfit. Make sure it fits you well. Look for a credit card that best meets your personal spending habits. If you tend towards carrying a monthly balance, find one that has the lowest possible interest rate. If you pay off your balance at the end of every month, the interest rate charged won't concern you, but stay away from those that do not provide a grace period (a period of time that a lender will allow before they start charging you interest).

Things to Think About

Taming Your Credit Card Habit

If you can't keep your credit cards in your wallet, if the ink wears off the numbers a few months after you get a card and the magnetic strip is worn out before you've paid the first month's balance, here are some helpful techniques to deal with your habit:

- Don't carry your cards with you. This way you'll have to go home before making a purchase—which may give you just the cooling off period you need.
- If that doesn't work, try putting all your cards in a bowl of water and freezing them in the freezer.
- If you find yourself charging a blow torch over the phone to get at those frozen cards, it may be time to cut them up.

Remember, for most of us, credit card debt is the most expensive debt we carry. If the cards are a convenience at a minor interest cost, that's great. But there's great danger in the freedom they give you.

If you do pay off your balance at the end of the month, look for cards with perks you can use, e.g., some cards offer frequent flyer miles that will credit you mileage for every dollar you charge.

121 Consider what you'll need to qualify for a credit card.

Only 4 out of 10 applicants for low-interest credit cards are actually approved to receive one. Here are some factors a lender will consider:

- **Annual pay:** Usually you'll need to earn a minimum of $10,000 per year.
- **Stability:** An issuer would prefer that you have been at your current job for at least one year. They also like to see that you have lived at the same residence for at least a year as well.
- **How much you owe:** They'll divide your monthly debt by your income (called debt to income ratio) to see where you stand. The average is about 35 to 45 percent (i.e., if your annual income is $35,000, and your total debt is $10,000, then your ratio would 29 percent).
- **Potential debt and amount of usage:** To figure this, issuers will calculate the ratio of your outstanding debt to your potential debt, i.e., the sum of the credit limits on all of your credit cards. (If your outstanding debt is $5,000, but you have limits for up to $10,000, then your usage ratio would be 50 percent.)
- **Credit history:** If you have a habit of paying your bills up to 30 days late or more, or if you were late more than 60 days in the past four years, your credit rating is tainted. Depending on the creditor, this will probably restrict you from getting a low-interest credit card.

"Life is short and so is money."

—Bertolt Brecht

Did You Know?

Pay Off Your Debts

At least two-thirds of credit card holders today tend to carry a monthly balance. Don't be one of those people. Set a goal now to pay off your debts as quickly as possible.

122 Credit card secrets for those in the know.

Here are a few pointers to help you get the most while spending the least on your credit card bills:

- Understand how your interest is being calculated. The typical method a lender will use in determining your interest charges is called the **average daily balance method**:

  If you owe \$3,000 at the beginning of the month, but pay off \$1,000 on the 15th, then your average balance was \$2,500 ((3,000 x ½) + (2,000 x ½)).

  If your annual credit card rate rate is 15 percent (1.25 percent per month) then your finance charge should be \$31.25.
- Another more expensive method is called the **previous balance method**:

  In the example above, your 1.25 percent interest would be calculated from your \$3,000 balance at the beginning of the month: 1.25% x \$3,000 = \$37.50.
- Pay off your monthly bill as soon as it arrives. If you do, you won't be charged any interest that month.
- Increase your monthly payments (pay more than just the minimum), and don't miss any payments.
- Most issuers offer low monthly minimum payments of about 2 percent to 3 percent of your monthly balance. But you should always pay more. Why? For instance, if you choose to pay only the 2 percent minimum each month on a \$1,000 balance at an interest rate of 20 percent (\$20 a month) it will take you more than 6 years to pay it off, and it will cost you \$580 in interest!

- If you do not qualify for a low-interest credit card, at least try to get one that offers a teaser rate, i.e., a lower rate for the first 6 to 12 months. After that time, the rate increases dramatically. But if you can pay off your debts before the higher rate kicks in, you'll be OK. If not, you might again be able to transfer your higher-interest debt to another card with a low teaser rate.
- Not worth the trouble? Consider this: if you transfer your $2,500 balance from your 18 percent credit card to the 5.9 percent teaser rate on a new one for even 6 months, you'll save about $150 in interest charges.

JUST THE FACTS

The Math: Calculating your Finance Charges

Balance at Beginning of Month:	$3,000
Payment on the 15th:	$1,000
Average Balance:	$2,500 [(3,000 x 1/2) + (2,000 x 1/2)]
Annual Credit Card Rate:	15%
Monthly Rate:	1.25% (15% ÷ 12)
Average Daily Balance Method:	**1.25% x $2,500 = $31.25**
Previous Balance Method:	**1.25% x $3,000 = $37.50**

123 Check out your credit card and charge card options.

Traditional credit cards such as Mastercard, Visa, Discover, and Optima allow you to charge purchases up to a set limit, which is called your credit limit. This amount can range from $500 to $1,000 or more for each credit card. Your available credit is your credit limit minus the amount you've spent (and haven't paid off) on the card so far. Credit cards allow you to carry a monthly balance and will charge you interest on that balance. Whenever your balance is paid in full, your credit limit is restored to its full amount.

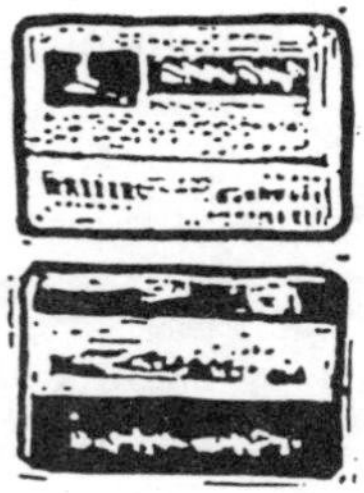

Travel and entertainment cards including American Express, Diners Club and Carte Blanche allow you to charge purchases, but require you to pay your bill in full each month. You are charged an annual maintenance fee for having the card. You can also get additional services with these types of cards, such as discounts on hotels and rental cars.

Department store cards are similar to credit cards, but are for use in a particular store. They allow you to make purchases in that store, carry a balance, and charge you interest. Most department stores today, however, also accept both traditional credit cards and travel and entertainment cards.

Tip

When evaluating a credit card, look at more than just interest rate and annual fee. Some cards offer frequent flyer miles for every dollar spent, credits toward gift items, and points toward a car purchase.

Other cards pile on extra charges for: late payments, immediate interest on cash advances, and a fee for exceeding your credit limit.

124 What about debit cards?

Debit cards aren't credit cards. They work more like paying by check. Using them wisely is a great way to discipline your spending. When you use a debit card, the retailer takes money directly out of your bank account for the amount of the purchase. A debit card looks and feels like a typical plastic credit card, but it's more like an ATM card, because your cash is taken at the point of sale.

You can use your debit card to withdraw cash from your ATM or to transfer money from one account to another, and you can use it to purchase goods and services, just like a checking account. There is usually no fee charged to use a debit card, and no interest is charged, since you are simply utilizing your own money. They are issued by a financial institution, usually your bank. Mastercard and Visa also offer debit cards.

125 There's always the secured credit card option.

If you don't have a credit history, or if you have defaulted on a loan or declared bankruptcy within the last few years, you probably won't be able to get a standard credit card approvedby a lender. Instead, consider a secured credit card, which allows you to provide collateral by depositing money into a special savings account to cover your credit card limit. In some cases, you'll only be permitted to charge what's in the savings account or less, but in others, you'll be allowed to charge more.

Secured cards charge higher interest rates, plus you may not receive any interest on your deposited money. But it can be a good way to build or rebuild a credit history. You should do your homework on this type of credit card if you're interested. Send $10 to RAM Research Special Report, Secured Credit cards, P.O. Box 1700, Frederick, MD 21702. Or for the short list, send $4 to Bankcard Holders of America, 524 Branch Drive, Salem, VA 24153.

126 Be smart about so-called rebate cards.

Used correctly, rebate cards can be a great way to save money. Most cards give you some kind of rebate based on your amount of purchases—say, 1 percent of every $1,000 you charge. But be careful: these kinds of cards often build in higher charges or fees which more than offset your "rebates."

Tip **For more info on various rebate card deals, visit: www.ramresearch.com/cardtrak/surveys/rebate.html or call RAM Research "CardTrak" at 1-800-344-7714 for a full report.**

127 Are "smart" cards really smart?

A smart card, also called a chip card, looks like a conventional plastic credit card, but instead of charging on it, you purchase it with a certain amount of money, then spend against it for up to the amount of money it holds. You've probably seen these around as "phone cards" that come in various denominations and allow the user to make long-distance phone calls and then either dispose of them or have them reactivated with a new dollar amount. For those who want to avoid the burden of credit, but want—and need—the convenience, smart cards offer a viable alternative.

ATMs, Checking, & Other Banking Perks

"Never ask of money spent/Where the spender thinks it went./Nobody was ever meant/To remember or invent/What he did with every cent."

— Robert Frost

Today, there are about 35 percent fewer banks in the United States, largely due to mergers, acquisitions, and consolidations. Deregulation allowed all kinds of financial institutions to offer the same type of services, so that now there is are few differences between a traditional commercial bank, a savings and loan, or thrift.

Today you can also go to other types of financial institutions that are non-banks to handle your money matters. But it's probably a good idea to have a relationship with a local bank in case you need a signature guarantee. Dropping by the neighborhood bank is very convenient.

128 Look closely at bank fees.

Since there are many different types of services you can obtain at a bank, you should check out the difference in fees from one type of service to another. Also, bear in mind that fees are not uniformly high at one bank and low at another. It makes sense to shop around.

129 Limit your ATM use.

Just as you probably need to cut back on your credit card spending, you should probably limit your use of the ATM, because all of these transactions can cost you money.

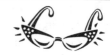

Personal Perspective

"For those of us on the run who don't like to wait, ATMs (Automated Teller Machines) have become part of our lives—just like cable TV, cellular phones, and the Internet. But ATMs actually began appearing on the scene over 20 years ago. At that time, banks begged their clients to try the new machines, because most people were very reluctant to trust their money to a newfangled machine rather than to a real live banker. Not only were your ATM transactions free, banks offered attractive premiums—from balloons for the kids, to hamburger coupons, to candy. It was a way to get us addicted, and it worked!"

130 Restrict your ATM visits.

Consider limiting yourself to using your ATM card once a week, or about 4 times per month, if possible. Depending on your bank, using the ATM can get expensive for each transaction, particularly if you have a habit of taking out only the money you need today. Try to gauge how much money you'll need for the week, and take just enough out of the ATM. Then promise yourself you'll spend only what you have.

131 Avoid using other banks' ATMs.

This little convenience can get very expensive. The charge for using an ATM outside of your own bank's network can be as high as $2 per transaction.

132 Look at specific ATM fees your bank might charge.

For instance, your bank might charge you for transferring money between your accounts. It can cost you from 25 cents to $1. Be sure to scan your monthly statement so you understand what you're charged for small services.

133 Explore ways to waive fees.

Just like a checking account can waive fees when you keep a minimum balance, by meeting certain criteria you might also be able to eliminate ATM fees.

Trap **If you have a tendency to withdraw money using the ATM twice a week, half at your bank, and half at a non-network bank, you could pay about $65 per year on ATM charges alone.**

134 Understand the art of checking.

Checks are at the center of the banking system. Your employer pays you by check, and you in turn probably pay most of your bills by check. Understanding how checking accounts work will help you better manage your money.

When you deposit a check into your account at the bank, it's sent to the bank on which it was drawn (to the bank that issued the check). That bank then debits (withdraws) money from the proper person's account (i.e., from the person who wrote you the check) and credits your account by transferring that amount electronically to your bank account. How quickly all of this happens depend on what type of banks are involved and on where they're located.

In general, these are the guidelines for clearance of a check deposited into your account.

Local Check	10% 1 day later	90% 2 days later
Non-local Check	10% 1 day later	90% 5 days later
Government check	100% 1 day later	
Check from your bank	100% 1 day later	
Bank or certified check	100% 1 day later	

135 Need a "special" check?

Sometimes a personal check just isn't good enough. For some reason, someone might want a guarantee. Usually this is true when a very large sum of money is involved—for instance, when you're buying a used car from a private party, making a down payment on a home, or when you're out of state and buying an expensive product. In cases like these, there are several types of special checks you can use.

- **Cashier's check:** This is also called a bank check, because it is drawn against a bank's account. You present the bank with the amount in cash for which you want them to write a bank check. A bank officer will draw out a bank check for that amount, sign it, and turn it over to you. You will have a carbon copy for your records. There is usually a nominal fee for a cashier's check.
- **Certified check:** This is your own personal check, which your bank guarantees to honor. After you write the check, your bank will freeze the amount in your checking account in order to cover the check, then stamp the face of your personal check "certified." You'll pay a small fee for this service.
- **Travelers' checks:** These are issued by travel companies (such as American Express), banks, and credit card companies (such as Visa) to be used in place of cash when you travel to places where personal checks might be difficult to use, and you don't want to be walking around with a large amount of cash on you. You can buy these checks in various dollar denominations, and even in foreign currencies. In order to secure these checks, you must sign your name immediately to the top of each check. At the time of a purchase or when you want cash them, you countersign at the bottom. Don't neglect to do this: if you don't sign at the top right away, these checks are like cash—anyone would be able to use them if they stole or found them.

Tip

If you're traveling out of the U.S., be sure to check and see if certain types of travelers' checks are preferred in the country you're visiting. For example, if you're going to France and the dollar is stronger than the franc at that time, merchants will be reluctant to accept travelers' checks in French currency—even though common sense would tell you that it's easier to navigate in the currency of the country. If the dollar is stronger, it's always advisable to get your travelers' check in American currency and then change over your cash money.

Get the most money for your money.

- **Money orders:** A money order is extremely useful if you don't have a personal checking account. The cost, about $3 at banks and about 85 cents through the U.S. Post Office, makes it the least expensive guaranteed check. You go to a teller, and pay in cash for the amount of the money order plus the fee. The amount is printed on the front of the money order, and you fill out the rest of the information (similar to a personal check), sign it, and send it.

Trap

There are some drawbacks to using a money order. For instance, it isn't returned to you, so you have no record of whether or not it was received or cashed. You can stop payment on it if it gets lost in the mail or stolen, but it is a complicated process. There are also limits on the maximum amount for a money order: The U.S. Post Office limits money orders to $700 each. Many banks cap money orders at $1,000 each. Beware: only purchase a money order from a bank or from the U.S. Post Office. A money order purchased elsewhere isn't necessarily protected, i.e., if the company goes out of business, your money order could be worthless.

"Money can't buy happiness.
It can, however, rent it."

—SOURCE UNKNOWN

THINGS TO THINK ABOUT

When checking out different types of accounts and services, look at:

- Money market/checking fees
- ATM/debit card fees
- Check order costs
- Stop payment orders, bounced check fees, money orders, and bank check fees
- Minimum balance fees
- Telephone inquiries
- Written or in-person inquiry charges
- Some banks charge a teller fee

THINGS TO THINK ABOUT

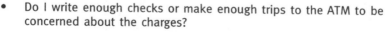

Bouncing Checks

Writing a check you're not sure about clearing? Consider the consequences. Returned checks are also known as *rubber checks* because they "bounce," or do not clear the bank, when there isn't sufficient money in your account to cover the amount of the check. If that's the case, your bank usually refuses to honor the check, and it will be returned unpaid. The person you paid the check to will not be happy: the check will be returned as a "bad check" (marked NSF or insufficient funds), and there will probably be an additional fee.

You yourself will also be charged a penalty for writing a check that didn't clear, sometimes as much as $30 for each bad check. If you write several bad checks in a single day, it can get very expensive. This can also have a negative effect on your credit rating.

To avoid rubber checks, apply for overdraft protection, which is a special line of credit (usually your savings account) that covers checks you write when there isn't enough money in your account. The bank will automatically transfer money into your checking account to cover the check, and charge you interest on the money transferred. Even so, overall you'll probably save money, and you'll also avoid the aggravation and bad feelings all around.

Stopping a Check

If you write a check and you decide you don't want the bank to pay it, or it gets lost, for an extra fee you can issue a *stop payment order* on that particular check. This order can be issued over the phone, in person, (good for 14 days) or in writing (good for 6 months). If you issue a stop payment order before the check is cashed, the bank must honor your instructions. Restrictions may vary depending on your financial institution, so be sure to clarify with a bank representative.

JUST THE FACTS

Questions to Ask Yourself

- Do I write enough checks or make enough trips to the ATM to be concerned about the charges?
- Have I shopped around to find the bank that will offer me the best deal?
- Would my money earn more (including the savings on the fees) if invested in a mutual fund, another savings account, or CD?

136 If you want a better deal on a checking account, you can probably get one.

Today there is a healthy competition among banks, so shop around. The first thing you need to do is assess your banking needs. Do you need a big bank with lots of ATMs, or can you manage with a bank that has fewer branches?

If you want to choose a larger bank, call a few of them and ask them if they'll waive their checking account fees. And since most banks would be thrilled to get your business, they're more than happy to accommodate your needs.

Smaller banks and credit unions offer you more personal service in banking. What's more, they are probably the best place to find lower interest rates and fees. Plus they'll know your name when you come into the bank.

137 Choose the right bank and save money.

If during a month you wrote 30 checks and used your ATM 25 times, and your fees were $10 per month plus 25 cents per transaction, it would cost you $24 per month or $288 per year to have that checking account. If your bank offers you free checking with a minimum balance, you'll save that money plus earn some interest.

138 Balance your checkbook.

Balancing your checkbook is a great way to keep an eye on how you're spending your money. Your monthly banking statement has become so sophisticated it can help you manage your finances. The statement will not only show your deposits and withdrawals—both cash and ATM transactions—it might also provide related information about when your Certificate of Deposit is coming due, or what the current interest rates are.

A relationship statement is a convenient snapshot of all of your banking activity, which some banks provide if you're a customer who does all of your banking with one institution. This all-in-one statement tracks all of your accounts with that

JUST THE FACTS

Checking Accounts Still #1

According to a Gallup Poll, 83 percent of consumers think checking accounts are the easiest way to pay their bills. Consumers believe that cash is the second, at about 8 percent, and electronic banking is third, at 4 percent. On average, consumers pay by check to make purchases about half the time. Women (53 percent) write more checks than do men (42 percent).

Senior Citizen Alert! There might be an inexpensive checking account waiting for you at your local bank. Banks are now offering basic banking accounts, sometimes called lifeline accounts. In some states they are required by law. Fees for opening an account can range from free to $25, and you're allowed 10 free withdrawals per month. The maximum monthly service charge is $3. In the majority of states that offer this service, you only have to keep a minimum monthly balance of $1! Whether or not your state offers this service, it might be worth your while to look for similar types of checking accounts in your area.

bank—checking, savings, CDs, credit cards, and loans. This is also part of the perks if you have a small business account.

139 Keep your record-keeping simple.

There are many different ways to keep track of your check writing: you can have a separate ledger booklet that fits into your checkbook; you can have checks that leave check stubs in a ring binder; or you can have carbon copies. You can even use computer software programs such as Quicken, which not only help you keep track of your checkbook balance and write checks for you, they can also print reports of your finances. But the bottom line is: keep it simple! Do what works for you (see Tip 142).

"You must get money to chase you,
but never let it catch up."

—DENIS WAITLEY

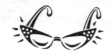

Personal Perspective

"Let's get real. While it isn't that difficult to take a few seconds to record the check you just wrote, many of us just don't do it. Since I'm one of those people, I finally decided, why not get the checkbooks that have the carbon copies of the checks attached. That way, now all I have to do is write a check—that's the easiest part—and it automatically keeps a record for me!"

140 Do the numbers—get your checkbook to balance.

Balance the pluses and the minuses. The bank even provides you with a worksheet on the back of your monthly statement. Use it. If the bank's balance doesn't match yours, here are some things to look for:

- Don't forget the bank's monthly fees and any check charges. They automatically deduct them from your monthly balance.
- Look for any checks (or withdrawals) you might have forgotten to record.
- You might have forgotten automatic payments, like your mortgage or 401k contribution.
- The most likely mistake is an adding or subtracting error, or a transposition of numbers—like instead of $56.50 you wrote $65.50—easy mistake, easily corrected.

Tip

Keep your receipts and canceled checks. You never know when you'll need them. These documents should be kept as long as you may need proof that deposits or payments were made. And remember, any canceled checks relating to your income taxes should be kept for at least seven years, and those for home improvements should be kept indefinitely (until you sell your home).

141 Consider banking from home.

Banking from home doesn't mean that you're putting your money under your pillow. Home banking allows you to electronically pay your bills, manage your accounts, and invest your money—by sitting at desk in your home office using a computer program. It is probably the wave of the future.

142 Bank on software.

Computer software programs, such as Quicken or Microsoft Money, can work together with your bank or an on-line service to help you get your finances in order and pay your bills. Electronic banking's biggest benefit is that it will provide you with accurate records of your transactions and will simplify your accounting at tax time.

Trap

Electronic banking may be the wave of the future, but it does have some drawbacks: You have to allow for five days' advance notice to send your money, days during which you won't be paid interest.

You'll be charged a monthly fee—a little under $10—for the service. Your bank might charge you an additional fee.

You must develop a new discipline to diligently check all data entries, recording and double-checking the details of every transaction. You'll be in charge of the accuracy of your records.

And of course, you'll also need to be computer literate—and have developed some computer savvy. So don't try this at home, folks, unless you're really ready!

Your bank and you: a win-win relationship

Learning to Save Like a Grown-up: Savings & CDs

"A penny saved is a penny earned."
—BEN FRANKLIN

143 Are savings accounts worth it?

The basis of all savings accounts is to earn money on what you're saving. Savings accounts are also called deposit accounts. The attraction of savings accounts continues to diminish, with so many other savings opportunities available inside and outside of banks. With banks offering to pay only about 2 percent interest in 1998 for putting your hard-earned money into their savings accounts, you might feel foolish when you can earn 10 percent or better in stocks, bonds and mutual funds, or even 5 percent or so in CDs or money market accounts.

Personal Perspective

"My youngest daughter is a psychology major at the University of Southern California, and a poet at heart. For years, whenever I'd tried to 'talk business' with her, I could sense her lack of interest.

"But one day, after she had worked all summer, she came to me and said, 'Mom, I need some advice.' As a parent, of course, I thought the worst. But was I surprised when she asked, 'How can I get more than 2 percent on my money from the bank?' I was so excited that I started to jump up and down and thought, 'Yes! We're talking money!' So we sat down and started to figure out that if she put away the $300 she'd made in a mutual fund earning 12 percent annual interest for 10 years, versus the 2 percent that she might be getting at a local bank, her $300 would grow to be worth $932 versus $366."

144 Find accounts you can bank on.

Some savings accounts are better than others. Here are some options:

- **Passbook accounts:** These are the traditional form of savings accounts. You get one of those little booklets when you open your account, with the amount you deposited stamped on the inside. Each time you make a deposit or withdrawal the teller will stamp the transaction to record it. When the teller records the transaction, the interest you've earned will also be calculated and added to your new balance.
- **Statement accounts:** These accounts are becoming more and more popular. Your deposits, withdrawals, and earned interest will show up either on a monthly or quarterly statement. If you have multiple accounts, the bank may combine your activities on one statement.
- **Holiday savings clubs:** These accounts are weekly deposits of a fixed amount of money, which you've determined in advance, so you can accumulate a particular amount for your holiday spending. You have the option of either making the weekly deposits yourself or you can have them transferred from another account. Some of these holiday clubs pay interest, some don't.
- **Money market accounts:** If your bank offers money market deposit accounts, it might pay you a higher rate of interest than a traditional savings account. Provided, that is, if you keep a required minimum balance. A money market account will also allow you to write checks against the account.

Tip

The advantage of a money market account at your bank versus a money market mutual fund account is that the bank account is guaranteed by the Federal Deposit Insurance Corporation (FDIC), and a mutual fund account is not. In addition, a mutual fund money market account requires you to pay fees, while the bank doesn't.

"There was a time when a fool and his money were soon parted, but now it happens to everybody."

—Adlai Stevenson

Trap

There's never a free lunch. Any time the government is involved, there will be rules and regulations. The case of bank money market accounts is no exception. A bank money market account will pay less interest than will a mutual fund money market account. Once again, you'll have to do your homework to decide which one is best for your needs.

145 Here's how banks calculate interest.

They use two basic methods:

- **Day-of-deposit to day-of-withdrawal:** This means all the money in your account earns money every single day it's there.
- **Average daily balance:** Simply stated, this means interest is paid on the average balance you keep in the account for each day during a given period.

Trap

Before you close an account, check to see when interest is credited. Otherwise, you can lose several months' of interest payments by taking your money out just before instead of after a quarterly interest payment.

Tip

Never, ever choose a savings account that offers the "lowest balance" method of interest. This pays interest on the smallest amount of money you have on deposit at a given time when interest is calculated.

JUST THE FACTS

The Math: Calculating Your Interest

Annual Interest Rate:	5%
Beginning Balance:	\$1,000
Deposit on the 15th:	\$1,000
End of Month Balance:	\$2,000
Daily Interest Rate:	5% ÷ 360* = .014%, or .00014 **Some banks may use 365-day year*
Method 1 Average Balance:	[(\$1,000 x 15) + (2,000 x 15)] ÷ 30 = \$1,500
Day of Deposit to Day of Withdrawal:	(15 x .00014 x \$1000) + (15 x .00014 x \$2000) = 2.08 + 4.20 = \$6.28
Method 2 Average Daily Balance Method:	[\$1,500 x .05] ÷ 12 = \$6.25

146 Look into credit unions.

A credit union is a nonprofit organization formed by a common group of people, such as employees of a particular company, or a group of neighbors.

Why sign up with a credit union?

Pros

- Credit unions tend to offer lower rates on loans and pay higher rates on savings accounts than do traditional banks and savings & loans.
- Two-thirds of all credit unions (versus about one-quarter of regular banks) offer free checking with no minimum balance.
- Credit unions charge lower fees for special checks and services, like cashier's checks, certified checks, money orders, and bounced checks.

Cons

- Most credit unions don't have ATMs, and those that do have limited free access to machines. While they offer a membership card to be used at other banks, the fees are much higher than if you had an ATM card with a traditional bank.
- At many credit unions, your canceled checks are not sent back to you.

147 Learn the tricks to getting favored treatment at your current bank.

Here are some things you can do now:

- Show your loyalty by doing all of your banking at one place. That includes your checking and savings accounts, safe-deposit boxes, CDs, and mortgages and loans.
- Bring in new business to your bank: get your friends or family to switch banks.
- Establish personal contact with the bankers. This will give you and them a chance to develop a relationship.

Like any relationship, being familiar with someone always makes doing business together more pleasant. Then when you ask for favors, like lower fees on your checking accounts, your bank is bound to be accommodating.

148 If you hate risk, consider investing in CDs (certificates of deposit).

The best investment is one that lives up to its promises. There is no better promise-keeper than a CD. This is a good place to help you learn some basic investment terms.

A certificate of deposit or CD is an instrument sold by your bank or broker that pays you a fixed interest rate for a predetermined amount of time. When you buy your bank's CD, you expect to get your money back (original investment or principal) after a specific length of time (at term or maturity), when it will pay you off in full (principal plus interest earned). Of course, there's a catch—to earn the interest on your money, the bank requires you to leave your money on deposit with them for a specific period of time—from 6 months to 5 years. The minimum deposit is usually about $500.

THINGS TO THINK ABOUT

How the Little Things Can Mean a Lot

Who cares about an ATM charge here or there—right? Well, all of those "here and there" charges can add up over time. Let's imagine a typical scenario for a year:

- **ATM:** $1.50 4 times a month $72
- **Credit Cards:** ($2,000 balance, 18 percent interest rate): $360 in interest charges, 3 $20 penalty fees for late payments. $420
- **Checking Accounts:** $20/month monthly fee, $10 charge for special services (certified checks, new checks, etc) 4 times during the year: $280

Grand Total $772

Before you know it, you've shelled out nearly $800 for the "little things." Wouldn't you rather have that in your account at the end of the year?

149 Don't buy the first CD deal you find.

Like any type of debt security (bills, notes, or bonds), when investing in a CD you should check out the interest rate being offered. And like most bonds, the longer the term, the higher the interest rate you'll be paid. Once again, do your homework if you want to find the best rates in town. You can also open up the *Wall Street Journal*, where you'll find lists of the best rates offered anywhere on CDs with comparable terms.

Tip

You don't have to buy (or sell) a CD at your neighborhood bank. Brokerage firms also offer CDs. You can buy them without any penalty or minimum deposit requirement attached. Of course, you may have to pay a premium for the CD or a commission to the broker for selling it to you—and that difference might wipe out your profit—but it's still worthwhile to find out.

150 Should you buy a CD?

Pros

- You'll receive a better interest rate (or yield) on your money than with a savings account. Of course, when banks need cash to make new loans, they'll be offering better yields on their CDs in order to attract new money like yours.
- Allows you to plan for your future by having a set maturity with a fixed interest rate, so you'll know how much you're going to have on a specific date.

Cons

- You're locked in at a specific rate, so if interest rates go up, you won't make any more money. (Of course if rates go down, you won't lose either!)
- You'll have to pay a penalty if you withdraw your money before maturity.
- When it's time roll over your CD at maturity, the new interest rates might be lower, offering lower overall yields.

Tip

You would be wise to ask this pertinent question before you buy a CD: what happens to your CD term or rate if your bank is merged or taken over by another bank? In the past, the terms have been allowed to change. You might want to do some homework about the risk factors involved should this happen to your bank.

Trap

When you buy a CD, remember that the bank gets to use your money for their long-term investments. That's why there are penalties for early withdrawal.

151 Need instant cash?

When you can turn an asset into cash immediately, this is called liquidity. A couple of examples:

- Western Union Money Transfer
- American Express Moneygram.

These aren't cheap by any standards. It usually costs around $20 to send $250, and close to $70 to send $1,000. That's quite a bit of money, so don't make it a habit. But it works when you desperately have to get money to someone fast.

Trap

Money transfers like Western Union should be a last resort only. The fees are steep—nearly 10 percent of money sent in some cases. It's funny how people don't mind paying a percentage like that (or 18 percent credit card fees), but panicked at a 5 percent market drop at the start of 1998.

152 Learn about wire transfers.

This is another method you have available to transfer money. It is quick and safe. To wire transfer funds you need to instruct your bank to transfer the money, providing them with full information on the name and number of the person's account being credited. A wire transfer transaction will be recorded at the end of the same business day on which you make the request. There is a fee of about $20, but that's about what it would cost you to send a check via overnight mail. The primary advantage with a wire transfer is that the recipient does not have to wait an extra 2 or 3 days or more for the money to clear.

153 Look into direct deposits.

Direct deposits will put your money to work faster and more efficiently than any other method of deposit. You can deposit your paycheck, investment earnings, pension, and Social Security payments. Banks welcome direct deposits, not only because they cut down on lines at the bank, but because they keep money coming into their institution on a regular basis.

How can you go about getting direct deposit? Simply sign up with your employer, brokerage firm, or the government, giving them your banking information and authorization to transfer your money into the specified bank account. You even have the option of splitting the money between different accounts, i.e., part in savings and part in checking.

Ask Lorraine Q&A

Q. *I don't agree with a charge on my last credit card bill. Can I refuse to pay it without damaging my credit?*

A. You may refuse to pay the amount in dispute only—pay the amount that you agree with. (Make sure you put all of your points in writing.)

Q. *All of my credit cards are pushing insurance—is that something I should consider?*

A. Probably not. You're not liable for any false charges if your credit card number is used without your authorization. Paying for insurance is really unnecessary.

Q. *I was irresponsible with my credit cards in college, but now I've cleaned up my act. How long will my credit history be tainted?*

A. Your credit history will generally extend back 7 years. But you may be able to take steps to clear you credit record sooner. Look under the phone book under "Credit Reporting Agencies"—there are several companies who can provide you a copy of your credit report for a very small charge. And even if your bad debts are still on your record, many new creditors will overlook them if you've shown responsible behavior for a few years.

Q. *I've gotten in too deep with my credit cards. Where can I turn for help?*

A. Try calling the National Foundation for Consumer Credit at 301-589-5600, 8701 Georgia Ave., Suite 507, Silver Spring, Maryland 20910. They won't pay your bills for you, but they'll give you valuable advice on important steps like negotiating with creditors, consolidating your debt, and budgeting. They can also help you decide if bankruptcy is the best option.

Q. *I want to earn the most on my money, but I also want to have enough reserve for emergencies. Is there a recommended amount to keep liquid?*

A. A rule of thumb that many people go by is 3 months' income. Keep it somewhere that you can get at immediately, like a savings or money market account.

Q. *My bank is offering me a variable rate CD. Should I consider it?*

A. That's a good option as long as you understand the details. Obviously, you should only choose a variable rate instrument if you believe that interest rates may move up before it expires. If they go down, then so will your payout. You should also check carefully into the way that the interest is adjusted—is it tied to well-followed benchmark like the treasury rate? That's the best kind, because you can track it easily. Never buy a CD where the adjustment criteria are up to the bank's management, or unclear in any way.

Q. *Why aren't CD rates more uniform?*

A. Simple. Some banks want the business more. If a bank is trying to attract deposits, then it's likely to offer better rates. But if a bank is essentially offering CDs as a service to customers, they won't have the best deals around.

Q. *I'll never learn to balance my checkbook. Every month I try to get around to it, but I never seem to have the time. How can I avoid bouncing checks?*

A. For die-hard procrastinators, I recommend that you get a overdraft line of credit at your bank. If possible, find a rate that's better than a standard credit card rate (around 17 percent). (Even better, find a bank that will notify you before they bounce a check.) This can turn into an expensive habit, however. At least try to scan your monthly statement for big charges for items like returned checks. It just may cure you of the habit.

Resource Guide

Credit Card Information

- Call RAM Research for a full report (research on rebate cards, secured cards and more):
  P.O. Box 1700
  Frederick, MD 21702
  1-800-344-7714
  www.ramresearch.com
- Or try the Bankcard Holders of America for more information on credit card deals.
  524 Branch Drive
  Salem, VA 24153
  703-389-5445
- Getting help with your credit card charges:

  National Foundation for Consumer Credit
  8701 Georgia Avenue, Suite 507
  Silver Spring, MD 20910
  301-589-5600

Certificates of Deposit

- To find the best rates, try:
  100 Highest Yields
  P.O. Box 088888
  North Palm Beach, FL 33408-9990
  1-800-327-7717
- For more information on different kinds of savings vehicles, contact:

  The Consumer Federation of America
  1424 16th Street NW
  Washington, DC 20036

  Send $0.25 and request the
  "Your Savings Options" pamphlet.

Section 4

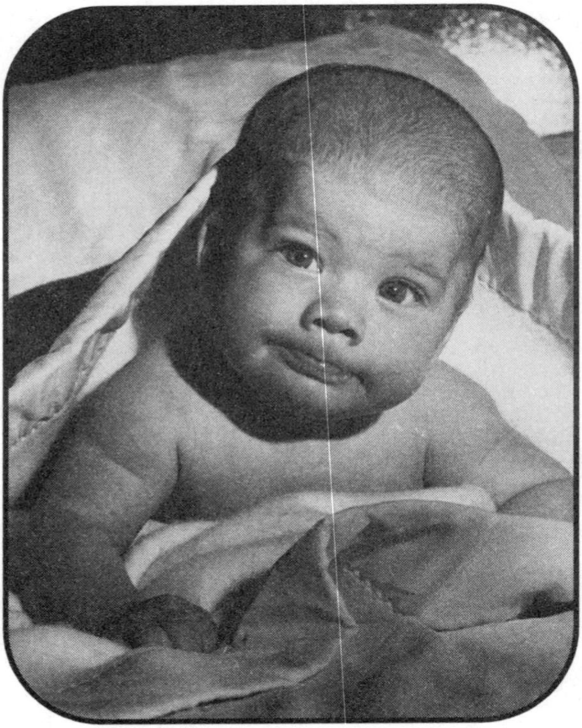
Eventually I'll assume responsibility for my financial future.

Teaching Kids About Money

Teaching your kids about money involves so much more than just counting pennies. Kids at any age can learn something about the value of a dollar: why it's important, when it isn't, and how to understand the difference. Money is a foundation for so many life lessons they'll need to learn—discipline, accomplishment, hope, values—even materialism.

Many times, parents underestimate the interest that kids have in money. I can remember getting out my small nest egg, which came to 8 bucks or so, and counting it over and over again. Not only did it strengthen my math skills—I learned to quickly calculate those nickels, dimes, and quarters—but it taught me how money is acquired. For many children, learning to save for something special, such as an outing or a toy, can illustrate the challenges and benefits of saving as well.

What's more—teaching your kids about money can't help but drive home a few lessons to yourself. It's harder to be a spendthrift when you're telling your kids to be responsible with their allowance. (Why should you get a brand-new car if they can't have a new bike?) If you really work at it, you and your kids can learn together!

A Run-Through of the Basics: The Allowance & Money Framework

"Children have never been very good at listening to their elders, but they have never failed to imitate them."

— James Baldwin

154 Set an example.

This lesson is the first of this section because it may very well be the most important. Kids absorb so much more than we think they do, and definitely more than what we tell them. If you tell your child to forget about those "cool" $200 sneakers that "all the kids have" but buy yourself expensive gadgets every time you have the chance, guess which lesson he'll learn?

Trap

Don't go overboard and set a price on every job around the house. Children should participate in household simply because it's part of normal family responsibilities. Don't teach your kids that the only reason to take out the trash is for cash.

Things to Think About

Talk Is Cheap

No matter the age, your actions are the most important influence on your child's attitude toward money. If you don't even look at a price tag before making a purchase, if your checking account is always overdrawn, if you live way beyond your means, the message you are sending to your child is that "money is no object." It can leave her with little respect for the value of a dollar.

155 Lay a strong foundation, and then give them some breathing room.

Figure out the basics of your system, like weekly allowance, extra jobs, etc. (see The Foundation worksheet, p. 150) and then step back and let your kids learn on their own. Sounds easy, but it means that you'll have to bite your tongue when your 5-year-old insists on spending his entire allowance on a cardboard plane that breaks the first day. But nothing teaches kids the value of money better than their own mistakes. The trick to this, of course, is having a system that can withstand the inevitable complaining. No advances on allowances.

Tip

Before your kids are money-savvy and old enough to manage their money (say 10 to 12 years old), you probably don't want their allowance to cover necessities like lunch money. Give them their lunch money every day, separate from their allowance. You don't want your second grader to learn about money the hard way by missing her lunch.

156 Talk to them in their language.

Don't try to explain annuities to your teenager, or the household finances to your 5-year-old: that's the surest way to lose their interest. Explain financial concepts in ways that they can understand: tell your toddler that he can't have a piece of candy that costs a dollar if he's only got a nickel to spend. It's the simple stuff that will stay with them.

Tip

A child under 5 may not be able to grasp the concept of "weekly" or "allowance," but you can build his money skills in other essential ways. Reinforcing sharing with others and assuming responsibility for his behavior will shape fundamental skills. These basics will be invaluable when he becomes an adult and has to manage his own spending money, share a phone bill with roommates, or handle an expense account.

First, teach them the value of the dollar.

157 Be firm, but don't rub in the hard lessons they'll learn.

When your child runs out of money because of poor planning, your "I told you so" won't make the experience more valuable. The mistake alone will be memorable enough.

Tip **A pre-schooler can learn the different values of coins and can give the clerk the money for small purchases. A play group can assemble some objects and open their own store. Using play money, they can decide what items should sell for a "big" amount ($5) and what should sell for a "small" amount ($1). Another idea is to take some of their story books and open a library—tots will love paying and collecting two real pennies for overdue books.**

158 Help them construct a budget.

This is an important first step to go through with a child of any age. Use the worksheet at the end of this section to give them guidelines for what they might spend on various items during a week.

Tip **To help your child learn how to manage money, her allowance should include some "free" money that she can spend on whatever she wants. Teach responsibility by letting her decide what part of that extra dollar each week goes to savings and what part goes to comic books or ice cream.**

159 Set a reasonable allowance and stick to it.

Make sure to pay your child promptly, on the same day of every week so they can effectively learn to budget their money.

Now the big question: what's a reasonable allowance? See the table (right) for national averages. Of course, it's up to you to determine how much your child can handle, or really needs.

Tip **If you catch yourself wanting to buy your kids extravagant gifts outside of birthdays and the holiday season, honestly evaluate what your reasons are. Are you trying to make up for something else you're not giving them, like time or attention?**

"Children need models rather than critics."

—JOSEPH JOUBERT

JUST THE FACTS

Weekly Allowance Averages

So what are other parents giving their kids? Here are some guidelines to give you some direction.

Age	Amount
6–8	$2.77
9–11	$3.72
12–13	$7.08
14–15	$8.91
16–17	$10.74

Source: Youth Monitor Survey, a syndicated service of Nickelodeon and Yankelovich Clancy Shulman

160 Give them the chance to earn more.

Once you've set a basic allowance, designate a few tasks or chores your kids can do to earn extra money up to a given limit. It may be small jobs like washing the car or trimming the lawn, or bigger ones like painting the garage. This gives them the chance to earn money for unexpected expenses like concert tickets or a very special plaything, while teaching them the tradeoff of time and money.

Tip

If you've set up designated jobs for set amounts of money, it gives you the perfect response to the next request for money.

Entrepreneurs can start young.

"Children are apt to live up to what you believe of them."

—Lady Bird Johnson

161 Don't forget that you're still the parent.

Carefully separate the money you spend on them during family outings from the money they get or earn on their own. For example, if you take your kids to the movies, you should pay. If you customarily buy from the concession stand when you're there, you should pick up the bill. If your kid decides she wants the extra super-dooper size popcorn with extra butter (something you don't normally spring for), she should pay for the extra charge, but otherwise it's your responsibility.

Teaching your kids to be smart with money doesn't mean that you play the role of head ogre. You can buy your kids an occasional ice cream cone, for Pete's sake, just because it's a fun thing to do. Or even manage a special allowance advance for the movies, as long as it's not a constant request and you take it out of the next week's allowance. Use your common sense: all kids are different, and only you know how much flexibility they can handle.

Tip

Expect kids to make mistakes when you give them increasing freedom and responsibility with money. A too-difficult video game that looked so enticing in the store, that fashionable T-shirt that didn't survive the washer, or one week's allowance blown on candy with no money left over for that compass he wanted for his camping trip can all be very valuable learning experiences. If you maintain a constructive, guiding attitude, your child should start to recognize the importance of planning.

THINGS TO THINK ABOUT

More Than Money

Just as with adults, a child's attitude toward money is an extension of how he or she has developed inner qualities. If you raise your children to be emotionally secure and to understand that they cannot have everything they want, you will have made an important contribution to how they later deal with money.

162 Make sure they know that money isn't the only point.

This can be the downside of educating kids about money: they become too interested in it. The first time that I collected my own nest egg (I think it was around 8 bucks), I was fascinated by it. I counted it endlessly, and was interested in the money rather than what it could buy. Soon enough, I discovered the joys of comic books and happily blew my stash. But the point is that you don't want to create hoarders—kids who value the money rather than its benefits. Encourage your kids to respect the savings in their savings accounts, but to wisely spend their spending money.

Tip **During the holidays, reemphasize the meaning of the occasion by having everybody chip in for a charity gift from your family.**

163 Teach your kids to be gracious about gifts.

Kids today receive so many presents on so many occasions that they often begin to assume that they're entitled to them. This is a dangerous precedent to set: instruct your kids to thank the gift-givers specifically, either in person or in a note.

164 Recruit extended family members to your plan.

How can you teach your 8-year-old to value his $3 allowance when Gramps is always slipping him a fiver? This is a tough one, but one to handle with some humor and grace. First of all remember: grandparents are supposed to spoil their grandkids; it's their right and their duty. So don't explode, just reason with them. Tell them you'd rather they kept their monetary gifts on the small side—that means pocket change, not bills. Even better, suggest a small present (not the Ultimate Nintendo Game Player you've been telling them they can't have for a year).

Tip **If grandparents or other relatives want to give your kids larger gifts of money, set up a savings account for their deposits, or better yet, a college fund.**

165 Try the allowance approach to forestall grocery store tantrums.

Unfortunately, every parent has to deal with the consequences of the consumer culture. Your child sees something that he wants and threatens to blow sky-high if he doesn't get it. Here's a tip: give him a small allowance before you go into the store (say, a quarter) and tell him he can buy whatever he wants with it. That way, you've shown some give but are also teaching the value of choices and money. You can even make this a game—find something you want for 25 cents.

166 Encourage your kids to comparison shop.

This can be a challenging trick: when a 9-year-old falls under the spell of an action-packed, super deluxe T.V. commercial, he's usually a lost cause. Still, you might have some room to point out other options: is this the CD-ROM that includes the new update? Would it be cheaper if he bought it through the Internet? Look for sales, store coupons, etc.

Tip

As your grade-schooler matures and has more experience with money, you can gradually increase her allowance to include money for school lunches, club dues, etc. As she gets older, let her select some of her own clothing purchases. Assist her in doing some comparison shopping. Together you can weigh the value of different items based on quality, price, and how much use she will get from them. Also, let her make gift purchases. Give her a spending limit and discuss what would be the best gift.

167 Teach them to be generous when it counts.

Too often, when kids first learn about money, they become hoarders. Remember, you want your kids to be responsible about money, not stingy. Encourage your kids to be gracious from time to time—that might mean buying a soda for their friend at the movies or springing for a present for Grandma.

"Children are completely egoistic; they feel their needs intensely and strive ruthlessly to satisfy them."

— Sigmund Freud

168 Don't lay money guilt on your kids.

Sure, you want to teach your kids the value of money, but your 10-year-old shouldn't feel guilty when you go out to buy school clothes. We've all heard the statistic—raising a child from birth to college costs an average of $250,000. Raising kids is an expensive undertaking, but it's your obligation (I would think privilege), never something that your kids should feel indebted to you for. And as long as you keep to a responsible spending pattern, this shouldn't really be a problem (i.e., that you haven't gone overboard on buying the luxuries).

169 An occasional reward is probably OK, but never a bribe.

Should you give your kids rewards for cleaning their room or for behaving at Aunt Thelma's? This is another gray area that still leaves the experts divided. Generally, most agree that an occasional small reward for a job well done—say, a quarter for diligently practicing piano for the whole allotted hour—is probably OK. But to offer your child the same quarter ahead of time would be a bribe, and sets a dangerous precedent.

170 Don't pay your kids for good grades.

I'm just going out on a limb here, because this is another one that the experts argue over endlessly. The ruling notion is that you never want to rob your kids of the personal satisfaction of an accomplishment. Besides, good grades build self-esteem and that's a reward in itself. Studies have shown that kids who are paid to perform a task have less personal satisfaction about doing that task.

Tip

Instead of paying your kids for good grades, make a point of celebrating when they do well in school. That could mean a night at the games parlor, or a day at the amusement park. (Both which cost money, by the way, but don't create the direct pay-for-grades expectation.) Or, let them choose their favorite food item for the family dinner—if you don't mind eating hamburgers or pizza instead of pasta and a salad.

171 Talk to your kids about family finances, but shield them from the worry.

This is a tricky balance. I think it's productive to talk to your kids about the family budget, but dangerous to involve them in the details. You never want to burden your kids with adult-size worries (your 8-year-old should never be worried about the mortgage). For example, you might explain that you can't by a new car until you've saved more money, but never that you can't make your car loan payment this month. The overall rule should be: convey careful planning about the future, but never communicate worry about the present.

This sounds like common sense, but so many parents cross this line unwittingly. Who hasn't wanted to blurt out "I'm trying to keep a roof over our heads and you want a new bike!?" from time to time?

172 Keep kids clear of spousal "disagreements" about money.

If you're steamed because your spouse decided to buy a speedboat without getting your final OK—save your blowup (if you must) until your kids aren't around. Even if the whole thing turns out to be a minor misunderstanding, the emotional repercussions can often be stressful for children.

173 Beware the favoritism trap.

Don't favor one kid over the other.

Anyone who grew up with siblings knows this is a powder keg of an issue. Most siblings live in a constant state of suspicion that they are being shortchanged somehow in relation to their brothers or sisters. I know my kids can hardly wait for the chance to scream "foul" whenever one received something the other didn't. A good way to avoid this pitfall is by setting up a system beforehand. Establish allowances for different ages from early on and don't vary from it. (Except for slight adjustments for inflation if your kids are very far apart in age. And explain why you are changing the amount.) Don't bend the rules for one child (say, saving her from shortfalls) and not for another.

It's easy to seem to favor one kid over another because of their different ways of handling money. Your first child, for example, may have been naturally responsible, never asking for exceptions to the rule. But the second may constantly look for loopholes that you occasionally give in to. Thus the birth of the "good kid penalty" that crops up in so many families.

Tip

Establishing equality between your kids usually has little to do with money spent. Think about the big "treats" that each of your kids got. Maybe one child got tap dance lessons, and another got rollerblades.

174 Don't confuse the "basics" and the "extras."

Every family struggles with this issue. What qualifies as an "extra" that your child should buy on her own? Only you, as a parent, really know the answer to that question, and it of course depends on your financial situation. Here a few questions I ask myself when I'm on the fence when deciding whether or not an item is a "basic" (one you should pay for) or an "extra":

- Is this item well above the average price? (i.e., a $40 pair of sneakers would be a "basic" while a $200 pair would definitely be an "extra")
- Is this a "staple" item that your kid will use every day? For example, a bicycle is probably something that your kid legitimately needs to get around. Spring for the bike. (But not the $500 one—see bullet #1 above)
- Is the "need" for this item strongly motivated by peer pressure? Advertising? Chances are, if your son wants something just because all the other guys have it, it's an extra. Same goes for the seemingly limitless Spice Girls merchandising items your daughter will want.

And remember—you *can* buy the luxuries occasionally—that's what birthdays are for!

I like you a lot but it's a mistake to spend my whole allowance on you.

Piggy Bank Dreams: Teaching Your Kids to Save

175 Encourage savings with a contribution plan.

If your children show the discipline and initiative to save some money, help them out with a set savings plan. For example, you might contribute $1 for every $10 they save. This is also a fair way to handle large items they may wish to purchase. If your daughter is pining for a $200 snowboard, you might offer to put up the last $50 if she can save the first $150.

176 Set realistic savings goals.

If you tell your 8-year-old that he can begin saving for his $20,000 college tuition, chances are he'll get discouraged pretty quickly. Start small: teach your kids to save up for things like their favorite toy, or an amusement park outing they've been pining for.

This much of my allowance for comic books and ice cream, the rest goes in the bank.

D-I-V-O-R-C-E

177 Your kid won't go to the highest bidder.

When you mix up the high emotions of a divorce and the strong feelings you have for your kids, there's bound to be some overspending going on. And if your kids are smart, they'll milk it for all it's worth. ("Daddy said he would buy me a pony if you'll pay for the upkeep.") This is an incredibly tempting impulse in any case: who doesn't want to see their kid's face light up at getting that gift they've been wanting? And during (or after) a divorce, when your kids may be upset or traumatized, it's an almost irresistible temptation.

But you *must* resist it, and so must your ex-spouse. Kids are so much smarter than we give them credit for—trust me, in the long run what will count with your kids are the big things: your dependability and your stability. Your being there for car-pool every day may not seem as glamorous as the mountain bike your spouse just gave your son, but it's so much more valuable over time, and your son knows it. (OK—maybe not in the halcyon days when the bike is still new, but he'll know it eventually.)

Tip **If you're the visiting parent, keep your spending in check. That doesn't mean you can't have a great time—go to the beach, but don't offer to take 10 of your son's friends to the amusement park, or take your daughter shopping on Rodeo Drive in Beverly Hills.**

Tip **If you can, talk to your ex-spouse about overspending and see if you can come up with guidelines for visits that are reasonable. Ask your ex to put a ceiling on spending so that your child can have a special time without breaking the bank.**

Tip

You could also consider setting up a "visit fund" that can apply to the upcoming activities. If you know in advance that your children are going on a special outing, allow them to earn extra spending money by doing extra chores around the house. That way the kids can take their own spending money to the amusement park, even though your ex-spouse will pick up the cost of going. This guideline can also apply to any special events.

178 Don't mix up your kids in the fight over money.

This is a close cousin to Tip 168—don't lay adult money problems on your kids. That means that if your ex-spouse is being a deadbeat about child support, it's between the two of you, and shouldn't involve your kids. Your children will have plenty of conflicted feelings about the split-up without hearing about who paid for the last school year and which "deadbeat" didn't.

"You know children are growing up when they start asking questions that have answers."

—John Plomp

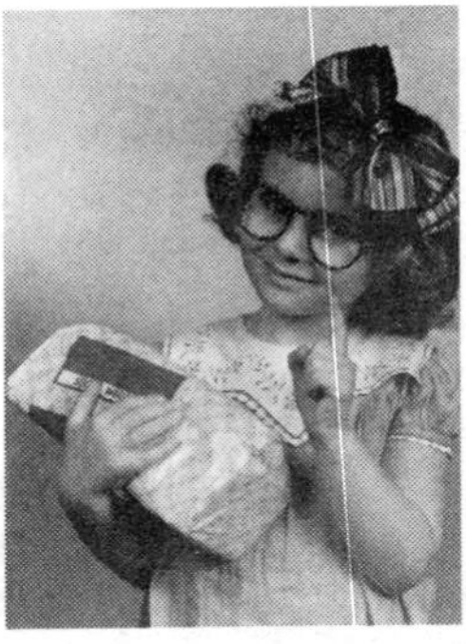

Before you spend it, is it worth the bread?

Junior Gets a Job

"In a world as empirical as ours, a youngster who does not know what he is good at will not be sure what he is good for."

—Edgar Z. Friedenberg

179 Encourage your kids to work, but keep it in check.

We all want our kids to have the initiative to pursue outside jobs, but not at the expense of their schoolwork, their family responsibilities, or just being a kid. Some kids become so enamored about earning extra money that they go overboard, working more and more hours so that they can buy more and more things. This is another gray area, admittedly, but these are a few questions you might ask yourself if you were worried about their working habits:

- Are their grades falling?
- Does their social life seem to have dropped off dramatically?
- Are they missing a majority of family gatherings or events?
- Are they spending a lot of money? (e.g., wearing nicer clothes than you?)

If your answer is yes to at least a couple of these questions, you should have a talk with your children. Explore ways to cut back on work hours. You might propose a way to earn money from *you*, which could give more flexibility for other interests.

Trap **Don't go overboard: your kids have plenty of time to work for a living. Don't let them miss out on playing on the soccer team because of a job.**

Tip **Don't underestimate the value of a mundane job. Even a job flipping burgers will teach your kid to be professional, on time, and respectful to customers. These are the building blocks of any great career.**

180 Bring up entrepreneurs.

Your daughter could mow a few lawns for extra cash, or she could start a lawn-mowing business. What's the difference? In the second case, she could really study the area, put up flyers, go door-to-door, even hire other kids, thus gaining an idea of what it's like to work for herself (and probably make more money). But more important than the money is the fact that you will encourage your child to think like an entrepreneur.

"Adults are obsolete children."

—Dr. Seuss

Time to start my own business.

THINGS TO THINK ABOUT

Should Your Kids Work in the Family Business?

To many parents, this seems like a natural progression: let your children take on duties at the family store or office, thus allowing them to learn about business under your guidance. This may work for many families, but I advise against it—at least for the first job after college. In their first full-time working experience kids learn about responsibility, but only if it is a truly independent experience. Calling in sick to your mom will never be the same as making excuses to the boss. And there will never be the same pressure to succeed (or possibility of failure) in a family environment as there would be in an outside job. Without being on their own, your children will never know whether or not their success was determined by their talent or by your money or influence.

181 Encourage your kids to do what they love.

Most kids think that the only way to earn money is by mowing lawns or babysitting. Although those are certainly two tried-and-true favorites, you should encourage your kids to think outside the box. If your son is a great writer, for example, help him come up with ideas to use his talent. Maybe it's publishing his own Web site, or selling articles to kid magazines. Show him how a writer might put together a query for an article and send it out to an editor at his favorite magazine. Or if your daughter loves horses, brainstorm with her about getting a job at a stable or starting a service where she cares for other people's horses.

Tip **If you show your kids early how to capitalize on their interests, you've taught them something a majority of adults don't know: your job should be your life, not a 9-to-5 trap.**

Tip **Don't worry if your kids' business ideas aren't financially successful. The most important thing they've learned is to take initiative.**

Personal Perspective

"A friend of mine brought her 14-year-old daughter by my publishing company one day. I carefully explained everything that we did, and asked her what she thought of a couple of our books. A few days later, she called me and presented me with a sophisticated analysis of our content, marketing, and packaging approach. I then learned that she had already started her own 'zine' by gathering interviews, writing stories, arranging the printing, and placing them in bookstores. This young girl knew more about the process than I had when I started my business. Even though she probably won't get rich from her venture, she'll be miles ahead when it comes time to choose and enter a career."

Investing for Babes

182 Teach your kids about investing early!!

I can't stress this point strongly enough. I think it's akin to learning a foreign language or skiing: so much easier than tackling it as an adult. Set up a modest investment account early—many brokerages allow you to start with small amounts like $1,000. You obviously don't want your child having that much money to play around with, but there's no reason why she can't be a part of the process. Show her the statement for the account. (Many now are set up so that you monitor them on-line.) Explain the different investing options that you have, and discuss one stock over another. Allow her to make at least one decision completely on her own—say, buy one share of Disney—or Apple. That way she'll be more interested in monitoring how it does afterward.

Tip

Some families start their own investment clubs. Once a month, the family sits down and picks stocks, and works on the portfolio—whether it's $50 or $5000. It's a great learning experience and an excellent way for the family to spend time together.

183 Teach investment savvy at a smaller level.

I think that kids can learn a lot by seeing something besides money sitting in an account increase in value. If your child is interested in baseball cards, for example, you might point out that they can sometimes be a good investment. Watching something that they can hold increase in value can be a powerful motivator for kids. This will not only be good for your child, it will give you insight into the next generation's thinking.

184 Teach the cash value of work.

Aside from tasks performed, kids can also learn a great deal by putting work into a *product* that increases its value. This might mean fixing up a bike, or repairing a radio, to be sold for a higher price.

185 Teach your kids to read the stock tables.

This simple exercise can open up a whole new world to a young teenager. I was fascinated when I understood that the jumble of numbers on those pages actually meant something that I could understand. Many kids enjoy the process of following a stock, especially if it's in competition with a sibling.

186 Take your kids with you on financial errands.

No, you don't want your 7-year-old disrupting your major client meeting, but there's no reason he can't go with you to see your broker or bank officer occasionally. It's a great way to introduce them casually to a world that many adults find intimidating.

"We worry about what a child will be tomorrow, yet we forget that he is someone today."

—Stacia Tauscher

I'm getting a headstart on investing.

Leaving the Nest

The independent lifestyle is a financial shock to most young adults who begin living on their own. There are so many expenses they had never thought about, much less thought to budget for. Suddenly, when the toothpaste isn't free, much less groceries, laundry, and cable bills, they see what making ends meet is all about.

187 Give them advice and emotional support, but not an open checkbook.

This is a stressful transition, and you can certainly help out by providing advice, information, and yes—the occasional bailout. But resist the temptation to give them money with no strings attached. If you've set up an allowance while they're in college, for example, then make it clear that any loans you give are just that—an advance on their allowance.

188 Base their allowance on a detailed budget.

If you are giving your children an allowance while in college, be sure that it's based on a real set of expenses. At the beginning of the year, sit down together and detail what the living expenses will be. That way you can't be accused of being unfair later on, and they have an idea of what it is you're willing to pay for (lunch at the student commons, yes, "beer bust" nights at the pub, no.)

189 Let them pay for extras.

The advantage of constructing a budget with your son or daughter is that it gives you the opportunity to point out the "extras" for which they should be responsible. Do they want a great new wardrobe for the new semester? It should be on them. How about a season tickets to the pro hockey league? Not your problem.

Tip

Have you ever tried to send money to a youngster studying abroad?

You can avoid the time it takes for a check to arrive and clear in a foreign bank, the cost of a direct money wire, or the risk of sending cash to a foreign location by using the cash advance function of your credit card. Simply make a payment of the amount desired on the card. Then, using your PIN, your child can get cash, in the foreign currency, at a credit-card ATM or office in the country where he is studying.

190 The credit card controversy—should you or shouldn't you?

Most parents believe that their child should have a emergency credit card. The problem is, of course, if that many college students consider things like an impromptu trip to Mardi Gras an emergency, and eventually run up a balance they can't handle. My advice? Give them the credit card in their name, explain all of the workings of the card, and let them go. Yes, many will get into a little trouble, but it's the only way to learn this lesson about debt.

Tip

- **Give them the card in their name. Most credit card companies today are willing issue new cards with low limits to young people. If it's in your child's name, you won't have the stress of late bills coming to your house, or the prospect of damaged credit.**
- **Keep the limit low. Let's face it—mistakes will probably be made with their first charge card. Make sure it's not a disaster by keeping the cap at a reasonable level—say $1,000 or $2,000.**
- **Explain how the card works. Tell them about the high interest rates, the penalties for late payments, and the importance of a good credit record.**
- **Consider giving them a debit card, which could be linked to a bank account with a minimal amount of money.**

"There are three ways to get something done: Do it yourself, employ someone, or forbid your children to do it."

—Monta Crane

"It is dangerous to confuse children with angels."

—David Fyfe

Things to Think About

Secured Cards

If you are a young person with no credit history who is having trouble getting a credit card, consider a secured card. The issuer will require you to put up a sum of money, say $500, which they will keep in an interest-bearing escrow account. They will then issue you a card with a $500 credit limit. If you miss a payment, the issuer will take the money from your escrow account. Your object here is to establish a good credit record by paying on time and not charging over your limit.

Time to venture out on our own.

Worksheet: The Foundation

Required Chores (unpaid)

What are the routine chores that you think each of your kids should be responsible for every week?

Extra Jobs (paid)

List extra tasks your kids could do to earn extra money. Think of the tasks you've been meaning to get to but never seem to have time for, as well as some longer-term tasks that could build a sense of responsibility.

Regular Allowance

(A) Together with your kid(s), list the expenses that they might have over a normal week.

Entertainment (movies, games)	$
Extras	
CDs	$
Computer games	$
Magazines/comics	$
Snacks	$
Other stuff	$

(B) Based on (A), calculate a reasonable allowance that your child can easily budget for an entire week—and that you can afford to give.

$

Ask Lorraine

Q&A

Q. *Should I get my kids involved in saving for their college costs?*

A. Probably not, unless they're in high school or older. Younger kids do better with more immediate goals, like saving for that new bike or video game.

Q. *My 12-year-old son has his heart set on an expensive new snowboard. I told him to save for it, but I know it will take him forever. How can I help without being a milquetoast?*

A. Plenty of ways. You might offer to match his savings in a small way—say giving him $1 for every $5 he accumulates. That way, you're encouraging his savings habit without being too indulgent. You might also offer to pay for the last portion of the board's cost—say the last $50—for an upcoming birthday or holiday.

Q. *I think I should pay for her bicycle, but she wants one that costs much more than I had expected. What should I do?*

A. That's easy. Offer to pay the amount up to what you had expected—pick out a "base bike" and use that figure. Then tell her that if she wants the one with the bells and whistles she can save toward the rest. If it's not too extravagant, you could help out by setting up a payment plan with her allowance or holiday money.

Q. *My 16-year-old son is working all the time, it seems. He spends the money on his car, going out, and new clothes. I don't want to discourage hard work, but I'm afraid that his priorities might be off. Should I limit his work hours?*

A. You're right to be concerned about discouraging his hard-working ways. The truth is that you've taught him a good lesson: if he wants the extras, then he'll have to work to get them. The key concern you should have is about his time: be sure that he's not neglecting his school work for the sake of his job, and still spends time with family and friends.

Q. *No matter how disciplined I am about teaching my 10-year-old son about money, he's hopelessly irresponsible. He's constantly asking me for "extra" money when his allowance has run out. I seldom give in, but I'm worried that he'll never learn!*

A. Don't worry if your kids don't seem be learning their financial lessons at a young age. All children are different, and most learn at very different paces. Just stick to your system—your son will come around when the things that he wants become more important to him.

Resource Guide

For Young Entrepreneurs

- If your kids are interested in setting up their own business, they might contact one of these groups for more information and help:

  The Center for Entrepreneurship
  Wichita State University
  1845 N. Fairmount
  Wichita, KS 67260
  316-689-3000

- Or for girls only, ask about Camp Start-Up, run by:
  An Income of Her Own
  1-800-350-2978
  www.anincomeofherown.com

Kid Resources for Money Education

- National Center for Financial Education
  Catalog costs about $2.00
  619-232-8811
  www.ncfe.org
- Consumer Federation of America
  Send a self-addressed envelope for brochures.
  124 16th Street NW, Suite 604
  Washington, DC 20036
  202-387-6121

Raising Young Investors

- Federal Reserve Bank of New York
  Publications Department
  (Comic books about money)
  212-720-6130
- Steinroe's Young Investor Fund
  (Minimum Investment $1,000)
  1-800-338-2550

Section 5

Start with a snapshot of your overall financial picture.

Growing Your Money

When should you start investing for the future? NOW. The first day you have extra money in your checking account, start putting money away in some sort of investment account other than your savings bank or CD.

Sounds easy, right? Well, the good news is: in today's marketplace, the options are enormous. The bad news: in today's marketplace, the options are enormous.

In fact, there are so many different ways to invest that it can blow your mind. And if you think mutual funds are an easy choice, try sorting through the thousands to find the best one(s) for your needs. So we're back to doing our homework. Remember there's no one formula that works for everyone. Your investment personality is unlike anyone else's—you have a different time frame, risk tolerance, and tax situation than the next person. That means that you should be calling the shots, or at least supervising them.

There are no quick fixes, no free lunches, and no sure things. That's a given. So let's get down to reality and work on keeping our money as well as growing it.

Investor, Know Thyself

191 Know what kind of investor you are.

Although the experts can probably do a better job choosing among different stocks and other investments, they still don't know YOU. That is: your personal goals, risk tolerance, and time frames. That's up to you to decide, and those decisions will help you choose the right type of fund in which to invest your hard-earned money.

The following are the essential questions you should ask yourself (and that a good mutual fund salesperson will ask you before accepting your money).

192 What kind of return are you looking for?

Oh sure, we all want the HIGHEST return. But this question looks at return from a different perspective. Are you interested in **current income** (i.e., collecting a dividend or interest payment) or in **capital growth** (i.e., watching your portfolio grow in value through the years)?

193 What's your risk tolerance?

Here's the real question to ask yourself: can you handle it when your portfolio drops in value by 10 or 20 percent? Does that thought leave you unaffected (you know it will come back even stronger), slightly queasy, or downright panicky? Sure you want to take a little risk in order to get a good return, but you shouldn't be losing sleep over it.

194 How liquid should you be?

Will you need cash in the near future for things like college tuition, loan payments, or taxes? Remember: one of the cardinal rules of investing is that you never want to HAVE to sell your investments. That could put you in the dreadful position of selling a stock, for example, when it has taken a dip. You may know that the dip is temporary, but that doesn't change the loss you'll take if you're forced to sell into it.

Add up your cash needs up front, and make sure that you have the money available when you need it. Keep in mind: the IRS won't put off April 15th while you wait for your stock to rebound.

195 What's your time frame?

Are you a 25-year-old with 40 years to retirement? Then you probably have the luxury of taking a long-term view, investing in stocks you know will give you a good return over 20 years, even if they have occasional yearly dips. Or are you on the edge of retiring and looking to live off your portfolio next year? In that case, you probably want to stick with less volatile investments to enjoy your golden years worry-free. Who wants to worry about their portfolio when they could be planning a safari?

Tip — **Remember that most of these factors in your investment character will change over time. Be sure to review and adjust them every 2 years or so.**

Trap — **Talk with your accountant. Too many times, investors rush into an investment plan without understanding all of the tax consequences. Then tax time reveals a grim reality: they should have invested in tax-free bonds, for example, or should have sold a losing stock earlier.**

196 Do you have special tax needs?

Nobody wants to think about taxes until they have to, but the truth is that taxes can make a huge impact on your investment decisions. If you don't want to face it, call your accountant. Ask her questions like: do you need tax shelters? Is there any reason why you should prefer dividend income, for example, over interest income? How will capital gains taxes affect your outlook?

197 Are there any other personality quirks, preferences, or propensities you'd like to indulge?

Lots of people neglect their heart in the investment process and then view investing as "cold" or "impersonal." It doesn't have to be. The investment process is a very personal one, and you can tailor your portfolio to your personality in many different ways. I know plenty of people who hate tobacco companies, but invest in them through mutual funds because they didn't know they could exclude them. In fact, that's an option you have with many mutual funds.

Or maybe you feel strongly about protecting the environment. There are plenty of "green" funds which concentrate on "green-friendly" companies. Most of these preferences fall under the umbrella of "socially conscious" investing—an increasingly common practice to which many mutual funds cater.

If you answer honestly all of these questions about your personal investment character, you'll have laid a great deal of the groundwork toward making your best investment decisions.

"One cannot raise the bottom of a society without benefiting everyone above."

—MICHAEL HARRINGTON

It's fun to watch your money grow when you invest it wisely.

Investing 101: Key Tenets

198 Never forget about inflation.

An annual inflation rate of 3.5 percent (the average since 1913) may not sound like much, but it's eating away at your savings faster than you think. Look at the chart below to see how inflation can erode a sizable investment. That's why your money sitting in a low-paying savings or checking account isn't really "safe."

It's never too early to start building a great portfolio.

This chart helps to illustrate the full effects of inflation: an item that cost $1 in 1913 would cost you more than $16 in 1997.

Effects of Inflation: Prices over Time*

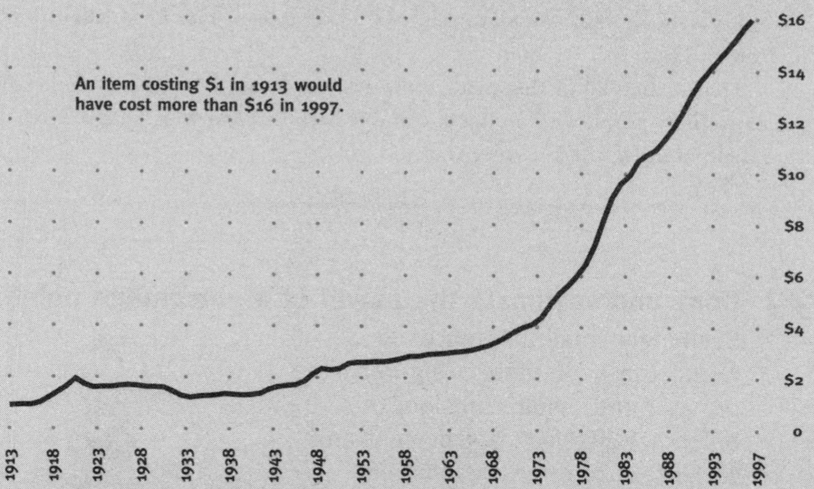

Source: Bureau of Labor Statistics

* Based on an item with a price of $1 in 1913, increasing by annual change in CPI.

Personal Perspective

"When I began working in 1969, Wall Street was the place to go for a good paying secretarial job with excellent benefits. I didn't know a thing about the stock market and truly believed that anything related to stocks or bonds was boring, and that whatever was happening on that trading floor had absolutely nothing to do with me and my life.

"It wasn't until 1980, when I moved my two children to Los Angeles and transferred out of an administrative position at Drexel Burnham Lambert to work for the High Yield & Convertible Bond Department under Michael Milken, that my perspective changed.

"There we helped finance young and growing companies and I got a firsthand look at how securities actually seed companies and, in some cases, an entire industry's growth.

"Now these securities had faces. People who had dreams and the money raised would help transform their dreams into realities. People like Ted Turner, who wanted to build Turner Broadcasting and CNN; Bill McGowan, continuing MCI's battle against AT&T for equal access to long-distance phone lines; Steven Wynn, transforming his vision for Las Vegas into more than just a mirage (no pun intended); Rupert Murdoch's passion for creating a viable fourth network through Fox TV. There are hundreds of examples. Many of the people you might not recognize, but the companies and their products are with us every day—United Airlines, Chrysler/Jeep, Revlon, Time-Warner, Mattel, Duracell, Pier One Imports, and on and on.

"That's when all of this made sense to me—when I transformed these securities into people and products—and it became clear to me the ones that had potential and the ones that did not."

199 Don't underestimate the power of a percentage point.

Seemingly small differences in return can have quite a big impact on your end result. Consider this difference between a 5 percent and 10 percent return over different time periods.

Compound Interest: Present Value

The formula is: $PV = FV \div (1+i)^n$

Interest Rate	Number of Years (n) 1	5	10	15	20	25	30	50
1%	$1,010	$1,051	$1,105	$1,161	$1,220	$1,282	$1,348	$1,645
2%	$1,020	$1,104	$1,219	$1,346	$1,486	$1,641	$1,811	$2,692
3%	$1,030	$1,159	$1,344	$1,558	$1,806	$2,094	$2,427	$4,384
4%	$1,040	$1,217	$1,480	$1,801	$2,191	$2,666	$3,243	$7,107
5%	$1,050	$1,276	$1,629	$2,079	$2,653	$3,386	$4,322	$11,467
6%	$1,060	$1,338	$1,791	$2,397	$3,207	$4,292	$5,743	$18,420
7%	$1,070	$1,403	$1,967	$2,759	$3,870	$5,427	$7,612	$29,457
8%	$1,080	$1,469	$2,159	$3,172	$4,661	$6,848	$10,063	$46,902
9%	$1,090	$1,539	$2,367	$3,642	$5,604	$8,623	$13,268	$74,358
10%	$1,100	$1,611	$2,594	$4,177	$6,727	$10,835	$17,449	$117,391
11%	$1,110	$1,685	$2,839	$4,785	$8,062	$13,585	$22,892	$184,565
12%	$1,120	$1,762	$3,106	$5,474	$9,646	$17,000	$29,960	$289,002
13%	$1,130	$1,842	$3,395	$6,254	$11,523	$21,231	$39,116	$450,736
14%	$1,140	$1,925	$3,707	$7,138	$13,743	$26,462	$50,950	$700,233
15%	$1,150	$2,011	$4,046	$8,137	$16,367	$32,919	$66,212	$1,083,657
16%	$1,160	$2,100	$4,411	$9,266	$19,461	$40,874	$85,850	$1,670,704
17%	$1,170	$2,192	$4,807	$10,539	$23,106	$50,658	$111,065	$2,566,215
18%	$1,180	$2,288	$5,234	$11,974	$27,393	$62,669	$143,371	$3,927,357
19%	$1,190	$2,386	$5,695	$13,590	$32,429	$77,388	$184,675	$5,988,914
20%	$1,200	$2,488	$6,192	$15,407	$38,338	$95,396	$237,376	$9,100,438
21%	$1,210	$2,594	$6,727	$17,449	$45,259	$117,391	$304,482	$13,780,612
22%	$1,220	$2,703	$7,305	$19,742	$53,358	$144,210	$389,758	$20,796,561
23%	$1,230	$2,815	$7,926	$22,314	$62,821	$176,859	$497,913	$31,279,195
24%	$1,240	$2,932	$8,594	$25,196	$73,864	$216,542	$634,820	$46,890,435
25%	$1,250	$3,052	$9,313	$28,422	$86,736	$264,698	$807,794	$70,064,923
26%	$1,260	$3,176	$10,086	$32,030	$101,721	$323,045	$1,025,927	$104,358,362
27%	$1,270	$3,304	$10,915	$36,062	$119,145	$393,634	$1,300,504	$154,948,026
28%	$1,280	$3,436	$11,806	$40,565	$139,380	$478,905	$1,645,505	$229,349,862
29%	$1,290	$3,527	$12,761	$45,587	$162,852	$581,759	$2,078,219	$338,442,984
30%	$1,300	$3,713	$13,786	$51,186	$190,050	$705,641	$2,619,996	$497,929,223

Note: Assumes $1,000 future value and annual compounding. For other future values, use table values as multiple factors divided by 1,000.
Example: If you were receiving $1,000 in 20 years, assuming a 6 percent compounding interest rate, the present value of your future cash receipt would be $312. If you were receiving $500, the present value would be $156 ($500 x 0.312).

200 Don't forget about compounding.

Similarly, many people don't understand what a difference compounding can make in their investment return. If your interest is compounded, it means that the base from which your interest is calculated grows throughout the year, or whatever your total time period is.

For example, suppose that you had a $10,000 in a CD earning 5 percent a year. If there were no compounding, you'd simply earn $500 ($10,000 x 5 percent), leaving you with $10,500 at the end of the year. But if your account compounded, say, quarterly, then your interest earnings would be calculated like this:

Beginning balance	**$10,000.00**
1st quarter interest : $10,000 x 1.25% = $125	
Balance end of 1st quarter	**$10,125.00**
2nd quarter interest : $10,125 x 1.25% = $126.56	
Balance end of 2nd quarter	**$10,251.56**
3rd quarter interest : $10,251.56 x 1.25% = $128.14	
Balance end of 3rd quarter	**$10,379.70**
4th quarter interest : $10,379.7 x 1.25% = $129.75	
Balance end of 4th quarter	**$10,509.45**

One example of the power of compounding is the famous "penny doubled." If you start with a penny, but double your investment every year, you'd end up with more than $5 million after 30 years, and a whopping $5.6 trillion by the time 50 years had passed.

Years	**Investment Values**
0	$0
5	$0
10	$5
15	$164
20	$5,243
25	$167,772
30	$5,368,709

201 Don't overrate or overestimate the experts.

Of course, financial advisors and analysts can be valuable sources of information, but the final investment decision should always be yours. Many of us are so intimidated by the investment world that we tend to give too much importance to investment gurus and advisors. (I think this is similar to the "God complex" we all tend to have about doctors).

There are several important rules to remember:

- **No one cares more about your money than you.** Sure, your broker may feel bad if you lose money on an investment, but you can bet he doesn't lose that same night's sleep that you do.
- **No one knows more about your investment situation than you.** The talking head on TV or editor of the newsletter may have a lot of good information, but they don't know anything about you. Consider their advice from within the framework of your own needs.
- **No one can predict the future.** No matter how respected is the analyst that you see quoted in the paper or interviewed on cable, remember—she's just guessing. Of course it can be an educated guess, but nobody ultimately knows what will happen with the economy, the stock market, or even acts of nature.

Tip **The analysts I tend to respect the most are those who spell out several scenarios rather than pretend that they can predict the future.**

202 Don't count on beating the experts, either.

It's not that they know that much more than you do (now that you've read this book), or that they're smarter, it's just that there are built-in advantages for the large investor. A mutual fund manager, for example, will get much lower commissions than you will, to start with. And her job allows her access to information much more quickly than you'll see it. If your company announces a merger, she'll get a call immediately, while you may find out on the evening news.

203 Diversify, diversify, diversify.

This is the rallying cry of small and large investors alike, and really is just a fancy way of saying don't put all your eggs in one basket. That doesn't mean spreading out your life savings between 3 or 4 stocks either. As painful as it may be, you have to think of the worst-case scenario. Imagine the consequences of one of them going way south if you've only got four: you'd lose a lot of money. Force yourself to consider how much you could lose without ruining your life: 5 percent? Then make sure you're in 20 different investments. Or is 10 percent your limit? Then find 10 investments you like.

When I say 10 investments, that means 10 *really different* investments—stocks which are relatively independent in their price movements. The key thing to remember here is that stocks within the same industry tend to move together. If you have 10 different stocks in the natural gas industry, for example, then you're not really diversified. If the price of natural gas plummets, you can bet that most of your stocks will, too.

Even farmers know money doesn't grow on trees.

Diversification

Cash $	10%	– Bank Accounts – Money Market Accounts
Bonds bond	40%	– Government – High-Grade – High-Yield
Stocks stock	50%	– Blue Chip – Small Stocks – International Stocks

In deciding among different investments, the principal categories most investors start with are Cash, Bonds, and Stocks. But within those categories are a number of different subcategories, which may also be a part of the diversification process.

204 Consider forming an investment club.

Many small investors today are forming investment clubs, which pool their money and make investment decisions together. Typically, investment clubs meet on a regular basis (say, once a month), and require a set investment amount from each member. Many investment clubs benefit from the discipline imposed by this structure, as well as from the "decision by committee" structure that governs them. It's also a great learning experience: investors become educated about the basics in a casual, social atmosphere. To start one, contact the National Association of Investors Corporation (NAIC) (see Resource Guide on page 210) for more information, and begin asking your friends and acquaintances if they'd be interested. You'd be surprised at how many people will respond, which is why you should give some thought to the number of people you'd like to include.

Did You Know?

The Math: Dividend Yields

If a stock is selling at $50 a share and has been paying a dividend of 25 cents a quarter, or $1 a year, then the dividend yield is 2 percent ($1 ÷ $50 = 0.02, or 2 percent).

205 Don't let the jargon scare you.

Do expressions like "preferred dividends" and "triple witching hour" make you break into a cold sweat? Well, rest easy—they do for most people. Most of us would rather ignore this complicated but critical part of our future because of the jargon that comes along with it. And sure—some parts of this terrain are bumpy. But the good news is that you don't need to master the really complicated stuff to be a responsible investor. Just wrap your mind around the basics and you've got enough to make a reasonably informed decision.

206 Don't lose your long-term perspective.

This is a classic trap that many investors fall into—being overly influenced by the recent performance of "the market." It's difficult not to get excited about a stock market that's been up 20+ percent for a couple of years, and even I begin wondering if I should reallocate more of my portfolio to stocks. But then I remind myself—the market almost always comes back to the long-term average of somewhere around 13 percent.

These last few years have been pretty impressive. But notice that the index always corrects itself over time. It's not a terrible thing—it's just correcting to its long-term average of 10 to 12 percent. (In this case, the average is a little better at 13.4 percent.) Of course, you don't want the down years to discourage you either. Consider a chart of the S&P 500 since 1975.

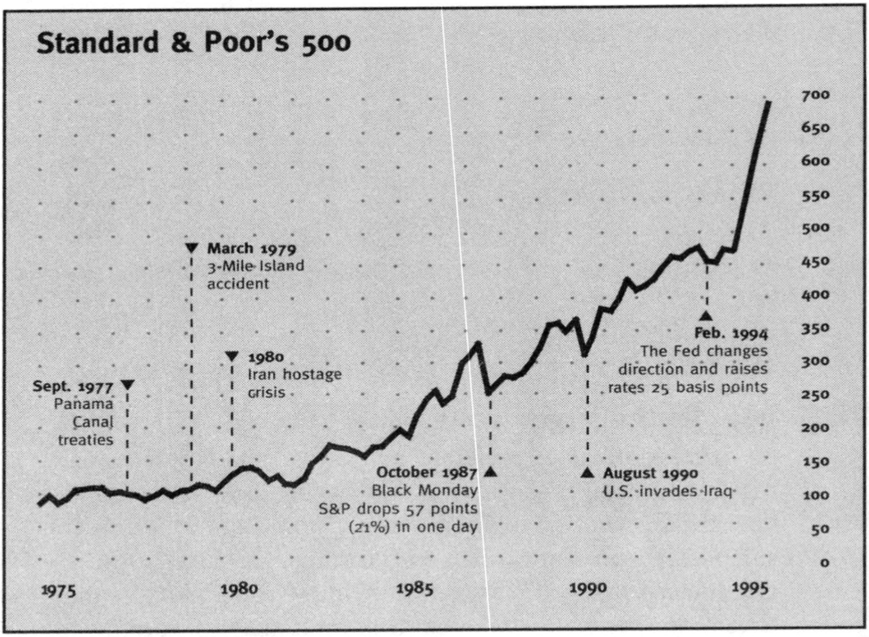

Here we see all of the major drops in the index for the last two decades. Many people panicked during those slides and sold their stock at huge losses. Let's look at the infamous "Black Monday" debacle (October 19, 1987, the day the market dropped by about 21%). If investors had simply held on to their stocks, they would have recouped their money and more. In fact, many investors recognized "Black Monday" as a buying opportunity. If you'd bought at the bottom of that dip, you would have made about 10% on your money by the end of the year (not bad in a year everyone else considered a disaster). By the end of 1988, after the market had largely recovered, your "fire sale" investment would have made you about 24% in a little less than 15 months.

Stocks & Bonds: Just Know the Basics

207 If you know the difference between a stock and a bond, you're further along than most investors.

Believe me—grasp these two concepts and you'll be able to hold your own in just about any cocktail party. There are a million different ways to invest, but almost all are derived from these 2 basic instruments. Here are the basic definitions:

Stocks

208 Simply stated, common stock is a share in a company's ownership.

It can also be called *capital stock* or *equity.*

As a stockholder, you provide the company with equity capital and, in turn, usually have the right to vote on certain matters—like electing a board of directors. As a majority (owning 51 percent or more), shareholders can indirectly control a company's business.

If you own shares in a company, you are directly linked to the company's fortunes. Your share will be reflected primarily through the price of your shares, otherwise known as capital appreciation. You may also benefit from dividend income which the company chooses to distribute to its shareholders.

"If stock market experts were so expert, they would be buying stock, not selling advice."

—Norman Augustine

Bonds

209 Think of a bond as a loan to a company.

With a bond, you have no ownership in the company, and it has a legal obligation to pay you back your money. It has agreed to pay you back on a given date, and to pay you a given interest rate in the interim. So if you own a $1,000 bond that has a 5-year life and a 10 percent interest rate, you're guaranteed to receive $100 per year, and get your $1,000 back in 5 years. (That's assuming that the company doesn't go into default, which is the only risk that bondholders take.)

Tip **Even in the event of bankruptcy, bondholders will often receive all or most of their money back.**

210 U.S. Government bonds (a.k.a. Treasury bonds) are obligations of the United States federal government.

From a credit standpoint, they're considered just about the safest securities you can buy. The interest you're paid is also exempt from state and local income taxes.

211 Municipal bonds are debt securities issued by state or local municipalities.

The money raised from the sale of these bonds can go towards housing developments, new roadways, sewage, etc. If you purchase a municipal bond, you are exempt from paying federal taxes on the interest received; if you are a resident of the particular state, you will be exempt from paying state and local taxes on the interest as well.

212 High-yield corporate bonds are those ranked below investment-grade by the rating agencies.

The "junk" status of these securities is usually overdramatized: most companies in the country don't qualify as investment grade, including those with millions of dollars in revenues.

213 Convertible bonds are bonds that can be converted into stock.

At some point these bonds may be converted into the company's shares (usually a higher price than the current market). Some investors like them because they offer the stability of the bond, but also give you some "play" on the company's stock price.

Tip **When you own a bond, you want interest rates to go down. That's because if your bond pays you, say, 8 percent a year and interest rates drop to 7 percent, then your bond is worth more because of its above-market coupon.**

Tip **Whether a security is a Treasury bill, note, or bond depends on its lifespan. If it's a year or less, it's a bill; between 1 and 5 years, a note; more than 5 years, a bond.**

Did You Know?

The Math: Convertible Bonds

If a \$1,000 bond is convertible into 40 shares of common stock at \$50 per share, then, the conversion price is:

$$\$1{,}000 \div 40 = \$25$$

If when the bond is issued, the stock is selling at \$40, then the conversion premium is:

$$(\$50 - \$40) \div \$40 = 25 \text{ percent}$$

Just the Facts

The Math: Bond Yields

Current bond yield = annual coupon payment ÷ bond price

Example: A $1,000 bond has a coupon rate of 7 percent, so it pays $70 a year. If you buy the bond for $900, your actual current yield is 7.78 percent ($70 ÷ $900 = .0778, or 7.78 percent).

If you buy the bond for $1,100, the current yield is 6.36 percent ($70 ÷ $1,100 = .0636, or 6.36 percent).

In any event, the 7 percent coupon rate does not change.

Tip

Bonds tend to move much more in sync with each other than other investments, because of their strong link to broader interest rates. If interest rates go up, chances are your bond's yield will too, which means its price will go down. (The exception is high-yield bonds, which have a stronger link to the fortunes of the company, similar to stocks.)

Things to Think About

Why would I buy bonds?

They're a good choice if you want your investment money to add to your annual income. Not only is this an excellent strategy for retirees, but it may also apply to younger investors in need of extra income. For example, when your kids are starting college, making those semi-annual tuition payments might be difficult if there's no additional money coming in each month. A bond's interest payments (or bond fund's distributions) can supplement your monthly income while keeping your original investment (principal) safely tucked away until the bond matures.

Bonds also tend to be less risky. Like a savings account, they will pay you interest—though usually quarterly or semi-annually. And if all goes well, they will pay you back their face (or principal) amount at the end of the term or at the maturity date.

So if you need a steady flow of income on your money, you might want to consider putting some of your investment dollars into a bond fund.

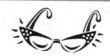

Personal Perspective

"Investment guru Peter Lynch, who successfully managed one of the greatest mutual funds in history—Fidelity's Magellan Fund—has often said, 'the time to buy may be when everyone else is running for the door; the time to sell may be when everyone is rushing in.'

"How exactly does this work? Well, during the end of the 1980s there was political and social pressure for new rules and regulations to limit investing of savings & loans and insurance companies in high-yield bonds. The pressure worked and these financial institutions were forced to sell their junk bond positions, and the Chicken Littles were running around yelling 'the sky is falling!' Even the pundits predicted widespread bankruptcies and other types of plagues would besiege us if we didn't wipe out high-yield bonds from the face of our capital markets.

"Well, lo and behold, by the early 1990s, can you make a guess at which securities were considered to be the best performers? High-yield bonds! Why? Because they had value. Value that could transcend negative publicity. And those that rushed in to buy (and not sell) their high- yield portfolios were paid off in spades."

"Let Wall Street have a nightmare and the whole country has to help get them back in bed again."

—WILL ROGERS

Making investment decisions isn't easy. You may want help.

JUST THE FACTS

Bond Ratings

The reason why some bonds pay higher interest rates than others is generally because of their bond rating, which attempts to measure the stability of the company. The highest rated bonds are rated AAA by Standard and Poor's (S&P), while the lowest rated bond gets a D rating. The two largest bond-ranking agencies are S&P and Moody's, and their ratings look like this:

Moody's	S&P	
Aaa	AAA	
Aa1	AA+	
Aa2	AA	
Aa3	AA-	
A1	A+	
A2	A	
A3	A-	
Baa	BBB+	
Baa2	BBB	
Baa3	BBB-	
Baa1–C	BB+–D	Non-investment grade

214 With a few exceptions, bank CDs are a poor excuse for an investment.

Sure they're safe, but so are plenty of other investments with a much higher return. Of course, banks love it—they pay you a tiny interest rate on your money, which they turn around an invest in much higher paying investments, like treasury bonds or bills.

THINGS TO THINK ABOUT

The Ups and Downs of Bonds

If interest rates go down, bond holders are generally happy, because it means that their bonds are worth more. (If you have a bond that pays you 10 percent when interest rates are 8 percent, you know you have a good deal.) That's why the bond market goes *up* when interest rates *fall*, and why it goes *down* when rates *rise*.

JUST THE FACTS

Over-The-Counter Stocks

OTC stocks are shares in companies traded outside of organized stock markets like the New York Stock Exchange (NYSE) and the American Stock Exchange (AMEX).

215 Preferred stocks are a more "bond-like" version of common stocks.

Preferred stock is a different way to own shares in a company. They're similar to common stock, but the most significant difference is in the dividends. Unlike with common dividends, the company is *obligated* to pay dividends to preferred shareholders. They also get a fixed dividend (unlike common dividends, which can vary depending on earnings), which is why they often trade more like bonds. (The dividends are kind of like interest payments.) On the other hand, preferred dividends are generally limited on the upside, while common dividends are not.

Trap

Just because your common stock reports a certain dividend payout, it doesn't mean that the company is obligated to pay it. Dividends are entirely at the discretion of management—if they hit a rough spot they can reduce or eliminate the dividend to common shareholders.

Did You Know?

The Efficient Market Theory

A fancy explanation for why it's nearly impossible to beat the market is the Efficient Market Theory widely taught in business schools. The idea is that the markets operate so efficiently that you can assume that everyone knows the same information and that it's already reflected in stock prices. Other experts make fun of the theory, telling the story of the man who wouldn't pick up the $20 bill on the street—surmising that it couldn't be there or someone would have already picked it up.

"An investor should act as though he has a lifetime decision card with just 20 punches on it. With every investment decision, his card is punched, and he has one fewer available for the rest of his life."

—WARREN BUFFET, CHAIRMAN AND CEO, BERKSHIRE HATHAWAY, IN *FORBES*, MAY 25, 1992

Average Investment Returns

	Average Return (1926–94)
U.S. Treasury Bills	3.7%
Government Bonds (Long-Term)	4.8%
Corporate Bonds (Long-Term)	5.4%
Large Company Stocks	10.2%
Small Company Stocks	12.2%

Source: Ibbotson Associates, Chicago

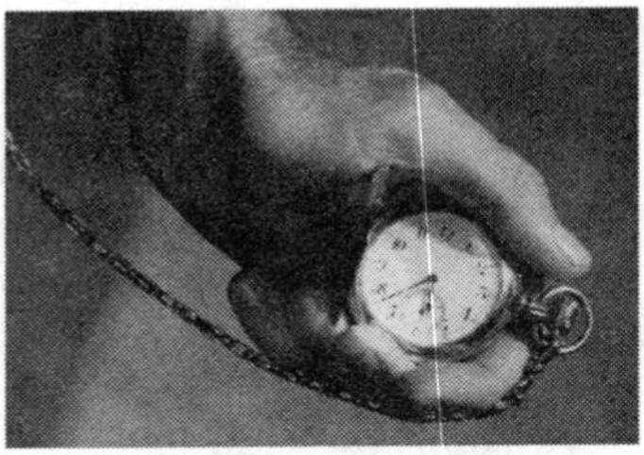

What to invest in depends on your time frame.

Sensible Strategies for the Do-It-Yourself Investor

"There are two times in a man's life when he should not speculate: when he can't afford it, and when he can."

—Mark Twain

216 Find strategies you understand and stick to them.

Let's say you've decided that you want to invest on your own. You're tired of mutual fund fees, and you hate calling your broker because she talks your ear off about her kids. You've read this book cover to cover, gotten a subscription to *Money* magazine, and are ready to take the plunge. How should you start picking your investments? Before we tackle stock picking, let's review more useful strategies for the beginning investor. These are a few tips that the pros on the street would rather you *not* know about.

217 Consider the "Dogs of the Dow."

The beauty of this strategy lies in its simplicity. This is the idea: at the beginning of every year, you pick the 10 stocks in the Dow Jones index (there are only thirty total) with the highest dividend yield. Dividend yield is calculated like this:

Dividend Yield = Annual Dividend ÷ Share Price

The Dogs have outperformed the averages over time, but underperform them in very good years. Thus, in 1997, when the Standard & Poor's (S&P) 500 was up 33.4 percent, the Dogs were up 22.2 percent. But over the past 5 years, when the S&P averaged an annual gain of 21 percent, the Dogs averaged 24.2 percent.

Again, this is an easy strategy to use. If, at the start of 1998 you wanted to use it, you would simply invest evenly in these 10 stocks, and hold them until 1999, when you would invest in the new Dogs.

1998 Dogs of the Dow

Symbol	Company	Price	Yield
MO	Philip Morris	45 1/4	3.54%
JPM	Morgan (J.P.)	112 7/8	3.37%
GM	General Motors	60 3/4	3.29%
CHV	Chevron	77	3.01%
EK	Eastman Kodak	60 9/16	2.91%
XON	Exxon	61 3/16	2.68%
MMM	Minn. Mining & Man	82 1/16	2.58%
IP	International Paper	43 1/8	2.32%
T	AT&T	61 5/16	2.15%
DD	DuPont	60 1/16	2.10%

See *www.DogsoftheDow.com* for more information and research on the Dogs of the Dow.

Did You Know?

How the Dogs Have Fared

The Dogs of the Dow have turned in an average 17.7 percent annual return since 1993, vs. 11.9 percent for the overall Dow Jones Index.

218 Dollar-cost averaging is also a tried and true favorite.

This is another simple investment technique, although it does require some stock picking at the outset. This strategy focuses more on *when* you buy your stocks rather than *what* stocks you buy. This is how it works: once you've picked a solid stock (or a few) you'd like to invest in, you invest the same amount of money at set time intervals.

That means that if you want to begin investing in General Motors, you might invest $100 in GM shares at the end of every month. The advantage behind this strategy is that you buy more shares when the stock is cheap, and less shares when the stock is expensive.

Here's a simple example tracking three months: Let's say that GM shares begin the first month at $50, so your $100 gets you two shares. The next month, the shares have fallen to $40, so you get 2.5 shares (most company investment plans allow you to buy fractions of shares). By the third month, the shares have bounced back up to $50, and before you even make your third investment you own 4.5 shares, worth $225. You've made $25, even though GM shares started at $50 and ended at $50.

Dollar-Cost Averaging: An Example

Month	Share Price	Amount Invested	# of Shares Bought	Portfolio Value
1	$50	$100	2	$100
2	$40	$100	2.5	$180
3	$50	n/a	n/a	$225

Things to Think About

The Disciplined Investor

You'll notice that a commonality between each of these strategies is an enforced discipline. That's because the most dangerous word in investing is "hunch." In fact, beware all references to "hunches," "good feelings," or even "gut instinct" about a stock. With these strategies, you'll never have the chance to fall in love with a stock ("I know it's down by half, but I just know it'll come back if I buy more...").

Stock Picking & Other Fun Sports

219 Understand the broad categories of stocks.

- **Blue Chip Stocks** are considered to be the most tried-and-true performers in the stock market. The nickname comes from the gambling chip having the highest value. These are companies with a long history of sustained earnings and uninterrupted dividends. They have been around long enough to show a good track record.

Trap

Even blue chips can steer you wrong. In the early 1970s, the "nifty fifty" as they were coined were a group of rapidly growing companies whose stocks were selling at high price earnings ratios. They were commonly believed to be the key to superior investment performance, but faltered by the end of the 1970s. From 1973 (near their peak) through 1981, 37 of the "nifty fifty" stocks actually fell in value. On average, these "blue chips" dropped 5% over that 9-year period—that was a 48% loss, accounting for inflation.

- **Growth Stocks** are those that have shown faster-than-average gains in earnings for the last few years, and are projected to continue doing so. While they outperform average stocks for the long-term, they do have a higher degree of risk. A growth stock usually doesn't pay its shareholders dividends.
- **Emerging Market Stocks** are those issued by countries with less developed, or "emerging," economies (e.g., Latin America, or Indonesia). The main idea here is that since the countries are so small, they have much more dramatic growth ahead. Of course, the downside is much higher risk, since so many important factors—like the economy and political risk—are so often uncertain.

Tip

Most investors buy individual foreign stocks through "ADRs," or American Depository Receipts. They trade on American exchanges in U.S. dollars.

Just the Facts

Where Do Stocks Trade?

- **New York Stock Exchange** (a.k.a. NYSE or the "Big Board") has the largest stock exchange in the world, with more than 2,700 companies listed. Many of them are the largest publicly traded companies in the country.
- **American Stock Exchange** (a.k.a. AMEX or The Curb): the third largest dollar volume stock exchange. It has more lenient listing requirements than the NYSE, so companies whose common shares are traded on the AMEX are usually smaller.
- **NASDAQ:** the world's first computerized stock market and second-largest market in the United States. Unlike the AMEX and NYSE, it is based in Washington, D.C.

Tip

Another alternative to "ADRs" are "country funds"—mutual funds which invest only in the stocks of a particular country.

"Change is the law of life.
And those who look only to the past or the present
are certain to miss the future."

—John F. Kennedy

Personal Perspective

"Why prices go up and down often seems like a mystery. And often they are just that! There are times when it is almost inconceivable why a particular company's stock price should go up and, conversely, when it goes down!

"The stock market is very temperamental and extremely vulnerable to good and bad news. It's not always logical, and that's vital to keep in mind. If stock prices can trade illogically, both up and down, there's even more reason to remain rational if you want to make money. Better still, if you chose wisely, just remain patient and stay calm until this irrationality passes."

220 Stick to the fundamentals.

- **Price:** The first thing you'll want to see before buying a stock is a price chart that goes back as far as possible. It gives you perspective on what the stock has done for the last few years, and how its recent performance stacks up. Has there been a run-up in the stock in recent months? How about a drop? Or is this a strong and steady performer?
- **Earnings:** What's the company's earnings history? Has it had shown consistent growth in the bottom line, or is it a more volatile performer? Consistent, increasing earnings are what investors look for more than anything else, and could justify a higher price.
- **P/E ratio:** The P/E ratio is simply the price of the stock divided by the most recent 4 quarters of earnings, and it's still the most widely used way of determining how a stock is valued by the market. The idea is that a stock price doesn't mean much if you don't know what you're paying for. So a stock may seem cheap because it's $40 versus $50 a year ago, but if the company's earnings are only half as much, then it's not such a great deal.

Trap

When reviewing statistics like past earnings and prices, keep in mind that the past doesn't always give good clues about the future.

For best results, take a long perspective.

Did You Know?

The Math: Price-Earnings Ratio

Price-Earnings (P/E Ratio) = Price $\div$ Earnings Per Share

Example: If a stock price is $50, and the Earnings Per Share for the past 4 quarters is $2.50, then the P/E ratio = $50 $\div$ $2.50 = 20

JUST THE FACTS

Stock Trading Jargon

- **Market Order:** A trade placed at the "market price" or at the stock's current price.
- **Stop Order:** An order that specifies a price at which you'd like to buy or sell. Investors usually use them to protect themselves in case of sudden market moves. You might put in a stop order to sell a stock if it dipped below a certain price—to limit your losses.
- **Day Order:** A trade that expires at the end of the day if not executed. If your stop order was also a day order, it would be canceled at the end of the day if the stop price was never reached.
- **Selling Short:** If you thought a stock was going to drop, you might sell it short. That means that you effectively "borrow" the stock so that you can "sell" it. Then if the price really does dip, you buy the shares at a lower price, replacing those that you've borrowed, and realize a profit between your buy and sell prices.
- **Buying on Margin:** Basically, you're borrowing from your broker to buy securities. If you're approved for this practice by your broker, you can generally "margin" your account for up to 50 percent of its cash value.

Personal Perspective

"Here's a good story that should give you an idea of the often irrational nature of the market. A few years ago, a national newspaper printed a story that made a very powerful (and wealthy) investor furious. In his anger, he instructed his advisors to begin buying up stock in the paper, with a vague intention to pose a hostile buyout. He had no other fundamental basis for his strategy, but because his purchases were so large they began to move the market. The stock moved higher because of the new demand, with many investors (especially small investors) not understanding why. Many of them assumed that something 'big' must be happening (e.g., some announcement was about to break) and began jumping into the stock. Finally, when this tycoon's temper cooled, he sold the stock and the market dropped again. Investors who believed there was a rationale behind the stock market lost money."

THINGS TO THINK ABOUT

How Margin Can Work For or Against You

A margin account is essentially a line of credit from your broker. That line of credit is limited by the Feds to 50 percent of the market value of your account for the initial transaction, and 25 percent going forward. Here's an example:

Suppose you had $2,000 to invest, and want to buy a particular stock at $20 per share. Rather than simply buying 100 shares, you decide to leverage your investment using margin and purchase 200 shares. Your account would look like this:

Market Value of Stocks ($20 x 200 shares)	$4,000
Margin (Market value less amount borrowed)	$2,000
Amount Borrowed	$2,000
Margin Percentage (margin balance ÷ market value of stocks)	50 percent

So now you satisfy the 50 percent margin limit. And if your stock increases, you'll make twice the profit.

But what if your stock price goes down? Let's say that it drops by $5. Your account would look like this:

Market Value of Stocks ($15 x 200 shares)	$3,000
Margin (Market value less amount borrowed)	$1,000
Amount Borrowed	$2,000
Margin Percentage (margin balance ÷ market value of stocks)	33.3 percent

Well, this is clearly a bad turn of events. Notice that you've lost $1,000 instead of the $500 you would have lost if you'd only invested $2,000. Still, you won't receive a margin call yet because your margin percentage is still above 25 percent.

But what if your stock continues to drop? Suppose it dived to $12 per share:

Market Value of Stocks ($12 x 200 shares)	$2,400
Margin (Market value less amount borrowed)	$400
Amount Borrowed	$2,000
Margin Percentage (margin balance ÷ market value of stocks)	16.7 percent

Uh-Oh. Now you'll receive a margin call. You'll be required to put enough money into your account to bring the margin percentage up to 25 percent. Even worse, you've essentially experienced an 80 percent loss ($1,600 ÷ $2,000 investment). And that's the important lesson to remember about margin accounts: they can leverage your gains and your losses.

That's how people got into so much trouble during big market drops in the past: In fact, before the 1929 market crash, banks would lend up to 90 percent of the value of client's holdings. That meant that a 5 percent decline can wipe out an investor—a phenomenon which many believe was responsible for amplifying the crash.

Even as recently as the 1987 crash (when the market lost more than 20 percent of its value), many investors were hit with big margin calls. Many large brokerage firms sent out representatives door-to-door to collect margin account monies due.

"I think knowing what you cannot do is more important than knowing what you can."

—Lucille Ball

221 Don't forget dividends.

There are 2 ways that your stock could make you money:

1 by selling your shares for more than you paid

2 by receiving dividend payments.

Dividends are most often paid in cash but they can be paid in other ways, such as additional securities. Companies that make regular dividend payments usually do so on a quarterly basis (every 3 months). Unlike preferred stock where the dividends are set, common stock dividends are made at management's sole discretion, so if your stock pays a dividend in the first quarter of the year, it may not pay in the second, and vice versa.

Not all companies make dividend payments, however. Some believe it is better for everyone to put profits back into the company to build the business.

222 Don't be afraid to admit your mistakes.

This is a lesson the pros live by. If you've picked a lemon of a stock and it's looking shaky, get out before it gets worse. New investors lose money by the boatloads before they learn this simple rule.

Tip **One way to tell if your stock is still solid after a dip is through asset value—literally the value of the hard assets owned by your company. Many analysts use asset value as a "bottom" for the share price.**

Did You Know?

The Math: Dividend Yields

If a stock is selling at $50 per share and has been paying a dividend of 25 cents a quarter, or $1 per year. The dividend yield is: ($1 ÷ $50 = 0.02, or 2 percent).

Things to Think About

Dividend Yield

A dividend yield is the return on your investment in a common stock or preferred stock based on current market prices. It is calculated by dividing the annual dividend payment by the market price.

For example: a stock is selling at $50 a share and has been paying a dividend of 25 cents a quarter or $1 for the year. The dividend yield is 2 percent ($1 ÷ $50 = 0.02 or 2 percent).

223 Hitting singles and doubles is better than swinging away at the home runs.

We all love those years when we get a 20 percent-plus return on our money. But you should never get so hooked that you begin taking chances in order to repeat that performance. Consider this table, which compares a volatile portfolio with a consistent one:

	Constant Singles		Home Runs and Strike-Outs	
1	10%	$11,000	25%	$12,500
2	10%	$12,100	5%	$13,125
3	10%	$13,310	–15%	$11,156
4	10%	$14,641	15%	$12,830
5	10%	$16,105	3%	$13,215
6	10%	$17,716	30%	$17,179
7	10%	$19,487	4%	$17,866
8	10%	$21,436	18%	$21,082
9	10%	$23,579	7%	$19,606
10	10%	$25,937	10%	$21,567

Personal Perspective

"In one of my first attempts at investing, I picked a stock I thought was a sure winner. When it dropped 30 percent in one year, not only did I refuse to sell the stock, I decided that I should buy more. Pretty dim, huh? I reasoned that the stock was an even better buy at the new, 'discounted' price. "Need I say more? The stock dropped another 30 percent before I cut my losses and tried to salvage my pride. Of course now I know that my judgment was seriously impaired by my inability to admit a faulty purchase.

"Let's face it—nobody likes to admit it when they've made a bad choice—it's human nature. I find that the best way to fight off this destructive (and expensive) tendency is to impose inflexible limits. It's easy: if any stock in your portfolio drops by a certain percentage—say 20 percent—sell it. It will be painful, and you will be tortured by thoughts of it coming back, but trust me, it will save you plenty of headaches in the long run.

"If it's easier, think of it this way. If your $1000 investment is now worth $800, you're out $200 and you want it back. But you don't have to make it back with that original stock. Ask yourself: is that stock really the best place for your $800? You could make back that $200 on another, better-chosen, investment."

224 Don't fall in love with a stock.

There was another dangerous tendancy lurking behind my expensive mistake in the above example. My reluctance to sell the stock was wrapped up in my pride, sure, but it was also because I had learned to love the stock. I read about the company, I visited its stores. The guys who ran the company seemed like really *nice* guys, and I was sure the whole thing was a winner. It was real romance and I had completely lost perspective. It's embarrassing, but it happens all the time. A certain industry or company just captures your interest: maybe you love the glamour of entertainment stocks, or anything to do with the Internet really floats your boat. BE CAREFUL. You have a built-in bias which should be carefully monitored and filtered out of your investment decisions.

Tip

But you shouldn't write off all stocks that have been on a downswing—there are situations in which a stock is undervalued by the market and can be snapped up at a good price. Just be sure that you do your homework on the fundamentals of the company, an that your emotions aren't driving your investment decisions. (See page 165 for discussion of buying opportunities during market dips.)

Did You Know?

What's an IPO Exactly?

What's the difference between an IPO (initial public offering) and the secondary market? An IPO is the first public sale of a company's stock—there are a set amount of shares which are sold into the market at a predetermined price. (That price is determined by the bankers, who generally try to get a "feel" for what the market will bear.)

225 A stock split doesn't double your money.

A stock split increases the number of shares a company has outstanding without changing shareholders' equity.

What does that mean? If you own 1 share of stock and it splits 2 for 1—you now own 2 shares of the same stock. The value of the stock does not change so if your 1 share of stock was worth $20, now you would own 2 shares of stock worth $10 each—therefore your shareholder's equity value remains the same.

The total number of shares currently trading in the market, however, has just doubled. So if before the stock split the company had 100,000 shares trading (or outstanding) it would now have 200,000 shares.

226 A reverse stock split works just the opposite of a stock split.

The company reduces the number of shares outstanding. In a 1-for-2 reverse split, shareholders get one new share for 2 of the pre-split ones, and the value doubles. So if you owned 2 shares at $10, and the company did a reverse split, you would now have 1 share worth $20.

Mutual Funds & You

227 If you're short on time, invest in mutual funds.

That may be the best advice you'll read in this entire book. Sure, that hot stock tip from your neighbor's cousin's best friend could pay off big-time, but do you really have the time to monitor a stock every day? Can you keep up with its day-to-day announcements, earnings, and management changes? Remember, there are thousands of professionals out there—essentially your competition—who do nothing but monitor that company all day for a living.

On a more encouraging note, those same investment professionals can also work for YOU, through the mutual funds you invest in. By buying shares in a fund, you are essentially buying the time and expertise of people who—let's face it—probably know a lot more about investing than you do. It's their job.

Tip

While there are many advantages to buying mutual funds, these are the most popular:

- **Convenience of buying and selling**
- **Diversity of investments**
- **Professional management**
- **Automatic reinvestments**
- **Distribution options**
- **Telephone redemptions and transfers**

228 Know the differences between the basic funds, particularly between bond and stock funds.

The bad news is that there are thousands of different types of mutual funds—nearly as many now as individual stocks. The good news is that you don't really need to know anything but the basics. If you don't know anything else, know the mix you'd like between stocks and bonds. This is the single most important distinction between mutual funds for the average investor.

This seems like a simple issue, but I know plenty of brainy types who haven't grasped this idea. If your money is in a all-stock fund, chances are you'll get more risk with more return over time. All bonds in your fund? Then you'll likely get less volatility with lower return.

Beyond that distinction, if you're feeling really ambitious, you can explore the other flavors of funds. Within the stock funds, for example, there are "high-growth" funds (read: more risk, with possibly more payoff) to "fixed" stock funds (read: blue chips with plenty of stability but not much movement). Or within the bond funds, you might choose between high-yield bonds (which are higher yielding), or government bonds, which are likely handing out lower interest payments but giving you more security.

JUST THE FACTS

What's a Mutual Fund Anyway?

- A mutual fund is a type of investment that pools together the money of thousands of people. At the helm is a fund manager—the person or company in charge of investing the money.

- There are more than 6,500 mutual funds to choose from—including Fidelity, Vanguard, and Capital Research. Depending on the type of fund you choose, your money can be invested in securities such as stocks, bonds, money markets, and commodities.

- When you invest in a mutual fund you are buying units—also called shares. It's very much like owning a stock: you become an owner of the mutual fund. The price you pay for the shares is called the net asset value or NAV. Remember this term and understand it well, it's key to your success in mutual funds.

- Because the fund makes many investments, rather than just a few, you get the advantage of diversification. This means that even if some of the investments are not performing as well than the manager expects, others are likely to do better. For example, a typical stock fund might be invested in more than 100 companies at a time. You can get even more diversity if you put your money into several different funds with different objectives.

And sure, if you want to really do your research, you can get into extremely specific funds, investing in Malaysia or Mexico, or focused commodities. But remember, once you've become that focused, you're moving away from the whole point of mutual funds: diversification. Put another way, if all of your money is in a fund investing in Indonesian stocks, then you'd better keep up with the news in Indonesia. Are you ready for that?

229 If you're really nervous, consider a money market fund.

Investing in money market funds is a good starter kit for first-time investors before plunging into stock or bond funds because you can get the "feel" for investing your money somewhere other than a bank account that is federally insured.

Money market funds are probably the safest, most stable of the mutual funds, and in many instances they pay returns that are 1 to 2 percentage points better than you'd receive on a bank savings account.

Tip

Try to save about 3 months' worth of living expenses in a money market fund before you even consider venturing out to other types of investments. The 3 months will give you a good emergency fund in case of a job loss or prolonged illness.

Did You Know?

Can Money Market Bonds or Funds Go Bust?

On the off chance that one of the bonds gets into default trouble, usually the manager of the money market funds makes up the difference to its shareholders. It's comforting to know that in the last 15 years, only one money fund ever lost money for its investors and even then, they only lost 4 percent of the total investment.

230 Index funds can save you some money.

An index fund simply invests in the same stocks in a major benchmark. For example, an S&P 500 index fund would consist of the same stocks held in the S&P 500 index, and in the same proportions. The idea is to mimic the performance of a key indicator as closely as possible. Because there is no real decision making in this process, they are not considered to be actively managed, and so usually have lower management fees.

Quite frankly, it has been proven (by academics and practitioners) that stock portfolios that are actively managed by "experts" (fund managers) do not actually perform any better on average than index funds. Go figure.

Things to Think About

Paying More for "Active" Management

Of course, there is one big difference between an expertly managed fund and an index fund. The fund manager charges a lot more for services than a stock index fund. So in the end not only do you do as well (or better) than the expert manager, but it costs you less!

You know that you're not going to read this in any advertisement for your friendly broker. While higher costs are bad for you, they're often good for the money managers who get compensated by how much money they bring into their funds.

"Never invest your money in anything that eats or needs repainting."

—Billy Rose

231 To load or not to load...

If you buy your fund through a brokerage—like Charles Schwab, Merrill Lynch, or Smith Barney—it will probably be a load fund—which means you will pay a commission.

If you know which fund you want to buy, you can save the commission by buying directly from the mutual fund company itself—that's called a no-load fund. Beware, however—even though you don't pay an up-front commission, there may be fees to cover sales and marketing costs.

While you can invest in mutual funds at any time, you might want to wait until the annual distribution is made—usually in December. If you buy before, it will cost more per share and you won't get any of the distribution benefits. Plus, the price of the mutual fund will drop after the distribution is made—so you may want to wait until then to buy.

Tip **A back-end load fund is not a no-load fund. In a back-end load fund, you are assessed a penalty fee if you get out of the fund before a certain period has elapsed. This penalty limits your freedom to change your mind about your investments and to move your money around freely.**

Trap **Some no-load funds charge a hefty fee for reinvesting your dividends. Find out if the fund you are interested in does this. You may want to avoid such a fund.**

Things to Think About

How Much Are You Investing in a No-Load?

When comparing a load fund with a no-load fund, be sure to consider that the amount of your initial investment will be reduced by the load fee. So if you invest $10,000 in a load fund which charges you 2 percent up front, then your initial investment will actually be $9,800.

Understanding Mutual Fund Claims

232 You can't eat relative performance.

OK—when you're looking at your mutual fund's performance, it's good to know the market benchmark to give you some perspective. On the other hand, a 2 percent return for the year will always be bad, even if the market fared worse. That's a classic angle that many mutual funds use during off years: their literature will say "outperformed the market by 2 percent" rather than "down 7 percent for the year." Remember, no matter how it's termed, it means you lose money.

233 What's the payoff anyway?

No one knows what will happen in the future, but we can get some helpful guidance by the information gathered in the past. These are the average performances of the key types of investments during the past 7 decades.

JUST THE FACTS

Average Investment Returns

Type	Average Return (1926–94)
U.S. Treasury Bills	3.7%
Government Bonds (Long-Term)	4.8%
Corporate Bonds (Long-Term)	5.4%
Large Company Stocks	10.2%
Small Company Stocks	12.2%

Source: Ibbotson Associates, Chicago

Nothing's Ever Free: The Risk versus Reward Tradeoff

"Anxiety is the space between the 'now' and the 'then.'"

—RICHARD ABELL

234 The offer of higher returns ALWAYS brings more risk. This is a critical truism to remember in the investment world, and probably the one most often forgotten or overlooked. Who isn't tempted by the idea of a "sure thing," as in "*There's just no way to lose on this deal, it's such a sure thing*"? Whenever you catch yourself caught up is this all-too-common trap, stop and repeat these 2 phrases to yourself as many times as it takes to come to your senses: "There are no sure things. The offer of a bigger payoff ALWAYS comes with more risk." Got that? Good.

Remember—when a deal seems too good to be true, it probably is!

THINGS TO THINK ABOUT

Understanding Risk

Risk isn't always such a terrible thing. On the contrary, nothing good comes without a little risk. For example, investing in stocks instead of bonds involves more risk, as we discuss in Tip 236. But a 20-year-old college student who kept her money in bonds for 50 years would be making an expensive mistake, given the higher average performance over time from stocks.

I would never imply that risk is bad per se. Only that the tradeoff between risk and reward be acknowledged and understood.

235 The longer your time frame, the lower the risk.

Because of the self-correcting nature of the major markets, time can cure almost any downdraft in the investment world. Consider the largest stock index—the Dow Jones Industrial Average (DJIA):

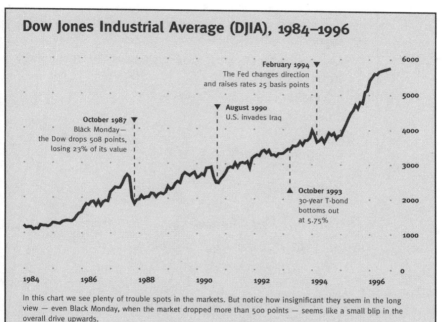

Dow Jones Industrial Average (DJIA), 1984–1996

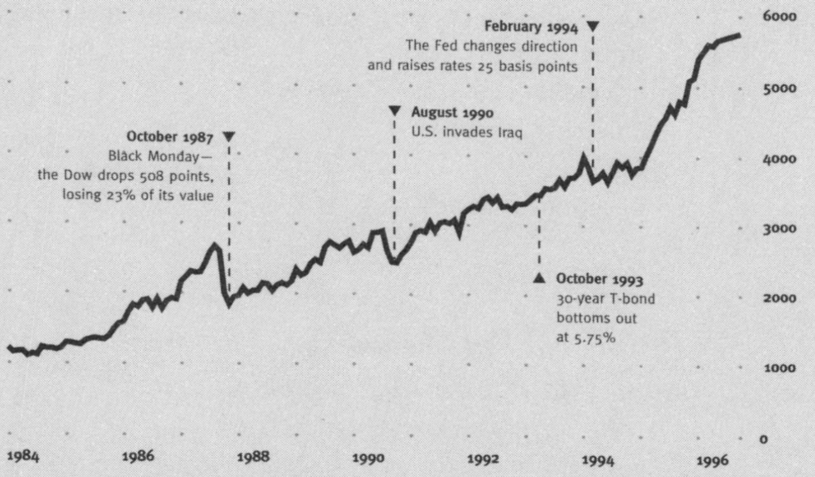

In this chart we see plenty of trouble spots in the markets. But notice how insignificant they seem in the long view — even Black Monday, when the market dropped more than 500 points — seems like a small blip in the overall drive upwards.

JUST THE FACTS

Kinds of Risk

Risk can come in many different forms:

- **Market Risk** arises from general swings in the market. In other words, your company might be fine, but if the market drops 20 percent, chances are your stock price will too.
- **Interest Rate Risk** is particularly applicable to bonds. When interest rates rise, for example, most bond prices fall since their coupon payments aren't worth as much money.
- **Individual Risk** is that which comes from your specific investment, i.e., a lousy earnings announcement that affects your company specifically.

236 Understand the basic risk/reward categories.

The risk/reward relationship is generally acknowledged to look something like this:

High Risk

- Derivative products like options and futures, speculative stocks (new or very small companies, or "penny stocks")
- Aggressive stocks (fast-growing stocks like technology stars)
- International stocks
- Blue chip stocks
- Bonds
- Government bonds

Low Risk

"Personally, I'm always ready to learn, although I do not always like being taught."

—Winston Churchill

Things to Think About

The Real Rise Behind Stocks

It's important to recognize that common stock is the riskiest investment in a company because in bankruptcy you get paid off last. And that's why its performance is usually higher than other types of investments.

While you could lose money in a single year or on a single stock, investors who have held a portfolio of stocks through any 15-year period since 1926 have always come out ahead.

If you're investing for your retirement or for any long-term need, the real risk may be *not* owning stocks.

Getting Fancy: Options, Futures

237 Leave the fancy stuff to the professionals.

In other words, my best advice to the average investor thinking of getting into options and other derivatives would be: *don't.* That is, unless you really want to devote the time to studying how they work (be prepared for long hours learning about strips, straddle strategies, and triple witching hours), and constantly monitoring their performance.

Remember the competition: legions of investment pros who've read lots of books—even *written* lots of books—on derivatives, and who have all day to keep an eye on them.

238 There are basically 2 flavors: a call option and a put option.

You would buy a call if you think the stock will go up, and a put when you expect it to go down.

If you buy a call option, you buy the right to buy it at a certain price within a certain amount of time. Let's look at a real-life example: Let's say that you decide that AT&T's share price is going to make a jump soon. On May 20, 1998 (the time of this writing) you look in the *New York Times* business section and see this:

MOST ACTIVE OPTIONS

Company	Date	Strike	Ty	Exc	Vol	Pr	Chg	% Chg	Pr	Chg	Compar
DellCptr	Jun 98	95	c	X	9,384	6 3/8	− 1 3/8	− 17.7	94 19/32	+ 3/32	
Pfizer	Jun 98	115	c	A	7,441	3 7/8	+ 5/8	+ 19.2	112 7/8	+ 2 3/16	DellCptr
AT&T	Jul 98	55	c	C	6,081	3 1/2	− 1/8	− 3.4	56 7/16	− 3/16	DellCptr
Micsft	Jul 98	75	c	P	5,973	12 7/8	+ 1/4	+ 2.0	86 39/64	+ 35/64	AmStrs
DellCptr	Jun 98	110	c	X	5,408	2	...	...	94 19/32	+ 3/32	Symntc
Terex	Jul 98	30	c	AX	5,340	2 1/8	+ 1/4	+ 13.3	30 15/16	+ 9/16	Symntc
Terex	Jan 99	35	c	AX	5,220	1 7/8	...	...	30 15/16	+ 9/16	Intuit
Lucent	Jun 98	75	c	ACX	5,041	1 7/8	+ 1/16	+ 3.4	72 1/8	+ 5/16	FileNt
DellCptr	Jun 98	90	c	X	4,720	9 1/4	− 1	− 9.8	94 19/32	+ 3/32	Intuit
											DayHud

You can buy a call option on AT&T stock for $3 ½, with a strike price of $55, and with an expiration date of July, 1998 (all options expire on the Saturday following the third Friday of the expiration month, so our calendar shows that this one expires on July 18, 1998). We also see that AT&T stock is selling for $56 7/16.

Now—let's say you buy the AT&T option. What has to happen for you to make any money? For you to break even, the stock needs to rise to $58 ½ before July 18. (That equals the $55 strike price plus the $3 ½ you shelled out for the option.) This is an important part of the equation that many first-time investors forget.

So what happens if the stock price does move "into the money"? Let's get really optimistic and say that AT&T takes a jump to $60. What should you do to lock in your profit? One of 2 things:

- You could exercise your option, buying the AT&T shares at the $55 strike price, and then immediately sell them for the market price of $60. Your profit would be $1.50 per AT&T share ($60 less $55 less $3 ½ price of the option.)
- Alternatively, you could sell your option, which will have risen in value by approximately the same amount.

On the other hand, what happens if the stock price drops or stays below our strike price? Nothing much, really. Your option will simply expire, worthless, on July 18, and you would chalk it up to a learning experience.

239 The flip side: buying a put.

A put works in exactly the same way, except that you're betting that the stock price will drop. From the same paper in which we took the AT&T example, we see that a July 1998 put on Microsoft with a strike price of $75 is selling for $12 7/8. We also see that Microsoft's shares are now trading at $86 38/64.

To make any money, Microsoft's shares would need to *drop* to $62 1/8 (the $75 strike price less the $12 7/8 price you paid for the option). That's about a 28 percent drop in Microsoft's stock that needs to happen during the course of the next month. (Remember: you're always working against the clock.) Wanna take that bet?

240 If you're looking for options with less time pressure, consider LEAPS.

There are longer-term options now that can relieve you of the extreme time pressure usually implied. These longer-term options are usually referred to as LEAPS, for Long-Term Equity AnticiPation Securities. LEAPS are put or call options with expiration dates set as far as 2 years into the future. Like standard options, each LEAPS contract represents 100 shares.

Consider commission costs carefully before executing a strategy. We've left commissions out of these calculations for simplicity's sake, but they can be a big part of the equation. A full-service broker can charge 3 to 5 percent on every trade, taking a big bite out of your profits.

A quick way to understand the derivatives markets is to look at it from this angle: they take risk away from those who don't want it (hedgers) and give it to those who do (speculators).

Did You Know?

Options Mean Bulk Buying

Options come in lots of 100, so if an option price is $2, then you'll have to spend $200 (not counting commissions), which will give you the option to buy 100 underlying shares.

241 If you must invest in derivatives, only bet what you can lose.

I know that's a rule that should apply to all investment strategies, but it's particularly relevant with derivatives. That's because with a derivative there is a much greater likelihood that you will lose your entire investment. Take options for example. If you were to buy 100 shares of Caffeine Cola stock for $10 per share, you'd have a total investment of $1,000. Now, as we know from our section on risk and reward, there is always a chance of the price dropping 10 to 20 percent, leaving you with a loss of $100 to $200. That's no fun, certainly, but we would be comforted by the possibility of the stock rebounding in the long run. Remember, until you sell the stock, it's only a loss on paper.

Not so with a call option. Let's say that instead of buying the 100 shares of stock, you decide to buy a call option giving us the right to buy the stock at $11. Your options only cost $100. (It is true that one of the advantages of an option is a lower initial investment.) You've decided that the stock is definitely set for an upswing to $12 or more. In this case, if the stock drops 10 to 20 percent, the options will expire worthless, and you'll lose the entire $100 investment. Since you never owned any shares, you have no long-term investment and no chance of recouping your loss should the stock rebound.

242 Remember, you're working against the clock.

All derivatives have some sort of expiration date, meaning that not only do you have to be right about the direction of the investment, *but about the time frame in which it will happen.* Most options, for instance, have a life of 3 months. That means that if you have a good hunch about Caffeine Cola stock, and decide to buy options, you've got 3 months (or less, depending on when you buy the option), for your hunch to pay off. If you buy the stock, you've got plenty of time to wait to be proven right.

Tip **Of course, you're not absolutely locked into an option until expiration date. You can always sell the option before it expires—hopefully for more than you paid for it!**

243 If you're looking for a faster way to lose your shirt, consider futures.

Because that would be the only reason you might begin trading futures. Really. This is a market that moves lightning fast, and offers incredibly high risk. Maybe you don't really want to trade futures, but you'd like to be able to brag about your conquests around the water cooler. Well, here's enough information to make you sound reasonably impressive to your coworkers.

Futures were originally developed in the agricultural market, when farmers wanted to lock in the price of their crops. So while his corn was growing, Farmer John would sell a futures contract at a certain price per bushel, thus protecting himself from a sudden drop in corn prices before he could get his crops to market. Today, many other types of companies use futures in much the same way.

But the futures market has expanded beyond the coverage of commodities, with contracts now written on financial instruments like foreign currencies and stock indices. An American company with a great deal of incoming revenue in Japanese yen, for example, might wish to sell a contract on yen, protecting themselves from a drop in the value of the Japanese currency. This kind of protective trading is known as *hedging.*

Did You Know?

Futures Delivery?

Although futures contracts carry an obligation to deliver the underlying goods on a given date, they are nearly always closed out with an opposing transaction before delivery date comes. Less than 5 percent of futures contracts actually result in delivery.

"The things which hurt, instruct."

—Benjamin Franklin

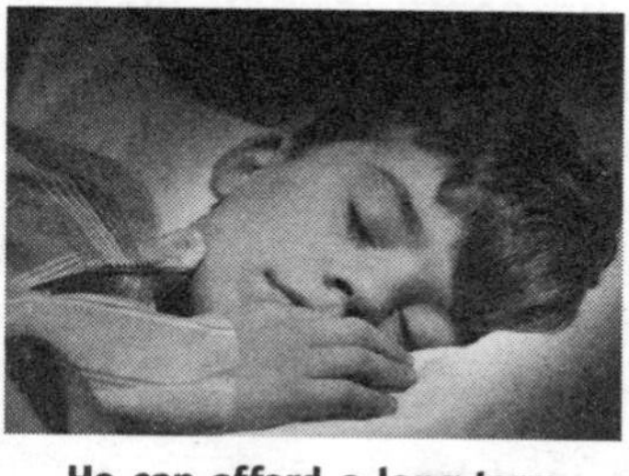

He can afford a long-term investment strategy, but can you?

Getting Wired: On-line Trading

244 Use the Internet for information, but be aware of its limitations.

One of the most important revolutions in the investment world has been caused by the explosion of Internet use. That's because the most important commodity in the investment world is information, and that's what the Internet is all about. Now, an investor at home can get much of the same information on the markets as investment professionals. Through a number of different sources, you can now get information like current stock prices, price history, and research reports on many different companies and securities.

There's no doubt that this development is tremendously helpful, but you should be careful of overestimating its benefits, and never for a minute think that it gives you the same advantages as the pros. Remember: the average Wall Street analyst or fund manager has information you'll never get from the Internet—conversations with company management, research reports, and more detailed data sources, to name just a few.

245 You might save some money by trading on-line.

If you feel comfortable making your own decisions, there are a number of on-line brokers which offer very low-cost trading alternatives. As with the discount brokers who were their low-cost predecessors, the tradeoff is a no-frills services package. Don't expect advice, research, or any hand-holding when you invest this way.

Popular on-line investment sites:

- eTrade: *www.etrade.com*
- eSchwab: *www.schwab.com*
- National Discount Brokers: *www.ndb.com*

246 Don't bet your portfolio on the Internet being up.

On-line banking is an ever-growing field with some glitches to work out. Keep in mind the headline-making outcry when America Online's (AOL) systems have gone down in the past. Of course, that could just be the equivalent of not being able to get your broker on the phone: it's your call.

Tip **Most companies have their annual reports and other helpful information on their Web sites.**

247 Beware of on-line rumor mills and "hot tips."

The unlimited ability to contact millions of people can be used unscrupulously by people with hidden agendas.

Trap **Remember that new access to information still doesn't put you on an even playing field with the pros. They have critical information—research reports, conversations with analysts and company managements—that the Internet can never give you.**

Things to Think About

Internet Resources

Here's what you can do when you surf the 'Net.

- Look up stock quotes, buy and sell securities, ask questions of experts, network with other investors, and do your homework to find answers to questions you need to know.
- Research company information, facts and figures—Hoover's is a great site to use.
- Review charts and graphs—Bloomberg, CNNfn, and Dow Jones Interactive might be your next stop.

You can even monitor your own personal portfolio—by inputting the stocks or funds you own—or those you want to—and quickly see how much money you would have made or lost.

Commissions & Other Sneaky Costs

"The only sure thing about luck is that it will change."

—BRET HARTE

248 Don't let commissions eat up your profits.

So many investors get so caught up in the excitement of trading that they lose much of their profit to commissions. Every trade you make will involve a cut going to your broker or online service.

249 Ask your broker for a discount.

Many brokers at full-service firms are empowered to apply discounted commission rates to various clients. Don't be the only sucker paying "retail" when you could be getting it "wholesale."

Personal Perspective

"When I opened up my first account with a full-service broker, I barely glanced at the commission rate, and jumped in feet-first to the stocks I'd been watching. I though I had done pretty well until I got my first statement: almost all of my profits were offset by commissions I'd paid. I was paying a whopping 4 percent commission. That may not sound like much, but consider that it adds up to about 8 percent for a round-trip trade, and you'll see that you start out with an 8 percent loss."

Help From the Pros

250 A good broker can be a blessing.

Sure a full-service broker is expensive, but a really good one may be worth the money. Remember, if you have a broker, you have a true advisor, as well as someone you can call during a worrisome time. If the biggest stock in your portfolio just took a nose-dive, it might be nice to have a broker to talk to rather than an on-line service.

Trap

NEVER go with brokers who contact you out of the blue. Chances are they're new, cold-calling brokers looking for clients. There's nothing wrong with that, of course, but wouldn't you rather have someone your friends and family have vouched for?

251 If you need more than an investment advisor and you've got a larger portfolio, consider using a financial planner.

If you have a large enough nest egg to warrant some extra help, ask around about a financial planner. Financial planners are combination brokers, accountants, and personal advisors. For a fee (usually anywhere from 2 to 4 percent of your portfolio) they'll help you with the larger, overall decisions about your money. For example, they will take stock of your personal investment needs and criteria and recommend a general investment plan, of which stock investing is only a small part. A good financial planner may recommend a percentage of your portfolio to invest in stocks, another portion to tax-free investments, and the rest to an all-bond mutual fund.

Don't get in the hole, start investing now.

252 Find your financial planner through referrals.

Never through advertisements or cold calls. When looking for a financial planner, ask your accountant and maybe your lawyer for recommendations. Many have a certification called a CFP (certified financial planner), which is some guarantee of a minimal level of knowledge about the investment world.

Trap: **Commissions are generated on trading, whether it's on a good stock or a lousy one. Your broker makes money based on the activity in your account—which has nothing to do with how profitable you are.**

Trap: **Beware of investments that your broker or advisor seem to be heavily biased towards. For example, an investment house may offer a higher commission on a mutual fund that they're trying to launch. High commission payouts like these can make your broker's or advisor's recommendation less than objective.**

JUST THE FACTS

Is Your Broker On the Up-and-Up?

Most are, but here are a few clues that should make you wary:

- **Excessive trading:** If your broker seems too eager to trade in your account, she may be guilty of churning. Don't get caught up in the excitement of the market, and let her talk you into more trading than you are comfortable with.
- **Misstatements or omissions:** Did your broker tell you that an investment would give you a 12 percent return, only to tell you later that it will be closer to 9 percent? Don't be afraid to ask exactly what the discrepancy was, and why she didn't tell you about it up-front. Or did she fail to tell you about an important fee involved in an investment? That's another good reason for a serious talk, and perhaps a new broker.
- **"Sure thing" talk:** Once any broker starts talking to you about "guaranteed" returns—especially high returns—you should hear alarm bells going off. No high returns are EVER guaranteed, and this is a good indication that you have a broker who's willing to play fast and loose with the truth for the sake of a trade.
- **Pressure to grant power of attorney:** Some clients with extremely long-term and trusting relationships grant their broker the right to trade their account on their behalf. If your broker starts angling for that right before you think it's appropriate, you should be suspicious of her motives.

Worksheet: What Kind of Investor Are You?

By filling out this worksheet honestly and completely, you'll have a great handle on your investment profile.

Return

What kind of return are you looking for?

Are you more interested in *current income* (i.e., collecting dividend or interest payments)?

Or would you rather have *capital growth* (i.e., watching your portfolio grow in value through the years)?

Risk

What's your risk tolerance?

How much of a loss in your portfolio would you find intolerable (i.e., would give you serious insomnia)?

5 percent?

10 percent?

20 percent?

20 percent+?

How much money could you lose in a year and still feel comfortable?

On paper (i.e., unrealized losses on investments you haven't sold)?

Realized losses?

Liquidity

How liquid do you need to be?

List below all the cash needs you have going forward. Think of big payments that might be due on house loans, to the IRS, etc.

Time Frame

When would you like to sell your investments?

How old are you?

How many years do you have until retirement?

How soon would you like to begin living off of your investments?

Taxes

Note: these are probably questions your accountant should help you with.

What's your tax situation?

What's your tax bracket?

Is your tax rate high enough to justify buying tax-free investments?

Do you need tax shelters?

Could realized investment losses help offset your tax bill?

Is there a reason to why you might prefer dividend income to interest income?

Personal Preferences

Do you have any other likes or dislikes you'd like to incorporate into your portfolio?

Are there any companies or industries you'd rather not invest in? (Some people, for example, would rather not invest in tobacco companies or the defense industry).

Are there any personal causes you'd like to consider (e.g., environmental, religious, pro-women or minorities)?

Ask Lorraine

Q&A

Q. *I'm young and have had no experience with the stock market. Now I have to choose an investment strategy for my retirement account at work. How should I start?*

A. You can begin by reading this section and becoming familiar with the basics of investing. I promise that if you get that far along you'll know more than the vast majority of your peers. Next—dive in and pick a mutual fund that fits your criteria. The great thing about being young is that you have lots of time and can probably absorb more risk than someone older. That means that you should have most of your long-term investments in common stock, which have a higher average return. You could even experiment with a couple of the riskier options (like foreign funds)—but only with a small portion of your account (say 5 percent). There's no better way to learn than by doing it and then watching the results.

Q. *Why do companies declare stock splits if the overall values do not change?*

A. Because companies believe that a lower stock price might psychologically encourage new investors to buy stock. It also makes stock ownership more affordable to a larger number of people. For instance you might not be able to afford a stock trading at $20, but when the price drops to $10 per share, it might be easier for you to take the chance.

Q. *My stock just went through a "reverse split"—what is that and why would they do it?*

A. Just like it sounds, a reverse split accomplishes the opposite of a regular stock split. So a company with 100,000 shares might wish to consolidate, and have only 50,000 shares outstanding. In that case they would complete a 1:2 stock split. A company might use this strategy for psychological reasons. If the price of the stock trading is higher, investors might consider it to be worth more. This is often the case when stocks are trading below $5. It also reduces the number of shares outstanding and saves the company administrative costs.

Q. *"I keep hearing the term NAV. What's a NAV?"*

A. Most mutual fund shares are bought based on a Net Asset Value (or NAV). The NAV is simply the total value of the fund's assets divided by the total number of shares.

Resource Guide

Investment Clubs

- The NAIC (National Association of Investors Corporation) can provide you with more information on starting your own investment club. Contact:

  NAIC
  P.O. Box 220
  Royal Oak, MI 48068
  Tel: 248-583-NAIC
  Fax: 248-583-4880
  www.better-investing.org

Socially-Conscious Investing

- 1998 Social Investment Forum
  1612 K Street NW, Suite 650,
  Washington, DC 20006
  Tel: 202-872-5319
  Fax: 202-822-8471
  e-mail: info@socialinvest.org
  www.socialinvest.org

Mutual Fund Resources

- *Morningstar* (newsletter ranking various mutual funds)

  Morningstar, Inc.
  225 W. Wacker Drive
  Chicago, IL 60606
  1-800-876-5005
- *Value Line Mutual Fund Investment Survey*
  1-800-284-7607
- *The Mutual Fund Encyclopedia*
  Dearborn Financial Publishing
  1-800-533-2665
- Lipper Analytical Services
  74 Trinity Place
  New York, NY 10006
  212-393-1300

Section 6

An excellent way to learn about investments is by reading the newspaper.

Understanding Information

In this age of information, there's no shortage of financial data. You can get it in the newspapers, buy specialized investing periodicals and books, subscribe to newsletters, watch TV, and even surf the Internet. Yet what good does this information do if you can't separate the quality from the quantity?

The key is being able to transform this information into knowledge. Which company announcements are truly newsworthy and which are simply public relations messages? Where should you really focus your attention in an annual report? And perhaps most importantly: what advice from the "experts" deserves real attention?

Once you understand how to apply the information you're reading—and overlook that which doesn't apply to you—you'll be well on your way to savvy financial planning.

Looking Up Your Stocks, Mutual Funds, Bonds, & Options

"All I know is what I read in the papers."

—WILL ROGERS

253 Learn to read the financial section of the newspaper. With the exception of the Internet, the newspaper will probably be the quickest and most convenient way to check out how your portfolio is doing on a daily basis. But the financial section can be confusing, as anybody who's ever tried to figure out the difference between a LIBOR rate and LEAPS option surely knows. Let's take a look at a few of the major sections from the pages of the *New York Times*. Your paper may look slightly different, but the essential information should be about the same as shown in the example on the right.

Generally, you will see that the stocks are split into 3 different sections: the New York Stock Exchange, the NASDAQ, and the American Stock Exchange. That's because different stocks are literally traded at different physical exchanges. Once you figure out what trades where, you'll be able to find each of your stocks fairly quickly.

Let's start with a NYSE section. On the next page is an actual excerpt from January 29, 1998. Let's take something familiar: AT&T.

Seem confusing? We'll take the headings one by one and see what they mean.

- **52-week high and low:** The first two numbers give us an idea of where the stock has been during the past year. Right from the start, we can see that AT&T has had quite a volatile year, with a high of $66 ½, and a low of $30 ¾.

- **Stock:** This is simply the abbreviation of the company's full name. It may take some searching in the beginning to find where your stocks appear in your paper, but you'll get the hang of it. (NOTE: AT&T's stock symbol, or "ticker," is actually "T", but most papers list stocks in alphabetical order by company name.)
- **"Div" or Dividend:** This column tells you what the annual dividend rate is. In most cases, this means that it's reporting the most recent quarterly declaration multiplied by 4. For AT&T, we see that dividend is $1.32 per year. (AT&T's most recent quarterly dividend was $0.33, so the annual rate is 33¢x4=$1.32.)
- **"Yld %" or Yield Percentage:** This is your dividend yield, which is calculated by dividing the share price by the annual dividend. Thus, for AT&T, the current price of $62 1/16 divided by $1.32 = 2.1 percent.

Looking Up Your Common Stocks

Excerpted from the *New York Times*, January 29, 1998.

10 1/4	8 7/8	ACM Sc	.90	9.0	q	1399	10	9 15/16	10	+ 1/16
7	6 1/4	ACMSp	.57	8.4	q	1675	6 13/16	6 3/4	6 13/16	+ 1/16
15	12 1/4	ACMMD	1.35 a	9.7	q	376	13 15/16	13 11/16	13 15/16	+ 3/8
10 9/16	9 3/8	ACM MI	.90 a	8.7	q	188	10 1/2	10 3/8	10 3/8	...
15 1/8	12 1/2	ACMMu	.90	6.1	q	89	14 15/16	14 13/16	14 7/8	+ 1/16
24 5/8	14	ACNiels	...	...	39	1352	21 5/16	20 3/4	21 3/16	+ 7/16
27 1/2	17 5/8	ACX Tech	...	...	cc	155	23 1/2	23 1/8	23 7/16	+ 3/8
49 5/8	27 1/2	AES Cp s	...	...	42	3910	42 1/16	40 3/4	41 3/16	− 1/8
73 5/8	48	AES pfT	2.69	4.1	...	8	65	65	65	...
57 7/8	37 1/2	AFLAC	.46	0.9	17	2495	49 5/8	48 15/16	49 1/4	+ 1/16
36 5/16	25	AGCO	.04	0.1	11	4862	27 3/8	27 3/16	27 3/8	+ 3/16
21 5/16	17 3/4	AGL Res	1.08	5.4	15	647	20 5/16	20	20 1/8	...
25 7/8	24 5/8	AICI pfT	2.25	8.8	...	73	25 5/8	25 59/128	25 5/8	...
19 1/4	10 1/4	AJL	1.44	11.4	...	x901	12 3/4	12 3/8	12 5/8	+ 3/8
24	16 1/16	AK Steel s	.50	2.8	7	10328	18 7/16	17 11/16	18	+ 9/16
25 1/8	22 1/4	AMB Pr n	.13 p	...	...	687	24 1/8	23 7/8	24	− 1/4
27 3/8	20	AMF n	...	...	...	1499	22 3/8	22	22 1/4	+ 1/8
24 3/4	21 1/2	AMLI Rs	1.76 f	7.5	18	463	23 7/8	23 1/2	23 9/16	− 1/8
136 1/2	78 1/4	AMR	...	...	12	6615	128	124 5/8	126 3/4	+ 3 1/16
19 3/8	9 7/8	APT Sat	...	...	...	256	13 1/8	11 7/8	12 5/8	+ 1/2
51 1/4	40 7/8	ARCOCh	2.80	5.8	42	297	48	47 13/16	48	+ 1/8
37 5/8	**19**	**ASA Ltd**	**1.20**	**5.0**	**q**	**1306**	**23 7/8**	**22 13/16**	**23 7/8**	**+ 1**
66 1/2	30 3/4	AT&T	1.32	2.1	22	89763	63 9/16	61 11/16	62 1/16	− 1 1/16
39 5/8	17 11/16	AVX Cp	.24	1.1	14	708	21	20 5/8	21	+ 1/4
40 3/4	29 1/4	^AXA UAP	.65 e	1.6	...	995	40 15/16	40 3/16	40 5/8	+ 1/4
32 3/8	9 5/8	Aames s	.13	1.1	10	2058	12	11 3/16	12	+ 9/16
26 15/16	24 1/2	AbbyNtl pf	2.16 e	8.1	...	2	26 11/16	26 11/16	26 11/16	− 1/16
71 47/64	52 7/8	^AbtLab	1.08	1.5	...	11187	72	70 7/8	70 15/16	+ 1/16
36 1/8	12 1/2	AberFitch	...	...	47	1607	30 7/8	30 3/16	30 11/16	+ 1 1/8
21	11 1/2	Abitibi g	.40	...	...	2318	14 1/4	13 7/8	14	...
28 5/8	17 3/4	AcptIns	...	...	11	192	23 5/8	22 15/16	23	− 3/8
32	**15 3/4**	**AccuStff**	**...**	**...**	**27**	**3511**	**25 13/16**	**24 1/8**	**25 3/4**	**+ 1 15/16**
18 1/2	10	AckGrp	.02	0.1	15	70	16 1/8	16	16 1/16	+ 1/16
9	4 5/8	AcmeE	...	...	39	70	5 9/16	5 7/16	5 1/2	+ 1/16
17 3/4	**8 1/2**	**AcmeMt**	**...**	**...**	**dd**	**173**	**10**	**9 1/8**	**9 7/8**	**+ 3/4**
29 3/4	15 1/16	Acuson	...	...	41	239	17 9/16	17 1/16	17 9/16	+ 1/2

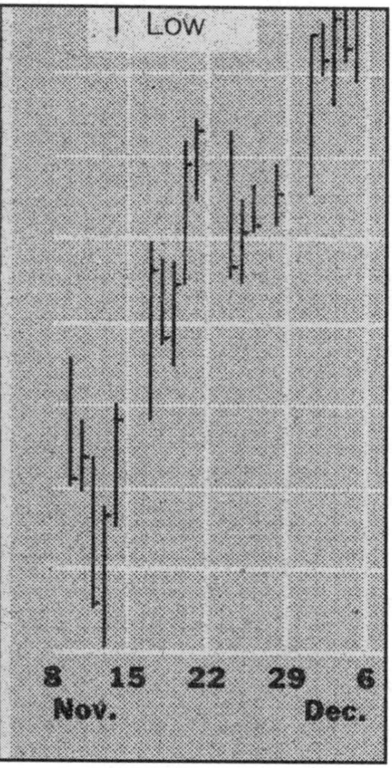

Slow-growth, steady stocks like utilities usually have high dividend yields—averaging close to 6 percent, versus 2.3 percent for the S&P 500 at the end of 1995. This is why they're attractive to "widows and orphans" investors, who are interested in dependable dividend payments over share price appreciation. The tradeoff for the higher payout is usually an unexciting stock performance.

- **"P/E" or Price to Earnings:** Most papers calculate the P/E ratio by dividing the current price by the earnings reported during the past four quarters. Since the P/E ratio is calculated like this: P/E = Current Share Price ÷ Earnings (last 4 quarters), we can calculate that AT&T's last 4 quarter's earnings were $2.82 (22 = $62 1/16 ÷ $2.82).

A high P/E ratio may indicate that a stock is overvalued, and a low ratio may mean that it's undervalued. But, as with all ratios, the P/E has to be considered in the context of the industry. P/Es tend to be much lower in basic industries like steel than in high-growth industries like software and technology.

- **"Sales" or Volume:** Simply put, this gives you an idea of how many shares were traded the day before—pretty useless information unless you know what the average is. In this case, we see that 89.7 million shares of AT&T were traded yesterday. If we happened to know that the daily average was 50 million shares, then you would have an idea that something newsworthy happened to instigate so much trading.
- **High and Low:** Just as you'd expect, these are the high and low prices for the stock during the course of trading yesterday. For AT&T, it was $63 9/16 and $61 11/16.
- **Last:** Finally—what you're most interested in: this is the price at which your stock closed the day before. In this case, AT&T price was $62 1/16 at the end of the trading day.
- **Change:** This tells you how much your stock price changed from the day before. Since AT&T's change is –1 1/16, then we know that the closing share price on the day before must have been $63 1/8.

254 What if you're looking up a mutual fund?

That's a pretty simple process, too. Most major papers now have a section devoted to mutual fund listings. Take this first section of the fund listings here:

Looking Up Your Mutual Funds

Excerpted from the *New York Times*, January 29, 1998.

AAL A				
Bond m	10.02	...	+ 0.4	+ 2.3
CapGrow m	25.89	+0.7	− 0.4	+ 7.0
EqInc m	12.99	+0.4	− 1.2	+10.2
HiYld m	10.36	+0.1	+ 1.4	+ 3.3
Intl m	10.37	+0.3	+ 2.6	+ 0.9
MidCap m	14.06	+1.1	− 3.0	− 2.5
MuniBond m	11.58	...	+ 0.5	+ 3.6
SmCapStk m	12.16	+1.4	− 2.3	− 4.3
AALCapGrB m	25.73	+0.7	− 0.5	+ 6.8
AARP Investment				
BalStkBd	20.61	+0.4	+ 0.2	+ 3.6
BdforInc	15.30	−0.1	...	+ 1.0
CapGrow	52.48	+1.1	+ 0.7	+ 3.3
DivrGrow	17.19	+0.4	+ 0.6	+ 4.1
DivrInc p	16.02	+0.1	+ 0.2	+ 3.0
GNMAUSTrs	15.22	...	+ 0.5	+ 2.2
GloGrow	18.15	+0.5	+ 0.9	+ 6.3
GrowInc	53.25	+0.7	+ 0.4	+ 4.7
HiQBd	16.23	−0.1	+ 0.2	+ 1.9
InsTaxFBd	18.67	...	+ 0.7	+ 3.5
SmCpStk	19.48	+1.1	− 2.3	+ 1.1
USStkIdx	18.47	+0.9	+ 1.0	+ 6.6
AHA				
Bal	13.91	+0.5	− 0.7	+ 3.7
DivrEq	18.46	+1.0	− 0.3	+ 4.8
FullMatFI	10.09	...	...	+ 2.8
LtdMatFI	10.24	...	+ 0.3	+ 1.8
AIM A				
AggGrow m	44.64	+2.2	− 3.4	− 6.6
Bal m	25.68	+0.7	− 0.4	+ 1.8
BlChip m	32.08	+0.8	+ 0.5	+ 5.4
EqGrow b	16.93	+1.9	− 1.9	+ 1.4
RetInc b	10.63	...	− 0.2	+ 3.4
Advantus				
CornrstA m	NA	NA	− 4.6	− 3.6
EnterprA m	14.10	+1.8	− 2.6	− 4.6
HorizonA m	21.32	+1.1	...	+ 9.1
IntlBal m	11.20	+0.3	− 0.7	+ 4.8
MtgSec A m	10.65	...	+ 0.7	+ 2.3
SpectrmA m	15.66	+0.7	...	+ 6.3
VentureA m	12.01	+1.0	− 3.8	+ 2.0
Aetna Select				
Aetna	NA	NA	− 0.3	+ 3.1
Bond	10.25	+0.1	+ 0.3	+ 1.9
Crossrds	11.53	+0.6	+ 0.5	+ 3.1
Grow	14.39	+1.3	+ 0.2	− 1.2
GrowInc	NA	NA	− 2.1	+ 0.3
IntlGrow	11.26	+0.5	+ 3.3	+ 7.6
Alger Group Class A				
Growth f	10.22	+1.4	+ 1.1	+ 1.2
SmCap f	9.41	+1.8	− 2.0	− 3.1
Alger Group Class B				
CapAppr m	24.18	+1.9	− 0.3	− 1.2
Grow m	10.12	+1.4	+ 1.0	+ 1.0
MidCapGr m	18.97	+1.5	− 1.1	− 3.5
SmCap m	9.32	+1.7	− 2.1	− 3.4
AlgeSmRet	17.63	+2.2	− 0.5	− 0.6
Alliance Capital A				
Alliance m	6.54	+2.5	− 2.2	− 3.0
BalShr m	14.81	+0.8	− 0.5	+ 3.5
BdCorpBd m	14.18	−0.1	− 0.6	+ 1.9
BdUSGovt m	7.57	...	+ 0.5	+ 2.5
GloDollr m	8.19	−0.3	− 3.5	+ 2.2

Largest Fu

Assets (mil.$)	Name
4,596	Vanguard
4,539	AARP GN
3,193	Fidelity In
2,783	PIMCo Ins
2,041	Strong Ad
1,414	Vanguard
1,352	American
1,321	Strong Sh
1,166	Scudder
994	Vanguard

Average perform
Number of fund

Fund Family Fund Name	NAV	Dly % Ret.	YTD % Ret
Amcore Vintage			
AggGrow b	15.20	+1.9	...
Bal b	14.16	...	+ 0.5
Equity b	19.22	+1.6	+ 2.0

Funds are listed by the company that issues them: the first here just happens to be the AAL Funds, abbreviation AALA. You'll learn to find your specific fund quickly beneath the listing. If you owned the Small Cap Stock fund, you'd simply go down to that listing.

- **"NAV" or Net Asset Value:** This is the number you'd likely be most interested in, and is the rough equivalent of the share price. In this case you'd see that the net asset value of your Small Cap fund is $12.16.

- **Daily, YTD, and 3-Month Return:** This listing gives you an idea of how your fund has performed over different time periods—in this case the previous day, the calendar year, and the past 3 months. This performance basically reveals the increase in net asset value—it includes any capital gains or losses in the stocks in the fund, as well as any reinvested dividends. In this example, you'd be happy to note that your fund was up a bit the previous day (1.4 percent), but would also see that it was down for the year to date (–2.3 percent), and even more for the past 3 months (–4.3 percent).

Tip

When evaluating the performance of a mutual fund, you should always look at its performance over various time periods—1 month, 1 year, even 5 years or longer.

Did You Know?

What's NAV Again?

Remember from Section 5, that the Net Asset Value (NAV) is really the total value of your fund's portfolio divided by the number of shares outstanding.

"Imagination is more important than knowledge."

—ALBERT EINSTEIN

The market has its ups and downs.

255 Options are a trickier investment to track in the daily papers.

Most newspapers won't have a comprehensive section devoted to stock options—the *New York Times* lists only the 10 most active. The *Wall Street Journal* is a better choice if you want to get specific prices on your option. Let's take a look at an excerpt from that section:

Looking Up Your Options

Excerpted from the *Wall Street Journal*, January 29, 1998.

Option/Strike		Exp.	–Call– Vol.	–Call– Last	–Put– Vol.	–Put– Last
ACC Cp	50	Jun	...	...	346	4
ADC Tel	15	May	...	...	1010	1
A S A	22 1/2	May	2200	3 3/8	...	...
AT&T	60	Feb	66	3 7/8	559	5/8
63	65	Feb	1099	7/8	40	2 5/8
63	65	Mar	274	2	10	3 7/8
Abbt L	70	Feb	290	3	65	13/16
71 7/8	75	Mar	118	1 1/4	225	4 1/8
AdvFibCm	35	Mar	562	1 11/16	...	...
A M D	20	Feb	1454	7/8	48	1 1/8
19 3/4	20	Mar	244	1 1/2	...	...
19 3/4	22 1/2	Mar	223	3/4	...	...
AgriBio	20	Jul	311	2 3/8	...	...
Airtch	45	Feb	919	1 3/8	35	1 13/16
44 3/8	45	Mar	3011	2 1/8	10	2 1/2
Albtsn	50	Mar	504	1 3/16	...	...
AlgLud	15	Feb	215	9 3/4	...	...
AlianP	7 1/2	May	282	1	...	...

Option/Strike		Exp.	–Call– Vol.	–Call– Last	–Put– Vol.	–Put– Last
BkrsTr	95	Feb	500	9 3/4	...	...
BarickG	17 1/2	Apr	1720	3	10	11/16
19 3/8	20	Apr	2052	1 1/2	65	1 13/16
19 3/8	22 1/2	Apr	949	3/4	2000	3 1/2
BayNwk	30	Feb	592	7/16	55	2 3/4
Benfcl	75	Feb	254	6 3/8	105	1 9/16
BergBrun	50	Mar	580	2 3/8	...	...
BestBuy	50	Feb	321	1 3/4	128	3 3/4
Beth S	10	Feb	466	3/8	...	...
9 13/16	10	Apr	881	3/4	27	7/8
Bill Info	45	Feb	202	3 1/2	57	3 1/8
BioPhar	17 1/2	Feb	...	...	250	3/16
22 7/16	22 1/2	Feb	1158	1 11/16	225	1 5/8
Biogen	40	Feb	322	3	209	7/8
BioTcG	10	Mar	177	3/4	250	1
9 1/2	12 1/2	Feb	393	1/8	135	2 7/8
Blk Dk	45	Feb	570	4 1/2	10	3/8
Boeing	42 1/2	Feb	...	...	1055	1/16

Option/S
ColumHCA
25 11/16
ColLb
CmpUSA
31 1/16
31 1/16
Compaq
30 1/8
30 1/8
30 1/8
30 1/8
30 1/8
30 1/8
30 1/8
30 1/8
30 1/8
30 1/8
30 1/8

Suppose you'd bought a call option on AT&T stock—a stock with a $65 strike price and a February expiration (review Section 5 for the lowdown on how options work). This is where you could see how your investment was doing. To find your option, you'd look to the first column: you'd see that the first column has the closing price of the underlying stock. (AT&T's last price is $63.)

The second 2 columns, strike and expiration, help you find your specific option. The following 2 columns apply to you only if you've placed a call option. They tell you the volume of your options (how many contracts were traded).

The column you'll be most interested in is the one with the "Last" heading, meaning last price. You'd see here that your option closed at "7/8," or $0.875. (If your option was a put option, you'd look to the last two columns, and find that your option was worth $2 5/8, or $2.625.)

256 Let's take a look at the bond section of the paper.

Again, this is from the *Wall Street Journal*, which is the most comprehensive newspaper for bond prices and yields.

Looking Up Your Government Bonds

Excerpted from the *Wall Street Journal*, January 29, 1998.

GOVT. BONDS & NOTES

Rate	Maturity Mo/Yr	Bid	Asked	Chg.	Ask Yld.
5	Jan 98n	99:30	100:00	....	4.88
5 5/8	Jan 98n	99:30	100:00	....	5.47
7 1/4	Feb 98n	100:00	100:02	....	5.62
8 1/8	Feb 98n	100:01	100:03	− 1	5.75
5 1/8	Feb 98n	99:29	99:31	....	5.40
5 1/8	Mar 98n	99:30	100:00	....	5.04
6 1/8	Mar 98n	100:03	100:05	....	5.07
7 7/8	Apr 98n	100:15	100:17	....	5.15
5 1/8	Apr 98n	99:29	99:31	....	5.19
5 7/8	Apr 98n	100:03	100:05	....	5.16
6 1/8	May 98n	100:06	100:08	....	5.18
9	May 98n	101:00	101:02	....	5.18
5 3/8	May 98n	99:31	100:01	+ 1	5.23
6	May 98n	100:05	100:07	....	5.28
5 1/8	Jun 98n	99:28	99:30	....	5.26
6 1/4	Jun 98n	100:11	100:13	....	5.23
8 1/4	Jul 98n	101:09	101:11	....	5.23

Rate	Maturity Mo/Yr	Bid	Asked	Chg.	Ask Yld.
13 3/4	Aug 04	144:13	144:19	+28	5.54
7 7/8	Nov 04n	113:00	113:04	+25	5.53
11 5/8	Nov 04	133:26	134:00	+28	5.54
7 1/2	Feb 05n	111:06	111:10	+25	5.54
6 1/2	May 05n	105:20	105:22	+26	5.54
8 1/4	May 00-05	105:24	105:26	+10	5.51
12	May 05	137:30	138:04	+30	5.56
6 1/2	Aug 05n	105:21	105:23	+26	5.56
10 3/4	Aug 05	131:09	131:15	+28	5.58
5 7/8	Nov 05n	101:27	101:29	+27	5.57
5 5/8	Feb 06n	100:09	100:11	+28	5.57
9 3/8	Feb 06	124:10	124:16	+32	5.56
6 7/8	May 06n	108:13	108:15	+29	5.58
7	Jul 06n	109:08	109:10	+29	5.60
6 1/2	Oct 06n	106:01	106:03	+29	5.60
3 3/8	Jan 07i	97:29	97:30	+ 4	3.65
6 1/4	Feb 07n	104:19	104:21	+30	5.59
7 5/8	Feb 02-07	106:31	107:01	+17	5.66

May	12
Aug	12
Nov	12
Feb	13
May	13
Aug	13
Nov	13
Feb	14
May	14
Aug	14
Nov	14
Feb	15
Feb	15
May	15
Aug	15
Aug	15
Nov	15
Nov	15
Feb	16
Feb	16

Treasury Bonds, Notes, and Bills

Here's where you can find your specific government bond. If you had a "9 3/8 Feb. '06" bond—meaning that your coupon was 9.375 percent and maturity date was February 2006, then you'd find it here (the bond listings are in order of maturity) by looking at the Rate and Maturity columns.

- **Bid and Asked:** The Bid and Asked columns tell you the price of your bond. In this case, the bid price on your bond is $124 10/32 (124.31), which is the price for each $100 in "face value" of your bond. (Since bonds are assumed to come in $1000 denominations, it actually means that the price is $1243.13 for each bond.) The asked price in this case is $124 16/32 ($124.50).
- **Change:** The next column, Change, does not refer to the change in price, but to the change in your bond's *yield*, which is listed in the last column (If you need a reminder of how bonds work, review Section 5). In this example, your yield is 5.56 percent. You'll notice that when the price of your bond moves up, its yield moves down. In general, you want the price to go up, and your yield to go down.

Corporate Bonds

Let's look at the first bond listed. The first column, which reads "ATT 4 3/4 '98," means that it's an AT&T bond with a 4 3/4 percent coupon and 1998 maturity. The second column gives you the current yield of your bond, in this case 4.8 percent. (Remember from Section 5 that your current yield is your annual coupon payment divided by your bond price.) The volume column gives you an idea of the activity in your bond (again, only useful if you know what the average is). The next 2 columns are your bond's price and net change. In this case, we see that the bond is selling for 99 17/32, or $99.53 per each $100 of face value. It's gone up by 1/32, or $0.03, since the day before.

Looking Up Your Corporate Bonds

Excerpted from the *New York Times*, January 29, 1998.

CORPORATION BONDS
Volume, $22,427,000

Bonds	Cur Yld	Vol	Close	Net Chg
ATT 4¾98	4.8	10	99 17/32	+ 1/32
ATT 4⅜99	4.4	75	98½	...
ATT 6s00	6.0	210	100⅛	+ ½
ATT 5⅛01	5.2	125	98⅛	+ ¼
ATT 7⅛02	6.8	70	104¼	+ ½
ATT 6¾04	6.5	92	103⅞	+ 1⅛
ATT 7s05	6.8	5	103½	+ ¼
ATT 8.2s05	7.8	5	104⅞	− ¾
ATT 7½06	6.9	70	108⅛	+ ⅝
ATT 8⅛22	7.5	58	107⅞	+ ⅜
ATT 8⅛24	7.5	27	107¾	+ ⅝
ATT 8.35s25	7.6	20	110	...
ATT 8⅝31	7.8	5	110½	− ¼
Aames 10½02	10.1	45	103½	...
AlskA 6⅞14cld	cv	17	144	− 1
AlldC zr2000	...	10	85⅞	+ ⅛
Allwst 7¼14	cv	2	87¾	− ¼
Alza 5s06	cv	36	113½	+ ½
Amoco 8⅝16	8.1	15	106	− 1¼
Amresco 8¾99	8.7	56	100¼	− ¼
Amresco 10s03	9.8	65	102	− ½
Amresco 10s04	9.5	10	104¾	+ ¾
Anhr 8⅝16	8.3	62	104½	− 1½
AnnTaylr 8¾00	8.7	50	100¾	+ ¼
Argosy 12s01	cv	81	90½	− ½
Argosy 13¼04	12.2	164	108⅞	+ ⅛
AubrnHl 12⅜20f	...	20	161	− ½

Bonds	Cur Yld	Vol	Close	Net Chg.
BethSt 8.45s05	8.3	189	101⅜	+ ⅝
Bevrly 9s06	8.4	3	107⅜	+ 1⅞
Bordn 8⅜16	8.2	27	102¾	+ ¼
BorgWS 9⅛03	8.8	60	104	+ ½
BoydGm 9¼03	8.6	110	107¾	+ ⅜
BrnGp 9½06	9.0	18	106	− ¾
BurNo 3.20s45	6.5	20	49	+ ½
CalEgy 10¼04	9.5	20	107½	+ ⅛
CamdPr 7.33s01	cv	10	125	− 5
CapsCap 6.55s02	cv	63	100	...
ChaseM 8s04	7.8	31	102¼	+ ¼
ChaseM 6½09	6.5	65	99⅝	+ ⅝
CPoWas 7¾	7.6	10	101½	+ ⅜
ChckFul 7s12	cv	4	100	...
ChryF 13¼99	11.6	10	113¾	+ 2¾
ChryF 12¾99	11.4	12	111¾	+ ½
Clardge 11¾02f	...	157	94	...
ClrkOil 9½04	9.1	33	104⅛	+ ⅛
ClevEl 8¾05	8.5	5	103⅛	...
ClevEl 8⅜11	8.1	42	103⅛	+ ⅛
Coeur 6⅜04	cv	75	78½	− ½
CmwE 7⅝03F	7.6	10	100¾	− 1
CmwE 8⅛07J	7.9	2	102⅝	+ ⅛
CompUSA 9½00	9.2	15	103½	...
CompMgt 8s03	cv	56	96	...
Consec 8⅛03	7.7	150	106¼	+ ⅜
ConPort 10½04	10.6	55	99½	+ ½
ConPort 10s06	10.0	10	100	+ ½
CntlHm 6⅞02	cv	7	185	− 1
CntlHm 10s06	9.3	30	108	− 1½
Convrse 7s04	cv	25	64¼	+ ¾

Vo
SAL
1998
$352,126
– 1997
High
105.13 10
102.89 9
107.49 10
Bonds

Tip

Remember that you want your bond's *price* to go up, not its yield. In fact, they tend to have an inverse relationship.

Other Indicators to Keep You on Top

"An ignorant person is one who doesn't know what you just found out."

—Will Rogers

257 Check the bellwether indices first.

Before I start checking for my specific investments, I always glance at the overall "market indicators" section to check the bellwether indices. For most people, that means a look at the Dow Jones and the S&P performance. It's worth seeing how it's done for the year, too, just to give you something to compare your investments with.

Trap

It never ceases to amaze me that the indicator which receives the most attention is the number of points the major indices move up or down, rather than the percentage change. Of course a 100-point movement sounds pretty dramatic—but it really only adds up to about a 1 percent change at the time of this writing. At the start of 1990, when the Dow was less than 3,000, a 100-point drop was nearly 4 percent of the market.

Did You Know?

Bellwether Background

The term "bellwether" comes from sheep farming: shepherds used to put a bell on the neck of the animal that led the flock so they would always know which direction the flock was heading. The wether, or lead sheep, would wear the bell.

The Key to Your Company: The Annual Report

"We're drowning in information and starving for knowledge."

—Rutherford D. Rogers

258 Read a company's annual report.

While they should always be read, it is true that annual reports, in many ways, are not an objective source of information. They're produced by the company and so tend to be biased toward the positive side of the company's performance. But they're also a valuable way to get an overview of the company's business, get a feel for management's plans going forward, and, of course, to take a look at the numbers.

Trap **Don't be too impressed by glossy reports with great design. It's all part of the game to make shareholders feel that their investment is solid. The professional packaging makes for easy reading, but shouldn't distract you from the main pieces of information you want to find.**

259 Learn what to look for in the financial statements.

Nobody expects you to understand all of the complex numbers and details of an income statement, but you're probably more capable than you think of understanding the basics. Let's take a look a the top 2: the *income statement* and the *balance sheet.*

- **Income Statement:** This is the key table within the annual report. It tells you how much your company earned in profits—which is really the bottom line, when you think about it. A typical income statement should look something like this:

Income Statement Sample (all numbers in $ millions)

Net Sales	$29,000
Cost of Products Sold	17,000
Selling, General, and Administrative Expenses	9,000
Operating Income	$3,000
Interest Expense	‹500›
Other Income ‹expense›, Net	100
Earnings Before Income Taxes	$2,600
Income Taxes	‹800›
Net Earnings	$1,800
Average Shares Outstanding (in millions)	600
Earnings per Share	$3.00

Although it's good to know what each of these major categories mean, you'll probably want to concentrate on the most important ones.

- **Net Sales:** This may be the best measure of your company's health. Are total sales going up or down? If they're going down, did management's overview give you any idea why? Are prices dropping, or are they selling fewer units?
- **Net Earnings:** Once again, are earnings moving up or down? What are the explanations given in the main text of the report?

Trap

There are often "extraordinary items" factored into a company's net earnings—like a big tax settlement, for example—that can distort the final numbers. Many companies show such special items separately, providing an "adjusted earnings" statement which is more indicative of the company's true operating performance.

- **Earnings Per Share:** This is how the net earnings get allocated to shareholders like you. (Of course, you won't actually receive them, but your claim to them is what gives your shares more value.) Exactly as you would expect, earnings per share are simply the earnings divided by the total number of shares outstanding.

Trap

Many investors may not realize that when a company issues new shares, they will be diluting your earnings per share. That's why a big new share issuance often has a depressive effect on the share price of a company.

Balance Sheet Sample (all numbers in $ millions)

Assets	
Current Assets	
Cash and Cash Equivalents	$2,300
Marketable Securities	200
Accounts Receivable	3,100
Inventories	2,800
Deferred Income Taxes	700
Prepaid Expenses and Other Current Assets	600
Total Current Assets	**9,700**
Properties, Plants, and Equipment	$11,000
Goodwill and Other Intangible Assets	3,700
Other Assets	1,500
Total Assets	**$25,900**
Liabilities and Shareholder's Equity	
Current Liabilities	
Accounts Payable	$2,600
Accrued Liabilities	2,900
Taxes Payable	500
Short-term Debt	1,300
Total Current Liabilities	**7,300**
Long-Term Debt	4,900
Other Liabilities	3,300
Deferred Income Taxes	300
Total Liabilities	**15,800**
Shareholder's Equity	
Preferred Stock	1,900
Common Stock—Shares Outstanding: 650,000,000	100
Additional Paid-in Capital	1,200
Retained Earnings	6,900
Total Shareholders' Equity	**10,100**
Total Liabilities and Shareholders' Equity	**$25,900**

More Sources for the Well-Rounded Investor

"Everyone knows that in research there are no final answers, only insights that allow one to formulate new questions."

—S. E. LURIA

260 Sign up for an on-line news service.

The Internet has brought an overwhelming amount of information to the small investor who has a computer and a modem. Services like "Hoover's Business Resources" or AOL's "Motley Fool" (see Resources at the end of this section) are handy ways to look up the basics about a stock—that means a good overview report about the company, and updated share price and ratios.

A word of warning—on-line services often focus on dramatic movements: the stocks that double, or the strategies with the 200 percent returns. That makes for a fun read, but don't be distracted from your (more prudent) basic investment plans.

261 Ask your broker for research reports.

Your broker has access to reports by her company's research analysts who cover the stock and its industry. They can be a valuable source of up-to-date information from an objective party. Ask your broker if she can send you what the company has provided.

262 Don't be afraid to ask the investor relations team.

A publicly traded company probably has an investor relations department to help shareholders just like you. They probably won't be equipped to answer detailed questions about the company's operations, but they can help with the basics, like interpreting a recent news event. In addition, with the development of e-mail and Web sites, you probably have a better chance of getting more in-depth queries addressed promptly.

Tip

Most companies now have Web sites where you can find out about recent news and company developments, as well as ask questions of the investor relations team. But keep in mind that they'll have an optimistic bias—think of the Web site as kind of a "live" annual report.

The more you know, the better you'll be at the game.

Personal Perspective

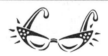

"My visits to a retail store virtually dictated my investment strategy toward its stock a few years ago. It was well-known women's clothing company which had done very well by catering to the growing numbers of professional women who needed well-priced, well-made, comfortable, fashionable clothes for work. There was a major management change, and a few months later I noticed that the clothes had taken a turn for the worse—the buyers seemed to have changed the styles that they were acquiring—including less-wearable, high-fashion knockoffs, and the quality of the clothes was suffering (buttons not sewn on well, or on backwards). I sold the stock a few months before it began to drop. And believe me, it dropped."

263 Ask to get on the mailing list for the company newsletter.

OK—we've all gotten the newsletters from companies where we work, and we know how pollyannaish they can be. But if you keep that bias firmly in mind, the newsletter can be a great way to figure out how the company communicates to its employees as well as tune in to future company plans.

264 Visit the stores!

I'm constantly amazed at the fact that so few investors think of this particular source of information—very possibly the best way of telling how your company is doing.

265 Ask the employees.

This is particularly helpful if it's a retail company with stores you can visit. Don't be afraid to ask general questions—How are sales? What's the mood with the workforce? Of course, you'll only be getting the opinion of one worker, but you'd be surprised how enlightening a few conversations like that can be. Many can tell you how the sales of their region, or even of all the stores, are stacking up for a particular season.

"I have never let my schooling interfere with my education."

—Mark Twain

Savvy investors use their brains.

Truth or Dare: Mutual Fund Claims & Other Tricky Details

Understanding Stories

266 For earnings reports, expected earnings mean everything.

This may be the number one complaint that I hear from investors: "My company just reported great earnings, but the stock went down. What gives?" Earnings by themselves mean almost nothing. What really matters are *expected earnings*. If your company's earnings went up 1000 percent, but the market was expecting 2000 percent, the stock will drop.

Tip **Thanks to the Internet, small investors can now see the expected earnings for many stocks. One of the most followed services is First Call, which is available through America Online. There you can see the median expected earnings based on the projections of a number of analysts closely following the stock.**

Trap **Don't get too cocky about being in on the expected earnings on "The Street." The small investor still isn't privy to "whisper earnings"—those talked about heavily between traders and analysts. They can affect the way the stock performs after a report, too.**

267 Determine if it's "new" news.

Figuring out if your stock will go up or down based on a specific piece of news can be frustrating. Consider this headline:

IN LONG AWAITED MOVE, CAFFEINE COLA'S
CHAIRMAN STEPS DOWN

In this case, you don't even have to determine whether this piece of information is good or bad, because it was expected.

In other words, the market already knew about it, and its effect had already been factored into the stock price.

268 It's hard to make a buck by reacting to news stories.

Suppose you've determined that the story that's just come out about your stock is definitely news—a surprise to the market. Your next question is, naturally, "What does it mean over the long term for the company?" Of course headlines like this are pretty easy to gauge:

CAFFEINE COLA'S BIGGEST PLANT EXPLODES

But what if it's something less clear-cut—like this?

CAFFEINE COLA SUDDENLY ANNOUNCES EXPANSION INTO SOUTH AMERICA

In this case, the story implies that this truly is newsworthy—but is it a negative announcement or a positive one? The answer is that it's nearly impossible for you to tell. On the one hand, it could be a wonderful thing that will add to earnings over time, pushing the stock up. On the other, it could require a large investment that will put a dent in earnings and cause the stock to drop. That's why I recommend that investors—if they choose to invest in individual stocks—focus on long-term fundamentals, not late-breaking announcements.

Tip **Remember, any of these newsbreaking announcements might have an short-term effect on the stock. But since you're a long-term investor you must think like one.**

Trap **Even if you know what to do, you might be too late to do it. This is really where the small investor is at the greatest disadvantage. Did you read the news in the morning paper? The big investors on Wall Street probably got the news within minutes of its release, via a phone call from a trader, perhaps a day or even a week ago.**

269 Mutual fund claims: look beyond the returns in the ads.

It's not that most funds will be dishonest (their claims are actually strictly monitored), just that they'll understandably focus on their best statistics. If a fund has a sub-par 5-year return, but a great 1-year return, guess which one will be highlighted in the ad? Use an objective source with standardized listings for all the funds (like *Morningstar* or *Value Line*) to compare the different fund returns.

Understanding Returns

270 Don't underestimate the power of a percentage point.

Seemingly small differences in return can have quite a big impact on your end result—especially over longer time periods. If you invest $1000 over 20 years with a 9 percent annual return, you'll end up with $5,604. But with a 10 percent annual return, you'd have $6,727—more than $1,100 in your pocket.

271 When in doubt, convert it to dollars.

If you're confused by the differences between cumulative returns versus standard returns and "annualized" returns and the like, ask yourself: how much money will I have at the end of 10 years at this rate? That's simple enough, right? Don't be embarrassed by the sheer simplicity of this inquiry: any advisor, broker, or fund salesman should be able to answer a question like that.

Tip

Although it's easier to leave the cost of commissions and fees out of your calculation, never forget what a bite it can take out of your end payout. Be sure to tell your broker or fund salesman to tell you what the end value of your investment will be *including* fees and commissions.

Tip

The Rule of 72

This is a handy way to understand what your return really means. If you want to know how soon your money will double at a given rate of return, divide 72 by it. So if your return is 5 percent, you know your money will take about 14 years to double (72 ÷ 5 = 14.4).

Ask Lorraine

Q&A

Q. *What if I can't find a paper that lists my option?*

A. If you can't get to a paper that has a specific price for your option, you can get a pretty good idea of how it did by looking up the price of the underlying stock. It won't be exact, of course, but should give you some guidance. (You can bet that if your stock went down, your option probably did too.)

Q. *What is the difference between the bid price and the asked price?*

A. The difference between "bid" and "asked" are just what you'd think. The bid price is what someone would give you for your security, and the asked price is what someone would sell it to you for. Brokers generally make the spread as compensation for providing the market (i.e., for providing a place for the stock to be bought and sold).

Q. *How do I get an annual report on a company's stock?*

A. You receive your annual report automatically as a shareholder. If you don't receive one in the mail, be sure to ask your broker or the company's investment relations department to send you one.

Q. *Should I consider a "hot tip" I get via the Internet?*

A. The on-line nature of the Internet can make its "hot tips" seem more alluring (i.e., they seem more timely). In fact, the anonymity of the Internet means you should be most skeptical about this source. Never act on advice from the Internet without finding more information in other places.

Q. *Where can I get more detailed financial information?*

A. Public companies are also required to file a 10K report, which is similar to an annual report but more detailed. (The quarterly version is called a "10Q".)

Shareholders love a bull market.

Resource Guide

On-line Investment Resources

- AOL's *Motley Fool* (available through AOL's on-line service).
  1-800-827-6364
- Hoover's Business Resources
  www.hoovers.com

Getting the Goods on the Best Newsletters:

- *Hulbert Financial Digest* tracks most financial newsletters and their performance
  316 Commerce Street
  Alexandria, VA 22314
  703-683-5905
- Recommended Periodicals
  Wall Street Journal
  On-line subscription $49/year; only $29/year for current print subscribers
  www.wsj.com
  1-800-369-2834

  Barron's available through *Wall Street Journal* subscription
  www.barrons.com

  Business Week
  www.businessweek.com
  1-888-878-5151
  P.O. Box 421
  Hightstown, NJ 08520

Section 7

Coping With Your Taxes

Frankly, few like to talk about taxes. Even fewer enjoy paying them. And although taxes are a necessary part of participating in our society, most of us tend to avoid even thinking about them until we're forced to on April 15th. However, tax planning can not only save you headaches, but plenty of money if you know what you're doing.

Who of us hasn't realized, too late, that we could have saved money if we'd only thought ahead? Or discovered a deduction we could have taken if we'd just planned for it? Those are the kinds of mistakes you can avoid if you start thinking about your taxes before the year begins.

So whether you're planning a system for your personal taxes or for your small business, remember: thinking ahead is the key to saving your hard-earned dollars from Uncle Sam. Take this opportunity to review your tax options and really understand the information that can save you money.

I won't try to tell you that your taxes will be a pleasant undertaking, but you might be surprised at how much better you'll feel about the process once you've done your homework. Remember: you can understand your taxes, or at least the basics. And even if it still makes you tense, the vacation you buy with your refund will be just the thing to help you relax.

Tax Tips to Save You Money

"Taxes are what we pay for civilized society."

—Oliver Wendell Holmes, Jr.

272 If you don't use tax-free savings accounts, you're throwing money away.

This is the easiest way that I know of to earn extra money. Not only is it the best way to save money (if you don't see it, you won't miss it), but it's the most efficient strategy for keeping your cash from Uncle Sam—who, by the way, is not your uncle. Essentially, with either a 401k or an IRA (the most popular tax-free savings plans), you can shield a portion of your income from taxes until you withdraw the funds (hopefully during retirement, when you're in a lower tax bracket).

Tip **Gone are the days of schlepping to the post office to get the right tax forms. Now you can download tax forms in a number of different places, including *www.ustreas.gov/*. America Online also has forms available for downloading.**

273 Make the most of your charitable contributions.

We all know that you can deduct the checks you write out to your favorite needy causes. But did you also know that you can deduct expenses involved in your volunteer time? For

Did You Know?

Tax-Free Savings

There's a limit to how much you can contribute tax-free. For 401k plans it depends on your salary (the top limit is $9,500), and for IRAs it's $2,000.

example, you can deduct your transportation costs related to a soup kitchen you helped staff. Also, if you "pledge" to public radio or television—like so many people do—your contributions are also tax deductible.

And don't forget to get a receipt for those bags of items you gave to Goodwill or similar groups—those contributions quickly add up.

274 Write off your school expenses!

If you're taking a class that's related to your job, most of your expenses are tax deductible (up to $5,250 in 1997—check with your accountant to know for sure). As anyone who's paid any tuition costs lately knows, this can be a huge tax break. (It may also affect which classes you take—if you're torn between taking the modern dance class that has nothing to do with your job, and the art history class which will make you a better curator, consider which one will give you the tax break.)

Let the government contribute to your education.

275 Deduct your job-search expenses.

Did you fly to another city to interview for a new job? Your expenses may be entirely tax deductible. (It doesn't even matter if you take the new job.) Did you take a workshop in career counseling to help you get your resume together? Write it off! I'm always surprised at the number of people who don't use this deduction opportunity to its fullest.

276 Keep track of your relocation expenses too.

If you got that job in another city, you can get a huge tax break on your relocation costs—even if your new employer helped out with some of them. Make sure to keep all receipts, from gasoline to burgers on the road, and present them to your tax person at the end of the year.

277 Don't forget about job-related expenses.

Be sure to track the unreimbursed expenses that you've had that were related to your job. Did you have to buy trade periodicals or newspapers? What about supplies to perform extra work at home? Do you belong to any special clubs or associations related to your job? If your employer doesn't pick up these costs, they're tax deductible.

Also consider the less obvious expenses. Did you have to buy special clothes (that you can't wear anywhere else) for your job? Or maybe you picked up a heater for your office to offset that pesky draft? All of those expenses are tax-deductible too.

278 Don't forget about any losses from casualty or theft.

In general, you can deduct any loss in value to your property that occurred because of fire, storm, or other casualty—including theft. Of course, your deduction would be reduced by any insurance reimbursement you received. There are some sticky details that you have to establish (check with your accountant) but it could be well worth your while if you experienced any thefts or property damage during the year to deduct them.

279 Check into writing off your home computer.

This is another big deduction that people often don't take advantage of. If it fits these 3 qualifications, your new $3,000 computer system could be a write-off:

- It's for the convenience of your employer
- It's a condition of your employment
- It's used more than half of the time for business

280 Heck—see if you can write off the whole home office!

In general, you can deduct expenses related to your home office if it is used exclusively on a regular basis as:

- your principal place of business
- a place of business for meeting or dealing with clients or customers

- a separate structure from your residence that is also used in connection with your business.

Trap **If you claim a home office, there may be some negative consequences to the value of your home. Check with a tax expert about all of the implications.**

281 Watch out for the 50 percent limit on entertainment.

This is a fairly large misperception among many people—particularly those who are self-employed. Although most of your travel expenses (such as airfare, auto rental, hotel rooms) are deductible, only 50 percent of your entertainment expenses (including meals) can be written off. That means that you should think twice before picking up that $250 tab—you can only write off half of it.

282 Can you write off your car?

Volunteers get to write off mileage.

Chances are that if you use your automobile more than half the time for your business, you can write off at least some expenses related to its upkeep. You can do that in 1 of 2 ways:

- **Actual expenses:** Under this method, you may be able to write off its depreciation value. Here are the standard limits for a car placed into service in 1997:

1st year	$3,160
2nd year	$5,000
3rd year	$3,050
4th year	$1,775

NOTE: There may be further restrictions if you use your car for both business and personal errands.

- **Standard rates:** Under this method, you simply deduct 31.5 cents for each mile you put on your car that is related to business. Keep track, because this can really add up.

283 Be smart about dependents.

This is really common sense, but we often forget to examine this tradeoff closely at tax time. You want to be sure of the decision between claiming a child as a dependent and letting them file a personal exemption on their own. If your child is young, chances are that your tax bracket is higher and there will be more overall savings by taking the deduction on your return. Or, if you're married but filing separately, be sure that the spouse in the higher tax bracket claims the dependents.

284 Get some tax help.

I hear this every year: "Once I've done all the work of finding my receipts, adding up expenses, and organizing my taxes, I don't know why I need a tax expert." Don't kid yourself. Tax advisors can save you money, and plenty of it. Of course you'll still have to do the grunt work of gathering the information, but a good tax advisor knows enough to be well worth the money. That includes deductions you probably hadn't thought of, tips on how to avoid an audit, and ideas for next year to save you money.

285 Consider donating stock instead of cash.

Stop! Before you give your favorite charity or alma mater a cash donation, consider giving them stock instead. If you have a stock that's made a profit, you could give away the same value while avoiding the capital gains tax of selling the stock yourself.

Trap **Don't bother going to a mass-market tax advisor where they basically retype what you've done onto a form and call it "advising." You'll notice that I recommend a GOOD tax advisor. Ask your friends or colleagues for a recommendation. Ideally, it will be someone who works with people in your field or industry.**

286 Check out tax software packages.

There are now a number of different tax preparation software programs that can help you get your taxes in order (but really don't take the place of a qualified tax advisor). More than simply entering your numbers onto the right forms, many of the better programs are written to "advise" you along the way. They might prompt you for extra deductions you may have missed, for example, or give you an average range for a specific deduction (to help you avoid red flags to the IRS). TurboTax, Kiplinger's TaxCut, and MacInTax (for Mac users) are just a few of the more well-established tax packages.

In a hurry for your refund? Many of the software packages offer the option of filing in EZ form, (kind of a shorthand version of your tax return, which is typically processed quicker). You can also speed things up by having the money directly deposited in to your account. Electronic filing is another new feature that gets you your money faster—just have your return transmitted by an IRS-approved transmitter.

287 Never use withholding as a savings plan.

This is a tempting psychological trick—who doesn't love the idea of a big tax refund at the end of a year? The problem is, of course, that you receive no interest on that money. Try to estimate your withholding more accurately, and put the extra money away in a plan that earns you interest instead.

Many companies offer flexible spending plans that allow you to use tax-free dollars toward child care and medical expenses. These plans can save you money! If you're in a 40 percent combined tax bracket, and pay $1,000 in medical expenses in a year, a flexible spending allowance (FSA) can save you $400.

288 Don't wait until April 15th.

I know from personal experience that this is how the sloppiest returns get filed. You rush to get it in on the last possible day, probably overlooking plenty of deductions that you didn't have the time to research. You should have all of your information to begin organizing your return by the end of January: why not start then? Remember: just because you've completed your tax return *doesn't mean you have to file it.* You can still put off writing that big check until the last minute, but this way you might have the time to figure out how to reduce it.

Worksheet: Estimate Your Taxes!

One of the problems with planning your tax strategy for the upcoming year is that you often don't know what your exact income will be. But you can make a good educated guess by starting with a worksheet like this. It will also help you to start thinking about ways to save on taxes *now*, while you can.

Gross Income	
Wages/Salary	$
Dividends	$
Interest Income	$
Capital Gains/Losses	$
Rents or Royalties	$
Pensions or Annuities	$
Other	$
	$
	$
	$
	$
	$

Subtract Deductions for Adjusted Gross Income	
IRA or 401k Payments	$
Other	$
	$
	$
	$
	$
Adjusted Gross Income (AGI)	$

Deductions

Medical Expenses* * Only in excess of 7.5 percent of AGI	$
State/Local Taxes	$
Interest Expenses* *up to the amount of your investment income	$
Charitable Contributions	$
	$
Casualty/Theft Losses* *in excess of 10 percent of AGI	$
Moving Expenses	$
Other: Unreimbursed business expenses, tax advisory fees	$
	$
	$
	$
	$
Total Itemized Deductions	$
3 percent AGI Adjustment* *applies only if your income is more than $121,200 ($60,600 if married filing separately)—if so, then you subtract 3 percent of the amount your gross income exceeds that amount, i.e., if you make $160,000, then you'd take off $1,164 (160,000–121,200) x 3 percent	$
Adjusted Itemized Deductions (1)	$
—OR—	
Less: Standard Deduction (2)* *for 1997: Single: $4,150; Head of Household: $6,050; Married Filing Jointly: $6,900; Married Filing Separately: $3,450	$
AGI less the larger of (1) or (2)	$
Less: Number of Exemptions x $2,650 (1997)	$
Taxable Income	$
Total Tax Payable* *see Tax Rate tables on next page	$

JUST THE FACTS

Tax Rate Tables

For 1997, tax rates were as follows:

Single

Taxable Income	The Tax is	Of Excess Over
0–$24,650	0+15%	$0
$24,650–$59,750	$3,697.50+28%	$24,650
$124,650–$271,050	$13,525+31%	$59,750
$124,650–$271,050	$33,644.50+36%	$124,650
$271,050+	$33,644.50+36%	$271,050

Example: If your taxable income is $55,000, then your tax would be $3,697.50+[28% x $30,350] = $12,195.50

Married Filing Jointly

Taxable Income	The Tax is	Of Excess Over
0–$41,200	0+15%	$0
$41,200–$99,600	$6,180+28%	$41,200
$99,600–$151,750	$22,532+31%	$99,600
$151,750–$271,050	$38,698+36%	$151,750
$271,050+	$81,646+39.6%	$271,050

Example: If your taxable income is $100,000, then your tax would be $22,532+[31% x $400] = $22,656.

Married Filing Separately

Taxable Income	The Tax is	Of Excess Over
0–$20,600	0+15%	$0
$20,600–$49,800	$3,090+28%	$20,600
$49,800–$75,875	$11,266+31%	$49,800
$75,875–$135,525	$19,349+36%	$75,875
$135,525+	$40,823+39.6%	$135,525

Example: If your taxable income is $75,000, then your tax would be $11,266+31% [$75,000–$49,800] = $19,078.

289 While you're filing for last year, begin planning for next.

This is the best way to plan ahead when you're smarting from the mistakes of the year before—figure out how to avoid them the next time around. Did you sell that high-flying stock at exactly the wrong time from a tax perspective? Make a note to yourself for the following year about your timing strategy. Or did you accept that bonus from your boss in December instead of January? Ask now to have the next year's put off.

Save on next year's taxes by planning ahead.

290 Sometimes it's all in the timing.

There are plenty of reasons to think twice about the timing of your income inflows and outflows from a tax perspective. The most obvious would be that you expect a large change in your tax circumstances from 1 year to the next.

- **Tax bracket increase:** Are you quitting your job to start a new business next year? Then chances are you'll earn less money next year and be in a lower tax bracket. That gives you good reason to shift as much income as possible to January 1 and beyond.
- **Tax bracket drop:** Or you may expect your income to be much higher next year, pushing you into a higher tax bracket. (Maybe you're selling a big investment, or starting a higher-paying job.) In that case, you should try to get as much income as possible *this* year (selling off profitable stocks, for example) while you're at the lower tax rate.
- **Minimum deductible cutoffs:** Maybe there's good reason to bunch certain expenses into 1 year in order to meet the minimum write-off requirement. For example, you can't deduct medical expenses unless they amount to 7.5 percent of your gross income. If you anticipate something close to that next year, it might be worth it to push off some payments until then so they can be written off.

Tip

Check with a tax advisor about new tax law changes. The implications might help you decide how to plan for the future.

Double Trouble: Taxes & Divorce

291 If you're the one paying, classify your expenses as alimony when you can.

Say that you're helping out your ex-spouse with medical expenses. You're better off classifying these payments as alimony—which is fully deductible—than as medical expenses—which are subject to the 7.5 percent minimum. Explore with your accountant all of your payments to your ex-spouse in this manner.

292 But if you're the one receiving, you'd rather call it child support.

On the other hand, keep in mind that you have to declare all alimony payments that you receive. Not so with child support, which your ex-spouse can't write off.

293 The best thing to do is work together.

Let's assume you're still speaking to each other. Clearly the best way to tackle the problem of minimizing your taxes is to coordinate your strategies. If you're in a higher tax bracket and are the one making the payments, then offer to increase them to a certain cutoff in exchange for the right to claim them as alimony. The point is to coordinate your 2 tax brackets in a way that means the *least combined* taxes paid out.

"Love is a fire. But whether it is going to warm your hearth or burn down your house, you can never tell."

—JOAN CRAWFORD

The Tax-Smart Investor

294 Factor taxes into all your investment decisions.

This is such an easy concept to overlook: who wants to think about the tedium of taxes when you're in the middle of a hot stock market? But you'll find exactly how important it is at the end of the year when the tax collector takes a bite out of the interest you've earned or your profits from capital gains returns.

295 Does your tax bracket point to taxable or tax-free?

When deciding whether to go with a taxable or tax-free investments, the experts point to these generally accepted guidelines. If your tax bracket is:

- **15 percent:** Tax-free investments probably won't help you much.
- **28 percent:** Some advantages from going tax-free. Consider each separately.
- **31 percent:** Go tax-free! You're crazy to produce more taxable income.

"There is one difference between a tax collector and a taxidermist—the taxidermist leaves the hide."

—Mortimer Caplin

THINGS TO THINK ABOUT

Taxable versus Tax-Free Investing

The reason why your tax bracket is important in making the taxable versus tax-free decision is this:

Say you have a choice between a 7 percent taxable investment and 5 percent tax-free one.

If you're in a combined **40 percent** tax bracket (federal and state):

- **Investment #1:** Approximate final return 4.2 percent. (7 percent x 0.6)
- **Investment #2:** Final return 5 percent.

Consider investment #2.

But if you're in a **20 percent** tax bracket, the first will return 5.6 percent.

- **Investment #1:** Approximate final return 5.6 percent. (7 percent x 0.8)
- **Investment #2:** Final return 5 percent.

Consider investment #1.

296 Know your tax-free options.

This can be confusing—there are seemingly so many different types of instruments with varying kinds of tax-free status. Let's review a quick rundown of the major instruments you should be aware of:

	Exempt From Federal?	Exempt From State/Local?
Treasury bills, notes, and bonds	No	Yes
GNMAs ("Ginnie Mae's")	No	No
U.S. savings bonds	No*	Yes
Municipal bonds	Yes	Yes**

*Possibly exempt if used to pay for higher education—check on restrictions.

** Only in state of issuance.

You should also explore your mutual fund options in the tax-free arena. They generally fall into 3 different categories:

- **Tax-Exempt Money Funds:** These funds generally invest in bonds and securities issued by states, counties, cities, and towns. The dividends paid by these funds are not subject to federal taxes. (Although they're probably subject to state and local taxes—check first.)
- **Double Tax-Exempt Money Funds:** Dividends from these funds are generally exempt from federal *and* state taxes.
- **Triple Tax-Exempt Money Funds:** You guessed it—these dividends are exempt from all the big tax threats—federal, state, and local.

JUST THE FACTS

Taxable Versus Tax-Free Tradeoff

For a quick check of which gives you the better yield, use this simple math:

- Divide the tax-free investment by 1–[your tax rate] to get its Taxable Equivalent Yield.
- So if you're in a 35 percent tax bracket and you're choosing between a 7.5 percent taxable bond and a 5.8 percent tax-free bond, you'd divide 5.8 percent by .65 (1–.35) to find your Taxable Equivalent Yield of 8.9 percent—clearly a better investment than the 7.5 percent taxable bond.

297 If you live in a high-tax area, give serious thought to "Muni bonds."

If you live in a city like New York, chances are you're paying federal, state, and city taxes, which means that your combined tax bracket could be close to 50 percent. That makes tax-free investments like municipal bonds especially appealing: your 6 percent tax-free bond would have a 12 percent taxable-equivalent yield.

Trap

Tax implications should just be one of the elements you factor into your investment decisions. Don't ever go with an investment just because it's good for your tax return.

298 Know the difference between capital gains and interest income.

This is a fairly simple distinction that can make a big difference in your investment strategy. That's because they're taxed in very different ways.

- **Capital Gains Profits**: Like the money you earned when you sold a stock at a higher price than you paid for it—taxed at a top 28 percent rate (or at the lower 15 percent rate if you're in a lower tax bracket).
- **Interest and Dividend Income**: Like the coupon payments you received from a bond or the dividends you got from a stock—taxed at your personal tax rate.

That means that if your tax rate is higher than 28 percent, then you should clearly choose investments that would give you capital gains profits over interest or dividend income (at least from a tax perspective).

299 Coordinate your capital gains and losses.

This is another easy strategy to employ, and it can save you a bundle. It's also something that your broker (if you're using one) can help you with. (She'll probably be glad to—tax trades are a great source of business for them.) Suppose you've got a $5,000 capital gain for the year (you've already bought and sold the stock). You'll likely be paying $1,400 (28 percent) of that profit to Uncle Sam unless you can come up with a loss to offset it.

Things to Think About

The Capital Gains War

The top capital gains tax now stands at 28 percent—that means that if you make a $100 profit on a stock, the most you'll have to pay to Uncle Sam is $28. (If your tax bracket is lower, it could be the 15 percent rate.) This has been a wildly contentious issue in recent years, with some people claiming that the tax discourages responsible investing while others fear that cutting the capital gains tax will benefit only the rich.

Take a look at your portfolio: if there's a loser there that you've been putting off selling this is the time to bite the bullet. In an ironic way, it might even make you feel better about the bad investment decision: now it can help you save a little money.

Did You Know?

Capital Loss Claims

If it's offset by a capital gain, there is no limit to the capital loss amount you can claim. But the maximum "straight" capital loss (that is, not offset by a gain) you could take in 1998 was $3,000. But don't panic—any overflow can be carried forward to future tax years.

300 Check into series EE bonds.

These are bonds issued directly by the U.S. government which sell at a discount and then they're redeemed at a higher value. You won't receive regular interest payments, but they will be building up in the value of the bond. For example, you might buy the bond for $7,500 and redeem it for $10,000—giving you a $2,500 implied interest income. The advantage of these bonds is that you don't pay taxes on that interest income until you redeem the bonds. Even better, if you use the proceeds to pay for educational expenses, the income may be entirely tax-free. (There are certain income restrictions and phase-outs—check with your accountant for details.)

301 Choose stock dividends over cash dividends.

There are certain times when you may receive additional shares of stock as dividends, rather than a cash payout. For the most part, this will mean a lower tax bill. (New stock is generally taxed at the lower capital gains rate.)

Keeping Your Business Tax-Savvy

302 Don't shirk on your self-employment tax duties.

If you decide to become self-employed (as a consultant, for example), you'll have more tax responsibilities to shoulder. Most important, since your income won't have taxes already taken out, you'll be responsible for estimating and paying your taxes every quarter. And you can forget about underestimating—there are stiff penalties for big understatements of your income.

303 Sit down with your tax advisor.

A seasoned tax person who specializes in working with people who have similar tax needs can be a lifesaver when you decide to go out on your own. Not only can she set you up with quarterly estimated tax payment amounts (based on projected earnings), but she can help you set up a filing system to best track your tax-deductible spending for the upcoming year.

304 Keep your personal and business records separate.

It sure sounds easy, but it's not. However, if by some fluke of the odds you get audited by the IRS, it's much easier to build your case when you can clearly distinguish between personal and business expenses. My tax person gave me the following easy tips:

- Start a new check register every January 1
- Keep a separate checking account for business and personal expenditures
- Use 1 credit card for business only
- Keep all your receipts until tax time, then determine what you'll need and what you can toss

Did You Know?

Calendar Watch for the Self-Employed

If you're responsible for filing an estimated tax return, these are the dates by which you'll need to get your payments in to the IRS:

- April 15
- June 15
- September 15
- January 15

305 Get out the aspirin: know about employee taxes.

Ready to take on employees in your business? Brace yourself—having employees can be a wonderful (and necessary) experience, but it also opens up new frontiers of accounting challenges and paperwork. Here are the main taxes that you'll need to set up and begin withholding:

Type	Who pays and how much?
Federal Income Tax	Employee Dependent on salary level (15 percent, 28 percent, or 31 percent)
State Income Tax	Employee Varies by state
Medicare	Employee half, employer half 2.9 percent (1.45 percent each—no limit)
Social Security	Employee half, employer half 12.4 percent (6.2 percent each—$60,600 limit)
Federal Unemployment	Employer, 6.2 percent
State Unemployment	Employer, varies by state

Once you've set up this system and begun withholding the correct amount of taxes, you don't just hang on to the difference until tax filing time. You'll need to start depositing those withheld taxes at your bank on a special form 8109 (see Resource Guide for more information).

Tip

Did that discussion of payroll taxes scare you to death? If the accounting side of your business gives you hives, you might want to use a payroll accounting service to handle this particular headache. Many accountants offer it as a standard service. At the very least, use a payroll tax software package to get everything organized.

Trap

Don't take your payroll taxes lightly. The IRS monitors these monies very closely (to protect your employees) and will shut down your business if you fall behind.

306 Keep taxes in mind when setting up your business entity.

Taxes are usually the critical consideration when deciding how to set up your business. The key question you'll want to ask yourself is this:

Do I want the profits (or losses) from the business to flow through to my personal return?

Yes. For example, maybe you're starting a business in the middle of the year, which you know will have start-up losses. You might want those losses to offset the income you made at the beginning of the year. These are a few of the entities you might consider:

- **Sole Proprietorship:** All legal and financial data are those of the owner, so all income is treated as personal income.
- **Limited Liability Partnership (LLP):** Profits and losses are passed on to the partners in proportion to their level of ownership.
- **S-Corporation:** Limited legal protection for the owners, but company income flows directly through to the tax returns of the owners.
- **Limited Liability Company (LLC):** Similar to an S-Corporation, except that you can have more shareholders, including some who aren't U.S. citizens. Again, income is taxed on the personal returns of shareholders.

No. Maybe you want to keep your company's taxes and your own separate. (Remember that you can still write off unreimbursed expenses for the company on your personal return.)

Then you might prefer to use a:

- **C-Corporation:** Since this type of company is an entirely different business entity, and the company is taxed separately.

Again, and I can't stress this enough, check with a qualified tax advisor or attorney before making these vital decisions—since they will impact your business for years to come.

One of the problems with a regular corporation is that profits going to shareholders are double-taxed. That is, they're taxed at the corporate level, and then if they're distributed to you, you'll have to pay a personal tax. One way to alleviate that pressure is to pay higher salaries to shareholders (particularly if they're also officers).

Tip

When deciding between an entity that would be taxed at your personal rate and one that would be taxed at the corporate level—say, deciding between a C-Corporation or an S-Corporation—keep in mind that, as of 1997 the top corporate tax rate was 35 percent, which is lower than the top personal rate of 39.6 percent.

"The income tax has made more liars out of the American people than golf has."

—Will Rogers

Things to Think About

Key Deductible Expenses

These are the key deductible expenses for a corporation (generally excluded from operating income on the income statement). Use this checklist to make sure that you're getting all the deductions you're entitled to.

- Salaries
- Rent
- Repairs
- Bad debts
- Interest
- Taxes
- Charitable contributions
- Casualty losses
- Depreciation and amortization
- Travel and entertainment
- Advertising
- Pension plan contributions

Tip

In general, a company can deduct an expense (i.e., include it "above the line" on its income statement) if the expense:

- **must be paid during the taxable year to carry on business**
- **is not a capital investment**
- **is "ordinary and necessary"**

JUST THE FACTS

Corporate Tax Rates

For 1997, the corporate tax rates were as follows:

Taxable Income	The Tax is	Of Excess Over
0–$50,000	0+15 percent	0
$50,000–75,000	$7,500+25 percent	$50,000
$75,000–100,000	$13,750+34 percent	$75,000
$100,000–335,000	$22,250+39 percent	$100,000

So if your taxable income is $85,000, then your tax would be
$13,750+[34 percent x $10,000] = $17,150
Note that the net tax rate comes out to about 20 percent.

If you're moving because of a job, save all your receipts.

Getting Organized! Tax Records & Receipts

307 Even disorganized people can organize their taxes.

Take me for instance. I can be terribly disorganized, usually because I don't want to take the time to handle something completely when it comes across my desk. We all have that problem—before you know it, things are lost in a pile in our inbox, or in the "mystery drawer" in the kitchen. This is how I've learned to manage: designate at least 1 big receptacle at the beginning of the year for your taxes. It might be a huge folder, envelope, or drawer that you can toss anything tax-related into for the entire year. That way, your receipts, investment records, and relevant notices are at least in one place where you can find them once you sit down to organize them.

Tip

Don't throw out those shoe boxes: hang on to your records for 7 years—that's how long the IRS has to audit you after you file your return. (You're usually in the clear after 3, but if you've underreported by 25 percent or more, they've got the full 7 to come after you.)

308 Set up your folders early and use them.

- Cash receipts
- Charitable contributions
- Business expenses
- Child care expenses
- IRAs
- Medical expenses
- Investment records
- Mortgage payments
- Miscellaneous expenses

These are the main categories you'll want to set up:

If you're not sure about whether an expense is deductible, throw it in the folder anyway—you can always look at it more closely at tax time.

309 Save those receipts!

No one likes to be the geek at the table who's jotting down notes for a tax return—and you don't have to be. Just get into the habit of grabbing the receipt and putting in the same place—say in the same pocket of your wallet. Once a week, when you pay your bills, go through them and jot down any details: who you were with, any extra tip, what you talked about. Then throw them in the same handy folder you've already got set up. This simple routine will save you loads of headaches, I guarantee, at tax time.

310 If your expenses are really complicated, keep a journal.

If you're the type who's traveling around the country, entertaining clients and picking up unreimbursed business expenses like there's no tomorrow, keep a diary. The IRS may need more than a receipt to substantiate a deduction—they'll need to know about the purpose, and the business relationships involved. Do yourself a favor and keep it all in one place—you can do a quick summary at the end of each day.

"It is best to do things systematically,
since we are only human,
and disorder is our worst enemy."

—HESIOD

When you're in over your head, consult a tax advisor.

Ask Lorraine

Q&A

Q. *Can't I buy investments in my kids' names?*

A. Yes! If you buy a bond for your children, they can cash them in once they're 14 years old and be taxed at the lower rate. The standard tax rate for kids under the age of fourteen is 15 percent, but before you transfer all of your income-earning assets to your kids—the limit they may earn is $1,300. Any amount over that limit will be taxed at the parent's tax rate.

Q. *Why should I wait to sell a profitable stock until next year? I know that my tax bracket will be the same, and maybe even higher.*

A. Your broker may be telling you to wait because there's a chance that you'll have losses next year to offset your gain, which you don't have this year. Remember, if you don't understand the advice you're given, *ask.*

Q. *I have a stock that I know will bounce back, but in the meantime has taken a big dip. Is there any way I can use that capital loss without losing my position?*

A. First of all, turn to Tip 222 ("Don't Be Afraid to Admit Your Mistakes"). If you're still devoted to hanging on to this stock, consider this slightly tricky strategy: you could sell the stock, take the loss, and then buy it again at least 31 days after you sold it. (Or you could buy more stock at least 31 days before you sell it.) That way you've maintained your position, with only the 31-day "down" period.

Another option is to sell the stock and buy another one you think is basically the same. For example, you could buy another mutual fund made up of essentially the same types of investments. (Although you can't be too close—the IRS does watch out for "substantially similar" tradeoffs.)

Q. *So I'm a little late on my taxes. How much could I get penalized, really?*

A. In general, the IRS charges 5 percent of the unpaid amount for each month (or part of a month) that you're late. That means that if you owed $1,000 in taxes, you'll be assessed $50 a month until you pay up.

Q. *Every year my broker starts pushing me to sell stocks for tax reasons. I'm never sure how to handle it—are there any guidelines?*

A. The essential point to remember is that you should never sell stocks for tax-related reasons alone. First ask yourself what you'd like to do regardless of tax considerations. THEN go back and reconsider your answer when tax issues are taken into account.

Q. *Why can't I call everyone who works for me an independent contractor?*

A. Sure that would be handy, since accounting for employees is a much bigger responsibility. You need to keep track of all kinds of payroll taxes and start filing with the IRS (see Tip 305 on Employee Taxes). With an independent contractor, you can probably simply issue a 1099 at the end of the year. Unfortunately, the IRS has strict criteria (20 in all) that you must meet to call someone a contractor.

These are the most critical:

- **Are the work-related activities of this person controlled by you?** To be an independent contractor, the person must have the flexibility to perform all duties necessary to run their business while also performing work for you.
- **Does this person work exclusively for you (versus working for other clients)?** To legitimately qualify as an independent contractor, the individual must have more than one client.
- **Does she have general duties within a set time frame every day (versus being hired for a specific project)?** If this person has specific hours and duties at your place of business, the IRS will consider her an employee, not an independent contractor.

Keep in mind, flexibility is key if you choose to work with an independent contractor. While there may be some set duties you would like her to perform, her situation must allow for her to come and go as she pleases and must enable her to provide for her own business well-being.

Resource Guide

Getting Help with Your Taxes

- The main number for the IRS is 1-800-829-1040. They can direct you to plenty of sources for tax help.

  IRS Web site: *www.irs.ustreas.gov/*
- Or you might ask for Publication 17, "Your Federal Income Tax," for general questions. (For small businesses, ask for Publication 334, "Tax Guide for Small Businesses.")
- For a listing of Enrolled Agents—who aren't quite CPAs but are good for moderately complicated tax-planning services, contact the

  National Association of Enrolled Agents
  1-800-424-4339
- To be sure your Social Security taxes are registered correctly in case of a name change, call the Social Security offices at:

  1-800-772-1213
- *Ernst & Young's Tax Saver's Guide* (published by John Wiley & Sons) is an excellent resource for comprehensive tax information. Check your local bookstore or library.

Setting Up Your Payroll Taxes

- Call the IRS to get an EIN (employee identification number) and receive your 8109 payroll deposit slip booklet.

  1-800-829-1040
- Automatic Data Processing (ADP) is the largest payroll processing company. They offer a free booklet on payroll information and IRS rules. Call and ask for the "Payroll Tax Guide."

  1-800-225-5237
- Paychex is another great resource for small businesses. They can give you plenty of information and literature on payroll issues.

  Paychex
  911 Panorama Trail
  Rochester, NY 14625
  1-800-322-7292

Section 8

It's never too early
to start planning
for the future.

Long-Term Planning

Planning for the future is something we seem to be able to put off endlessly. After all, who wants to think about retirement when they're at the peak of their career? Or has time to set up a college fund for a toddler? Even worse, who wants to write a will or think about life insurance while still in the prime of life? Not me, I know.

But I've learned to deal with all of those issues in a responsible way by simply thinking of them as tasks. Just like with my taxes, I review all of my long-range plans for my family once a year. And I'm happy to say that it's become easier every year because of the routine. Once the system is set up, it's easier to review plans without becoming bogged down in unpleasant implications—getting older, children leaving—even facing the grim reaper.

But if you still have problems planning far into the future, consider the more pleasant aspects of the process. I like to point out the advantage that time gives people in saving, for example. When you've got 40 years on your side, you can build up a sizeable nest egg with a very small monthly investment. That means that $25 a month could pay for your 2-year-old's Ivy League education. Or better yet, it might just buy that villa in the South of France you've always dreamed about.

Planning for the Big Bite: College Tuition

311 Start by adding up the costs.

Ouch. College costs are becoming an increasingly painful reality in the financial lives of American families. Costs vary widely among schools, but the average projected costs for the year 2000 are about $125,000 for a private college, $60,000 for a public one. Those numbers disturb the sleep of parents everywhere, but it's important to face them early so you won't be caught without a plan before it's too late.

Tip **Use the Present Value Table in Section 5 (p. 52) to determine the amount you'll need to start putting away now to save enough for college.**

312 Explore tax-friendly ways to save.

The government looks kindly on savings used for education (see, for example, Tip 300 for a discussion on EE bonds). Talk to your accountant to be sure that you're taking advantage of all of the education loopholes.

Tip **Save in your kids' names when you can. There are cash benefits to setting up savings accounts in the names of your kids. Before the age of 14, your child can earn the $650 in interest and dividends tax-free. And the second $650 will be taxed at the child rate—currently 15 percent.**

Trap **Although saving in your kid's names can be tax-savvy, it can backfire when they go to apply for student financial aid one day. Be aware that their investment accounts can hurt their eligibility for college loans when the time comes. (IRAs or 401k's can be a good way around this problem—see page 265.)**

313 Start early and increase your annual return.

Remember: the earlier you start, the more aggressive you can be in your investment vehicles. If you begin saving when your kids are toddlers, you can put more money into higher-yielding (on average) investments like stocks.

314 Consider zero-coupon bonds.

With zero-coupon bonds, you'll basically buy a bond at a deep discount and receive its full face value later. So you might pay $500 for a bond that will pay you $1,000 in 20 years—the trick is that you don't receive interest payments, because they're "implied" in your final payoff. The actual annual return is usually in the same ballpark as other bonds, but many investors like the structure—especially when saving for a specific goal, like college.

Trap **One of the drawbacks to zero-coupon bonds is that you have to pay taxes on the implied interest payments, even though you're not really receiving them. It's referred to as a "phantom tax."**

Tip **If you want to escape the phantom tax, you can buy municipal zero-coupon bonds—the interest is deductible from federal and state taxes (see Section 7 for more discussion of tax-free bonds).**

315 Recruit relatives to the cause.

Don't be shy about telling grandparents or other relatives and friends about the college savings accounts you've set up for your kids. They'll probably like having the option of contributing to your child's college fund at birthday time, so educational savings could get a nice boost.

316 Know the ins and outs of financial aid.

There are countless sources of help for tuition money—scholarships, loans, grants. But many of the applications processes are complicated, so it's a good idea to start becoming familiar with terrain early—definitely by your child's high school years. A good start is the CASHE system (College Aid Sources for Higher Education)—a database on thousands of different types of financial aid for college (see Resource Guide for contact information).

317 Explore ways to improve your eligibility for money.

Follow the College Money Checklist to financial aid.

If you're looking for financial aid, you'll also become acquainted with the FAFSA (Free Application for Federal Student Aid). Prepare yourself—it's no picnic. You'll need to provide tax returns and other information about your financial status. How much money you could receive will depend on your eligibility, so think about some strategies that could help:

- Don't take any big payouts (like selling property or stock) if you don't have to.
- Consider taking any income reductions in the year you'll be reviewed.

Trap **One of the downsides to saving in your kids' names is that it can hurt their eligibility for student loans when the time comes. You might consider setting them up with IRAs and 401k's—these investments are not taken into account in the government's eligibility review.**

JUST THE FACTS

College Money Checklist

(Contact the Federal Student Aid Information Center for all, 1-800-433-3243)

- Federal Grants
- Pell Grants
- State Grants
- SEOG (Supplemental Educational Opportunity Grants)
- Student Loans
- Stafford Student Loan Program (undergraduate)
- Perkins Loans (graduate)
- PLUS (Parent Loan for Undergraduate Students)

Staying on Top of Your Student Loans

318 Consider consolidating.

If you have more than 1 student loan, it might pay to combine them. It could simplify your payments, and possibly lower your interest costs, depending on the levels at which you start.

319 Be conservative in choosing your payback plan.

Your handling of a student loan will reflect on your credit record for years, so you want to set up schedule you can meet. Take the lowest monthly payment, at least in the beginning—you can always adjust it later.

Sallie Mae has a number of different payback plans for student loans, which vary the interest you'll pay during different segments of the loan period. Call 1-800-524-9100 for details.

320 Prioritize your payback by interest-rate level.

Take a look at your loans and determine which ones are costing you the most money in interest. If you can, pay off the more expensive loans first.

321 Think hard before you pay off your student loans.

Excited about getting rid of that debt? That's admirable, but take a good hard look at your other debt first. Student loans generally have some of the lowest interest rates and flexible terms of any consumer debt. I've seen too many people pay off their student loans ahead of time, only to run up a 18 percent-rate credit card balance the next year.

322 Can you cut your interest rate even more?

Sallie Mae offers "good behavior" discounts for those who pay their first 48 payments on time. You might be able to lower your interest rate by up to 2 percentage points if you qualify. Or if you agree to have your payments automatically deducted from your checking account, your interest rate could be reduced even more (usually 1/4 of a percentage point).

Strapped for your payments? You might be able to defer your loan payments, depending on your situation. Many lenders allow breaks for periods of unemployment or time as a student. Check with your lender for their standards.

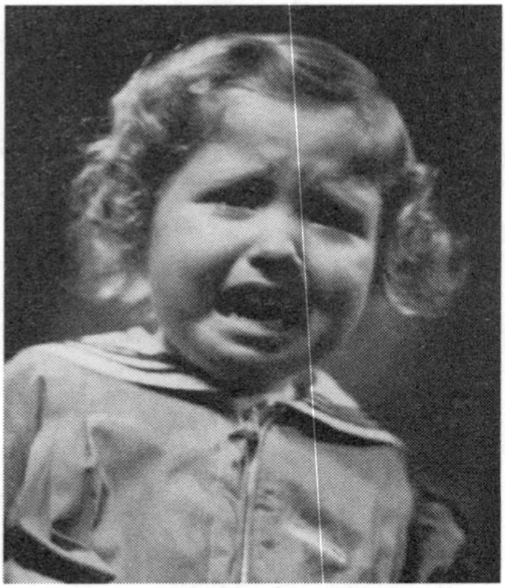

Have you seen the projected cost of a college education?

Making Your Olden Years Golden: IRAs, 401k's, Annuities

"You can be young without money but you can't be old without it."

—Tennessee Williams

323 Start now.

So, what if you're 25 years old and can't imagine where you'll be this weekend, much less in 40 years. Find out what kind of retirement plan your company has and begin contributing to it. It will be a great way to start saving, and you'll hardly notice the money that will begin coming out of your paycheck. Even if it's a minimal amount—say $25 per month—you'll be amazed at how quickly it will pile up. Once you acquire this discipline, you'll find that it's something you don't even think about it anymore during your career. Remember—your contributions might be tiny, but you have time on your side, which means decades of compounding. At a 10 percent annual return, your $25 per month will grow into a nest egg worth $132,777 in 40 years.

324 Find out about your employer's retirement plan and use it to the max.

We've already made this point to some degree when we discussed savings in Section 5, but we focused on personal savings plans like 401k's and Keogh's. Many companies also offer more traditional retirement plans, although it's becoming less common (and you must be cautious, in the event that your company becomes insolvent later on). There are a few different types of retirement plans your organization might have—here are the main categories:

- **Defined Benefit Plan:** Your employer commits to giving you a specific dollar amount when you retire.
- **Defined Contribution Plan:** You (and maybe your employer) set aside a specific amount in the the account. The end benefit will vary depending on the way it's invested.
- **Profit-sharing Plan:** A profit-sharing plan is funded by your company, and is essentially a bonus based on the company's good fortunes.

JUST THE FACTS

Different Types of Retirement Plans

- **401k Plan:** This plan is the IRS-designated name for a type of salary-reduction plan private companies offer employees as a retirement benefit. Similar plans are offered by non-for-profit organizations and are called 403b's; 457 plans are for state and local government employees.
- **IRA:** An IRA is a tax-deferred retirement savings plan available to everyone whether employed or self-employed.
- **Keogh:** A Keogh plan is of special interest to entrepreneurs, self-employed people, and employed people who have income from a free-lance or side business. It's a tax-deferred retirement nest-egg-growing program with tax-deductible contributions.

325 Don't be afraid of stocks.

This is one of the most important points I can make to young people who want advice about their retirement plan: investing in stocks will give you a much higher return in the long run. Yes, they can be more volatile from year to year. Everyone has a personal risk profile that they can live with. But the extra 5 percent or so that stocks have returned historically over bonds can make a huge difference in your retirement nest egg. Let's say that you manage to put away $200 per month for 20 years. If you earn a 5 percent return you'll have $79,356 versus the $137,460 you'd have with a 10 percent return.

"If you can count your money, you don't have a billion dollars."

—J. PAUL GETTY

326 Just because you can't withdraw your money doesn't mean you can't enjoy its benefits.

What scares many people (especially young people) away from plans like a 401k is the permanence of the arrangement. What if you need that money—then you'll get stuck with that ugly 10 percent penalty, right?

Not necessarily. Many plans allow you to borrow against your 401k account—usually up to half of the total value. Check with your employer about their specific plan.

Trap

Be careful not to contribute money you might need later. It's true that you will pay a penalty on any savings that you withdraw from tax-free plans like IRAs.

327 Vesting is a beautiful thing.

Many employers now have matching savings plans—which means that they'll contribute to your savings based on your contributions. They're basically giving you money, and you'd be foolish not to take it.

328 Aim for bare-bones expenses in your golden years.

For most people, this means having your house paid off by the time you retire. Along with your Social Security benefits, this will also give a good boost to your monthly income. (And leave more for scuba diving lessons.) Keep this goal when you set up your mortgage.

329 Figure out what your expenses will be now.

Not only is this a handy way to calculate what you should be saving, but I think it's important from a psychological perspective. By doing the math and some of the planning today, the prospect of your retirement can become more real to you.

Add up your projected expenses on the worksheet on the next page, and come up with a realistic amount that you'd like to live on when you've retired.

330 Retiring doesn't mean just surviving.

I see this classic scenario played out all the time. To get the bare minimum that they'll have to save, many people figure out only what they'll need to *survive* after retirement. That means rent, food, and utilities. Well, I know that when I retire I plan on doing plenty more than sitting home making the occasional pot roast. I plan on doing everything I don't have the time for now: that means African safaris, tango lessons, and that sporty convertible I always wanted to drive down the Autobahn. And that takes money.

A worksheet like this is helpful: calculate what you might need for at least 2 different "lifestyle" levels.

Monthly Expenses for the Swingin' Retiree

	Survival	**Living!**
Rent	$	$
Utilities	$	$
Entertainment	$	$
Medical	$	$
Travel	$	$
Extras	$	$
Gifts	$	$
Less Social Security payments	$	$
Total Income Needed	$	$

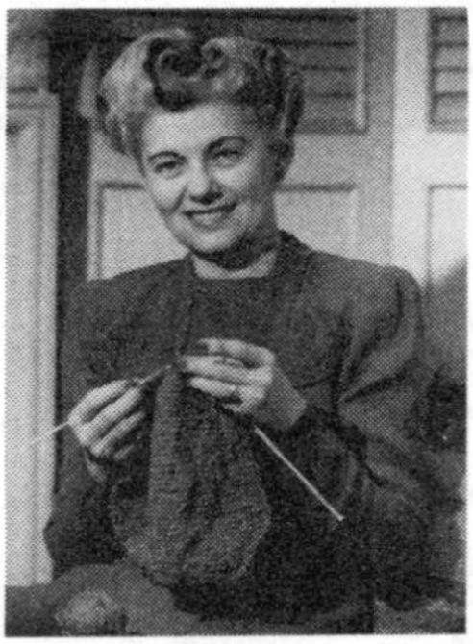

It's wise to have a retirement plan all your own.

331 Figure out how much savings you'll need.

Now that you have an idea of what your expenses will be, how much do you need to save? Most banks (or your accountant) will calculate this for you, but the following table that will give you an idea of what you'll need (see next page).

These calculations assume that you retire at age 65 and live until age 90. It also assumes 10 percent return on your savings, 4 percent annual inflation, and a 4 percent annual income growth rate.

Monthly Amount You Should Be Saving

Total Yearly Expenses	Current Age 20	30	40	50
$30,000	$255	$457	$851	$1,780
$50,000	$425	$762	$1419	$2967
$75,000	$638	$1143	$2128	$4451
$100,000	$850	$1524	$2838	$5935

332 If you've got more than $2,000 a year to sock away, look into annuities.

Annuities are special instruments offered by insurance companies and are the best way to get tax-deferred returns saved up for your retirement. This is basically how it works: you give the insurance company a lump sum of money and they invest it according to your instructions—the gains are entirely tax-free. There are 2 key types of tax-deferred annuities:

- **Guaranteed Rate:** A guaranteed-rate annuity, as you might think, gives you a fixed rate of return on your money—"guaranteed" by the insurance company.
- **Variable:** A variable annuity allows you to invest your money in a wide range of mutual funds—bond, stock, or money markets. It gives you much more flexibility, although the trade-off is a more volatile year-to-year performance.

"Buy an annuity cheap, and make your life interesting to yourself and everybody else that watches the speculation."

—CHARLES DICKENS

Tip **In general, if you've got a longer time horizon (i.e., 10 years or more until retirement), a variable annuity is the best bet. You may have more volatile yearly performance, but you'll probably get higher returns over time.**

Trap **Just as with IRAs and 401k's, there's a penalty for withdrawing your money from an annuity before you're 59 1/2. The government will charge you 10 percent of the interest earned so far, and the mutual fund will probably have a "surrender charge."**

333 If you're self-employed, check out a Keogh or SEP-IRA plan.

The great thing about setting up your own retirement plans like these is that the limits allowed are much higher. With these plans, your company can generally contribute up to $22,500 per year, or 15 percent of earned income (whichever is smaller) to a retirement account for that employee. If you're the only employee, then your company would simply be paying into the account for you. The amount you contribute to the plan is completely deductible from your company's taxes.

334 Don't count on your spouse!

Some people will call this a cynical point, but I have seen too many women become financially devastated after their husband left them (or passed away). This doesn't mean that you start planning your separation, simply that you take simple steps to find independence and security. Think about these points:

- **Pay attention to your own retirement plan.** Many women have retirement plans but don't accumulate as much, for a number of reasons. Either they move in and out of the work force more often, or simply contribute less because they assume that their husband's plan will be plenty for them both.
- **Be prepared to live on your own.** Women tend to outlive their husbands, and many, unfortunately, take a big financial hit in their widowed years. Be sure that your retirement plans provide enough income for your life expectancy.

Tip

The Keogh and SEP accounts are pretty similar. The Keogh is a bit more complicated to set up, but it offers a few advantages (like flexibility about which employees to include and the possibility of a higher maximum). Ask your accountant about your specific situation.

"I think the only reason you should retire is if you can find something you enjoy doing more than what you're doing now. I happen to be in love with show business, and I can't think of anything I'd enjoy more than that. So I guess I've been retired all my life."

—George Burns

Plan ahead and reap the rewards in your golden years.

Health Insurance, HMOs, & Other Mysteries

335 To HMO or not to HMO?

HMO plans vary widely, depending on your employer (if you have one), the company, and your situation. For many people HMOs offer an excellent alternative: low-cost treatment for the occasional ailment or illness. For others, it's an inadequate approach to a serious illness. Before making a decision about your employer's HMO, ask your coworkers about their experience with the plan. Have they been happy with the coverage? Have they had trouble getting appointments? Are there any payments or fees they hadn't expected?

Also be sure to pose the situations that are most likely to happen to you: is there a certain doctor who you would hate to give up? Then find out what it would take for you continue seeing her. Might you (or your wife) become pregnant in the near future? Ask about OB-GYN doctors and programs. The point is to understand that not all plans are alike, and that they can have a major impact on your life. Once you've asked these questions, you might find that the HMO will be fine, or that it may end up being more expensive than the full coverage of another option. Understand the tradeoffs.

336 If you're young and uninsured, be resourceful.

We all know how expensive health insurance can be when you're not under the protective umbrella of an employer. Chances are that an HMO will be your best bet (see Resource Guide for numbers to call), but there might be other ways to find an affordable plan. Consider:

- **Parental Coverage:** If you're young enough, you might be eligible for coverage through your family's plan. This is often the cheapest way to be insured. Ask your parents, and offer to pay your share of the total premium.

Just the Facts

There Are Basically Two Kinds of Health Insurance

- **Fee for Service:** Typically, you can go to any doctor you want and this plan will cover it. But you'll have a deductible (say, \$1000–\$2000 for the year), and probably a co-payment (usually 10 percent to 20 percent of your total medical costs up to a certain limit).
- **Managed Care (HMOs):** These plans vary widely, but you'll probably be limited to healthcare providers who are part of the plan. It usually costs less than a fee-for-service plan (lower premiums, copayments, and deductibles). But you might find the restrictions bothersome, and some patients complain about waiting periods for the doctor they want.

- **Trade Associations:** There are many organizations that offer group plans for members. Is there a group affiliated with your profession, or even a hobby, which you might be able to join?
- **School Coverage:** If you've recently graduated, ask your administrative office about ways to continue your coverage. You might be able to maintain a minimum amount of hours, or to extend your coverage through COBRA for a certain number of months.

Tip

If you've just graduated or are between jobs, you might be able to get temporary health insurance. It can last up to 8 months and it's usually relatively cheap. See Resource Guide for more information.

Things to Think About

The Questions You Should Ask About HMOs

- What happens if you want to see a doctor outside the HMO?
- What's your co-payment?
- Are all the doctors within the plan generally available?

337 Don't buy into a plan that won't cover your chronic ailments.

This is a classic maneuver of many insurance companies—refusing to insure "pre-existing conditions." For example, they may refuse to cover costs related to your chronic back pain or that trick knee. Ask your prospective insurer carefully about any exclusions or limits in their plan. If they won't cover your problem right away, see if you can start a waiting period. They may agree to cover it after a period of a year, for instance.

338 Don't forget about disability insurance.

No one likes to think about the unthinkable: some tragic accident that leaves you unable to work. Your health insurance will pay your medical bills, but what will you live on?

That's where disability insurance comes in. Many employer plans include this in basic coverage—usually it will pay around 60 percent of your income (up to a limit) in case you suffer a disability. If your employer doesn't offer disability coverage, check into individual policies that will cover a minimum amount of your income (see Resource Guide).

THINGS TO THINK ABOUT

Disability Coverage Checklist

Be sure your disability coverage has these features:

- **Non-cancellation Clause:** make sure that your insurer can't cancel your policy for any reason.
- **Illness and Accident Coverage:** "Disability" should mean a serious illness or accident. Your insurer's definition should be all-inclusive.
- **Renewability:** You shouldn't have to go through medical exams every year to renew your policy, or face a rate increase if you've made a number of claims. Be careful of any clauses that might give them this right.

Insuring Your Stuff: Property & Casualty

339 Check your insurance rates before you buy the house.

This is an imporant step that many home buyers forget. Be sure to find out what your insurance will cost you before you sign on the dotted line. You don't want to find out about that fire-prone canyon when it's too late.

340 Do your homework before insuring your home.

Sure it's a headache, but there's no way you can get around it if you own your home. You might as well make it the least expensive you can. The first thing you'll want to do is determine the amount of coverage you need. There are standard categories that your insurance company will present and ask you to choose from.

For example, the "HO-1" category will cover the 11 most common perils, like fire, theft, and smoke damage. The HO-2 category will go further to protect you from frozen water pipes or roof collapse from snow. Evaluate your situation carefully, and buy only the amount of coverage that you need.

Tip **Make a video of your house and its contents. It can be done in just a few minutes and make all the difference in whether you get paid in a disaster.**

341 Renters need insurance too.

If you rent your house or apartment, renter's insurance is a great (and relatively cheap) way to protect your belongings. Premiums are generally less than $200 per year and can cover more than you might think.

For example, most policies will cover damage that occurs outside your home. If you accidentally damage something in a store, your policy may cover it. And if you think the belongings inside your apartment aren't worth insuring, sit down and add up the cost of replacing your T.V., stereo, VCR, and microwave.

For all insurance policies, be sure you'll receive the *replacement value* (as opposed to the cash value) of your belongings. If your 5-year-old VCR is stolen, regardless of how much it was worth, you'll need the money for a new one.

Insurance you might not have thought of: don't forget about the insurance benefits you get from other places:

- **Many credit cards offer insurance to members. American Express, for example, offers car rental and travel insurance, as well as insurance on items bought with the card (the Purchase Protection and Buyer's Assurance plans).**
- **Renter's and homeowner's insurance often insure items outside of the home, such as those in your car, or on your person when you're out and about. Ask your agent about your specific plan.**

THINGS TO THINK ABOUT

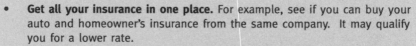

Bringing Down that Home Insurance Premium

Try some of these tips to cut your insurance bill:

- **Get all your insurance in one place.** For example, see if you can buy your auto and homeowner's insurance from the same company. It may qualify you for a lower rate.
- **Check into protective measure discounts.** Many insurance plans offer discounts for features like smoke detectors or burglar alarms. Ask your insurance company about your options.
- **Take the highest deductible you can afford.** This will definitely lower your premium, and chances are you won't ever have to pay the deductible. (Of course, never get a deductible that you can't cover from your savings.)

Facing the Inevitable: Getting the Life Insurance You Need

342 Don't be stingy about your life insurance.

This also goes under the category of things we don't like to think about and so often don't prepare for. Nobody likes to imagine that they'll be taken away suddenly, much less the pain it could cause their family and friends. But this is an exercise that responsible adults must go through for the sake of their loved ones.

Trap

Don't buy life insurance if you don't need it. In general, you only need life insurance if you have people depending on you for income. If you're single and 25, chances are you don't need it.

343 Base your insurance decision on reason.

So many of us pick insurance benefits in a completely arbitrary way: $25,000? Sounds reasonable. No. There are 2 ways to come up with a better benchmark: based on your *income*, or on your family's *expenses*. The first approach is probably a good shorthand way to start: most advisors recommend that you aim to provide your family with 75 percent of your after-tax income.

"Insurance. An ingenious modern game of chance in which the player is permitted to enjoy the comfortable conviction that he is beating the man who keeps the table."

—Ambrose Bierce

344 In most cases, term insurance is the way to go.

There are 2 basic types of life insurance.

- **Term Insurance:** Term insurance is the simplest brand—you simply make your payments and your beneficiaries collect in case of your early demise. But if the policy expires while you're alive, that's it—it has no value.
- **Cash Value Insurance:** With cash value insurance, part of your payments add up, although you'll pay dearly for that benefit. The amount that you could get while you're still alive is referred to as the *cash surrender* value of your policy.

Although you should obviously discuss the options with your accountant and your insurance advisor, cash value insurance is often so much more expensive (*sometimes 10 times more than term insurance!*) that it's simply prohibitive to buy. Chances are that you're better off investing your money somewhere else than in your insurance plan.

345 Skip the insurance broker and save some dough.

If you buy your insurance directly from an insurance company rather than through a broker, you can avoid paying the broker's fees. There are also discount insurance brokers who can get you a reduced rate.

JUST THE FACTS

Pick Your Brand of Life Insurance

There are thousands of different insurance products, but there are 3 different essential types of cash value policies.

- **Whole or Straight Life:** Your premiums are consistent, you build up a cash reserve, although you have no control over how it's invested.
- **Universal Life:** The amount of the premium can vary as you use your cash reserve to cover the costs. You can also change the amount of the final death benefit, and there's a guaranteed investment return. But there are also higher fees involved for these benefits.
- **Variable Life:** Essentially an investment product. You can choose from a variety of products to control how your cash reserve is invested.

Did You Know?

Renewable or Level Plan?

You have the option of buying 2 types of term insurance: either *annual renewable* or *level premium policy*. With the first type, you have the option of renewing your policy every year, but at increasing premiums. A level premium plan, on the other hand, will have the same premium for a fixed number of years. The tradeoff is that the premium will likely be a bit higher at first.

346 One person doesn't have half the expenses of two.

One of the most common mistakes I see in survivor benefits decisions is the assumption that the surviving spouse will need only half the money the couple did. This perception, for example, leads many spouses to choose the "50 percent" option as the appropriate pension payment in the event of their death. But many of the expenses of the surviving spouse will be the same as that of the couple: house payments, utilities, car payments, health insurance, gifts for family—all will involve just as much money.

I had great luck with a discount insurance broker.

Estates & Wills & More Stuff We'd Rather Avoid

Whoa. If you thought retirement was a difficult thing to think about, then it's probably even tougher to face this next subject. That's why this is the area where people are often most negligent: who wants to think about their own death?

347 Do your will. Now!

If you can't get motivated for this particular task, visualize the scenarios which would make you the most unhappy. That's it: imagine that aunt of yours with the hideous taste getting your treasured antique vase from Indonesia and using it for an ashtray. Or your well-meaning brother throwing your perfect cashmere scarf into his garage, never knowing that you always wanted to give it to your favorite niece. Worse yet, many families are torn apart by petty bickerings over who gets what. Don't let this happen to your family.

Trap **A common misconception about wills is that you can do it yourself. On the contrary, handwritten wills are not recognized in most states. Get a qualified lawyer to put yours together.**

Trap **Trusts aren't just for rich people!! Setting up a basic trust should cost you $1,000-$2,000, and could save your family tens of thousands later.**

"Death and taxes and childbirth! There's never any convenient time for any of them!"

—MARGARET MITCHELL

THINGS TO THINK ABOUT

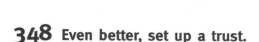

A Checklist for Your Will

There are 4 critical things a good will should accomplish:

1. Explain who gets what.
2. Designate who gets to distribute the rest.
3. Explain who gets your kids (and pets, too).
4. Limit your estate's tax liability.

348 Even better, set up a trust.

Trusts aren't just for rich people anymore, and they can make life a heck of a lot easier for those you leave behind. The main reason is that a trust can transfer all of your legal authority to another person in a way that a will can't. The provisions of a will (generally transferring assets) have to be carried out by court order—a process referred to as *probate*. Probate can be a long, expensive, and arduous procedure. If you set up a trust, you can save your beneficiary plenty of headaches and money.

You don't have to be rich to benefit from a trust.

Did You Know?

Getting Around Probate Fees

Probate fees are generally standard—and expensive—in most states. For example, for a $100,000 estate, your beneficiaries will need to pay the court a $6,300 probate fee before they can have your assets transferred into their names according to your will. If it's a $1,000,000 estate, they'll be charged a whopping $46,300. If you establish a trust (which transfers your legal rights automatically), you can avoid those fees.

Beating the Tax Man From Beyond: Estate Taxes

349 Don't put your family through the estate tax cash crunch.

Estate taxes in the U.S. are currently enormous, and the government wants the money from your beneficiary 9 months after your death. That means that on top of having to deal with the grief of your demise, your spouse and family will have a huge financial burden that could have been so easily avoided. Here are a couple strategies that could save your family the anguish of having to sell off the family home:

- **Leave as much as possible to your spouse:** You can give as much of your estate as you want to your spouse—free of estate taxes. By that reasoning, you have much more incentive to leave money to your spouse than to other family members. (Ask your accountant about legal ways your spouse could use the money to support them.)
- **Give it away before you die:** You can reduce your estate by making gifts now of up to $10,000—they are tax-free. (Above that amount, it's still considered to be a part of your estate and taxed accordingly.) If you plan ahead, you can start an annual gift-giving schedule now that could reduce your estate taxes considerably. Besides, you'll be around to see all the joy it brings to the recipients.

Tip

You can give even more than $10,000 if you pay the money directly to a college in the form of tuition, or directly to a health care institution for medical expenses. Some charities are also allowed to receive unlimited tax-free gifts—check with your accountant.

350 Reducing estate taxes: don't own your own insurance.

If you assign the ownership of your life insurance to someone else or let someone else buy the policy, it won't be added to the value of your estate upon your death. That way your beneficiary won't have to pay taxes on it.

Did You Know?

The Estate Tax Crunch

OK, one more time!! If you leave your family an estate with a certain dollar value, they'll have to pay up to 55 percent of that value to the IRS—IN CASH. That means that if you leave your beautiful house to your favorite daughter and the IRS values it at $1,000,000, your daughter will need to come up with up to $550,000 within 9 months after your death, and will most likely lose the house you wanted her to have.

351 Consider setting up an A-B trust.

This kind of trust is an excellent way to save your family an enormous amount of money—essentially doubling the $600,000 tax-exempt amount. Here's how it works: while both spouses are alive, they set up an A-B trust, basically dividing their combined estate into halves. When one spouse dies, the surviving spouse simply becomes a trustee of the "A" portion of the estate—with all relevant rights. If the surviving spouse uses up the "B" half, he or she may dip into the "A" half. But the critical advantage of the A-B trust comes when the second spouse dies—both halves now pass to the family, but each under a separate $600,000 tax-free limit.

Tip **You don't even have to be a married couple to set up an A-B trust. Two friends or any kind of couple can set one up legally.**

352 Don't underestimate the value of your estate.

Think there's no way your estate could be worth more than $600,000 (the limit that's exempt from federal taxes)? You'd better be sure: many families' homes have multiplied in market value, not to mention investment accounts and funds which have done very well. Throw in the value of a couple of cars and insurance payouts, and many middle-class families are at the $600,000 threshold. Go through a reasonable market valuation with your accountant at least every few years to determine the extent of your estate tax liability. NOTE: That exempt amount will be rising to $1,000,000 by the year 2006.

Worksheet: Estate Value

Review this worksheet annually to make sure that increased market valuations don't change your financial circumstances.

Here's a checklist to help you estimate the value of your estate

Real Estate (homes, properties)	$
	$
	$
	$
	$
Cash and Investments	$
	$
	$
	$
	$
	$
Life Insurance Proceeds	$
	$
Employee Benefits (pension plans, retirement plans)	$
	$
	$
	$
Other Property (automobiles, collections, etc.)	$
	$
	$
	$
	$
	$
	$
Total Value of Estate	**$**

The Insurance No One Plans For: Long-Term Disability Care

353 One out of 3 of us will end up in a nursing home.

Ugh—nobody likes to think about spending their golden years in an institutional setting. But the reality is that a large percentage of people do—not because there was no one to take care of them—but because they didn't plan ahead. Long-term health care is extremely expensive and we all need to prepare for it, just as we buy normal health or life insurance.

JUST THE FACTS

The Aging U.S. Population

Care for the elderly is becoming even more critical issue as the U.S. population continues to age—thanks to longer life expectancies and healthier lifestyles. According to the U.S. Census Bureau:

- The elderly population increased 11-fold from 1900 to 1994, compared with only a 3-fold increase for those under 65.
- From 1960 to 1994, the "oldest old" (persons aged 85 and over) increased by 274 percent, compared with 100 percent for the 65 and over, and 45 percent for the total population.

354 Don't count on Medicare.

This is the biggest misconception about long-term health care. Medicare pays for an extremely limited amount of service. Basically it covers 20 days of "skilled nursing care," then you pay $81.50 per day for the next 80 days, and then you're on your own. That's right, about 100 days of financial help. Just to put that in perspective, the average nursing home resident stays there for about *3 years*.

JUST THE FACTS

So What Does It Cost?

Plans and premiums vary widely, but here's a table based on a standard plan:

If your're in your...	Your annual premiums will be about...
40s*	$750
50s	$1,000–$1,250
60s	$1,500–$2,500
70s	$3,750–$8,000

*You can't buy an LTC plan until you're 45 years old.

355 Medicaid can help, but only if you agree to become destitute.

This is a terrible alternative that many senior citizens turn to: "spending down" their assets so that they can qualify for Medicaid. This strategy can be particularly devastating for the spouse, who is left with almost nothing to live on.

356 Your family can help, but do you really want to burden them?

The reality of this scenario is that your family will often take on the burden of your health care. It may seem ideal, but it can place enormous financial and emotional strain on them—particularly if money is tight and they are trying to invest their time and funds in a new generation of kids. For example, if you had sufficient money, you could still live with your family but afford a nurse to help you as well. That takes lots of responsibility off your loved ones' shoulders and leaves you with more time to enjoy each other's company.

357 Find the right plan.

Long-term care (LTC) plans are essentially defined by 2 characteristics:

- **The daily benefits** (how much money your plan will offer a day). They range from about $50 to $250 per day for a nursing home, and $40 to $150 for home health care.

- **The benefit period** or how many years your plan will pay for. As mentioned, the average nursing home stay is about 3 years, so many people gravitate toward that benchmark.

358 If you're young, consider getting an inflation option.

Your $100 per day won't do you much good in 30 years if good healthcare costs $500 per day. An inflation option allows your benefits to increase according to inflation, usually with a 5 percent cap per year. As we've seen in our section on inflation (see Section 5), this can make a huge difference in your end result. To give you an idea of the benefits, after 30 years, a $100 payment with a 5 percent compounded inflation option would be worth nearly $700 per day.

359 Be sure your plan includes a home health care option.

There is a definite trend toward more medical care at home, and just about everyone would prefer this alternative. Most LTC plans allow for a home health care option that's anywhere from 50 to 80 percent of your "skilled health care" option.

THINGS TO THINK ABOUT

The Long-Term Health Care Checklist

Here's a quick rundown of things you should check out before buying an LTC Plan:

- **Restrictions on home health care:** Be sure that it doesn't have to be administered by a professional health care worker—this can make it difficult to get your benefits.
- **Waiver of premium:** Once you begin collecting benefits, you shouldn't have to pay premiums anymore.
- **Restrictions on qualifications:** Your plan shouldn't require a hospital stay, for example, for you to start receiving benefits. Be sure that there are no other important qualifiers that could keep you from becoming eligible.
- **Renewability:** Your plan should be guaranteed renewable.
- **Restrictions on preexisting conditions:** Check this clause carefully—most plans should have nothing prohibitive here outside of a standard 6-month clause.

The Shaky Safety Net: Social Security

360 Figure out your Social Security benefits now.

This is an easy process to go through and could help you in your retirement planning. I also think it's invaluable in helping you to understand the reality of your retirement—something so many of us have difficulty comprehending. You can find out your benefits by filing a "Request for Earnings and Benefit Estimate Statement" from the Social Security office (see Resource Guide for information).

361 Don't count on Social Security.

Social Security funding is in a precarious state. Will it be there for you when you're ready to retire? More important, will your benefits be enough to support you? No! The maximum monthly benefit in 1997 was $1,326.50—definitely not enough to support the life you'd like to lead in your golden years.

JUST THE FACTS

Early Withdrawal

You also have the option of drawing your Social Security payments as early as age 62. In that case, your benefits would be reduced according to the following schedule:

Benefit Reduction	Age
20%	62
$13\frac{1}{3}$%	63
$6\frac{2}{3}$%	64
0%	65

In other words, if your regular benefit were $1,000, but you chose to begin drawing when you were 62, then you would receive a 20 percent reduction, or $800 per month.

362 Make sure you're getting proper credit with Social Security.

Be sure that you're registered properly with the Social Security office so that your work credits are going to your account. This is a particularly important issue for people who've gone through name changes.

363 Consider taking early benefits.

Mathematically, this is an attractive deal from the government. Sure your benefits will be less, but you'll be getting 3 extra years of payments, which works out to be beneficial. In other words, if your trade-off is $800 early versus $1,000 in 3 years, it probably makes more sense to take the first option. That's because you'll be receiving $28,800 during those 3 years ($800 x 36). The extra $200 you'd receive per month under the second option wouldn't equal that for 12 years. ($28,800 ÷ $200 ÷ 12 months).

Tip

The Social Security penalties against earned income don't apply to dividends and interest. You can make as much money as you are able from those sources without being docked.

"I cried all the way to the bank."

—Liberace

Don't forget the home health care option!

364 Take the benefits even if you think you might go back to work.

There's really no harm in starting and stopping Social Security, and there could be a lot of benefit. If you decide to go back to work (making enough money to completely disqualify you from all Social Security payments), you have 2 options:

1. You can ask to be placed on "work suspense," which means that you won't receive benefits but you'll begin to accrue credits again. Once you retire again, your benefits will be recalculated.
2. Withdraw your application and pay the money back. The beauty of this option is that no interest is owed on the money you've had. In other words, you could have been earning interest on the that money during your temporary retirement, which you get to keep when you pay the principal back. Pretty nice, huh?

365 Be sure that your spouse can get your payments.

A surviving spouse can collect the Social Security benefits if certain conditions are met. The surviving spouse:

- must be at least 60 years old
- must have been married to the deceased for at least 9 months
- must be unmarried at the time of application

Tip

If you're divorced or widowed but were married to your spouse for at least 10 years, you can qualify for additional benefits—if your spouse's Social Security benefit is larger than yours. This is particularly helpful for women who may not have worked for as many years as their husbands and now find themselves with less-than-acceptable Social Security checks.

Ask Lorraine

Q&A

Q. *What happens to my retirement plan money if I move to another company?*

A. Generally, you'll be able to take your own savings with you. But the amount that your employer has contributed on your behalf will depend on whether you're vested. The rates vary between companies, but the standard is a 100 percent vesting after 5 years, and 20 percent vesting after 3 years.

Q. *I work but my spouse doesn't. Am I still subject to the $2,000 IRA limit?*

A. Your spouse can contribute an additional $250 per year (bringing your total together to $2,250) by setting up a "spousal IRA."

Q. *So, what would have to happen for me to begin receiving long-term insurance benefits?*

A. Most plans require you to meet certain standards, often determined by qualifiers or gatekeepers. A qualifier can determine that long-term health care has become a medical necessity, for example. They often use a checklist of "ADLs" (activities of daily living) to determine your eligibility. If you can't perform 2 of the 6 main ADLs (like bathing or feeding yourself), you would be eligible.

Q. *What if I decide to go back to work after I'm already receiving Social Security?*

A. Social Security will dock your payments as follows:*

- If you're between 62 and 65, you'll lose $1 for every $2 you make over $8,640
- If you're between 65 and 70, you'll lose $1 for every $3 you make over $13,500
- If you're 70 or older, there will be no change.

*As of 1997; may be adjusted from year to year

Q. *Are my Social Security payments taxed?*

A. Of course—you didn't think Uncle Sam would miss out on that opportunity did you? Your benefits will be taxed based on certain thresholds for your provisional income. Consult your accountant for details.

Resource Guide

For Student Loan Help

- Sallie Mae
  1-800-524-9100
- Department of Education
  1-800-455-5889
- CASHE (College Aid Sources for Higher Education)
  301-258-0717

Saving for Retirement and Insurance

- Financial Aid Hotline
  1-800-4-FED-AID
- National Council on Aging
  409 3rd Street SW, Suite 200
  Washington, DC 20024
  202-479-1200
- National Council of Senior Citizens
  8403 Colesville Road, Suite 1200
  Silver Spring, Maryland 20910
  301-578-8800
  Fax: 301-578-8911
  www.ncscinc.org
- Insurance Information Institute
  110 William Street
  New York, NY 10038
  212-669-9200
  www.iii.org

Social Security Help

- Social Security Administration
  1-800-772-1213
  www.ssa.gov

Shopping for Health Insurance

- USAA (insurance company selling directly to consumers)
  1-800-531-8000
- Quotesmith (database of insurance companies)
  1-800-556-9393

Glossary

10-K Annual filing that publicly traded corporations make with the Securities and Exchange Commission (SEC).

10-Q Quarterly filing that publicly traded corporations make with the Securities and Exchange Commission (SEC).

401k plan A type of pension plan that allows you to set aside money for retirement. The key advantage to a 401k plan is that it is a tax-free vehicle. That means you don't pay taxes on the money that goes into your 401k account until you withdraw it (hopefully after you've retired and you're in a lower tax bracket).

account executive (AE) A retail *broker* at an investment firm.

accrued interest Earned interest that hasn't been paid to you yet. For example, if you sell a *bond* with accrued interest, the buyer pays the amount that's accrued as well as the market price of the *security*.

active portfolio management Investment strategy—the opposite of *passive portfolio management*.

An active strategy can include changing the *asset* mix during cycles in the investment markets, shifting between *stocks* in different industries, and buying and selling individual *shares* based on under- and overvalued target prices.

In contrast, *passive portfolio management* involves less decision making on the part of the manager—it is often a "buy and hold" or *indexing strategy*, in which the portfolio is simply constructed to match a popular index.

adjustable rate Interest rate that changes periodically. The adjustments are based on a standard market rate, such as the *prime rate*, or the rate on Treasury bills. Also called a *floating rate*, or *increasing rate*, the rate can change quarterly, monthly, or semiannually. A floor puts a limit on how low the interest rate can fall; a ceiling limits the rise.

adjustable rate mortgage (ARM) A loan (also called a variable rate, or *floating rate* mortgage) whose interest rate fluctuates with prevailing market rates.

affinity card Credit card that offers some reward for its use, such as frequent flyer mileage or cash rebates.

American Depository Receipt (ADR) Certificate representing stake in a foreign company held in the United States.

ADRs are traded on U.S. stock exchanges and through U.S. *brokers*, eliminating the need for U.S. residents to deal in foreign currencies on foreign markets. Transactions are the same as for U.S. *shares*, although one ADR does not necessarily represent one share; it can correspond to multiple shares or fractional shares.

American option See *options*.

American Stock Exchange (AMEX) The smaller of New York City's two stock exchanges. Also known as "The Curb" until 1953. Because of more lenient listing requirements than those of the *New York Stock Exchange (NYSE)*, the companies whose *common stock* is traded on the AMEX are usually smaller.

annual percentage rate (APR) Measurement of the true cost of credit. The APR is more exact and higher than the stated interest rate for installment loans because it considers the compounding of interest during the loan period.

annuity An investment contract sold by an insurance company that guarantees future payments to the buyer on a monthly, quarterly, or annual basis. Annuities are often used to provide retirement income.

applicable federal rate (AFR) Set by the IRS, this is the minimum interest rate that family members and friends are required to charge each other on personal loans.

arbitrage Buying a *security*, currency, or *commodity* on one market and simultaneously selling it (or an equivalent) at a higher price on another market.

arbitration Submitting a dispute for settlement by an impartial individual or panel.

assets In accounting, a company's resources that have future value. Tangible assets include such things as: cash, buildings, inventories, land, supplies and vehicles. Intangible assets include: copyrights, goodwill, and patents.

asset allocation A method of diversifying investments by keeping a set percentage of the value of a portfolio in *stocks*, *bonds*, cash, and other investment vehicles.

asset-backed security A form of borrowing secured by *assets* and the income attached to them. *Mortgage-backed* bonds may be considered a form of asset-backed security.

baby bond A *bond* with a *par value* of less than $1,000. Baby bonds open the bond market to small investors, but they can be more expensive relative to the dollar value because of the higher administrative costs.

back-end load A *mutual fund* in which a penalty charge is assessed if sold before a certain period has elapsed.

balloon payment A loan payment that is particularly large relative to any other payments. A balloon payment is usually the last payment on a loan and retires the balance of the loan.

bankruptcy When an individual or a company is insolvent, i.e., unable to pay debts as they come due. See also *Chapter 7*, *Chapter 11*, and *Chapter 13*.

basis point Measure of yield or interest rate that is equal to 0.01 percent. For example, if a bond's yield moves from 8.25 percent to 8.50 percent, it has moved 25 basis points.

bearer bond A *bond* not registered to a specific holder. Rather, these *securities* have coupons attached, and each interest payment is paid to whomever presents the coupon for that payment.

bellwether *Security* whose price is widely viewed as an indicator of a market's direction.

beta (b) Measure of a security's volatility, or how much its price moves in relation to the overall stock market. A *security* with a beta of 1.0 carries exactly the same risk as the market in general. When the market rises 4 percent, a *stock* with a beta of 1.0 is expected to rise 4 percent as well. But a security with a beta of 2.0 would rise twice as much, or 8 percent.

Big Board Nickname for the *New York Stock Exchange*.

blind pool An offering by a company or *limited partnership* that does not list the specific properties to be acquired. (An industry is usually indicated, such as oil and gas, real estate, or technology.)

blue chip Considered to be the most tried-and-true performers among stocks. (In the U.K., blue chips are called "alpha stocks.")

bond Debt *security* issued by a corporation or government entity, usually in multiples of $1,000, obligating the issuer to pay bondholders a fixed amount of interest at specific intervals, usually semiannually, and to repay the principal of the loan at maturity.

bond ratings Classifying *bonds* by sizing up their risk of default. Several organizations publish bond ratings, most prominently *Moody's Investment Service* and *Standard & Poor's (S&P)*.

bond/warrant unit *Security* in which a *bond* and a set number of equity *warrants* are sold as a unit. Sometimes called a "synthetic convertible."

bond yield Return an investor gets on a bond investment, expressed as an annual percentage.

Bond Yield = Yearly Coupon Payments ÷ Bond Price

book value (1) In accounting, the original cost of an *asset* (plant or equipment) less its accumulated depreciation, sometimes called the "carrying amount." (2) In securities analysis, the valuation of the *equity* that holders of *common stock* have in a company. See also *book value per share*.

book value per share Book value of a company divided by the number of outstanding shares.

Book Value per Share = Shareholders' Equity ÷ Total Number of Outstanding Shares

broker In finance, the salesperson who deals with a brokerage firm's customers.

buyback Company's purchase of its own *securities*. A company might decide to buy back some of its *common stock* if it thinks that the price is too low, and that a buy-back is the most efficient use of its money.

cafeteria plan Employee benefits package that lets workers pick and choose among a "menu" of benefits, so that those with different goals can better accomplish their objectives.

call feature Provision of a *bond* agreement that allows the issuing company to repurchase the bond before it matures.

call option Gives the holder of a *stock* the right to buy an *asset* at a particular price before a certain date. See also *options* and *derivatives.*

capital gain The money you make when you sell an investment for more than you paid.

capital loss The money you lose when you sell something for less than you paid.

capital stock The amount of money or property contributed by stockholders to be used as the financial foundation for a corporation; includes all classes of *common stock* and *preferred stock.*

capitalization ratio A way of measuring how debt-laden a company is. It's calculated by adding up the proportions of *common stock, preferred stock,* and debt that make up a company's capital structure.

EXAMPLE: Your company has a total debt of $500 million, preferred stock valued on the balance sheet at $150 million, and common stock valued at $350 million. So its capitalization ratio is 50 percent debt, 15 percent preferred stock, and 35 percent common stock.

certificate of deposit (CD) Debt instrument issued by a bank to individuals and institutions that lend it money for a set period of time. CDs are time deposits, meaning they can't be withdrawn until their term is up.

certified financial planner (CFP) Person who has passed a two-year tax planning and personal finance program from the College of Financial Planning in Denver, Colorado.

certified public accountant (CPA) An accountant who has passed certain exams, achieved a certain amount of experience, reached a certain age, and met all other statutory and licensing requirements of the U.S. state in which he or she works. In addition to accounting and auditing, CPAs prepare tax returns for corporations and individuals.

Chapter 7 Most common form of *bankruptcy* for individuals and privately owned companies.

Chapter 11 *Bankruptcy* filing involving an attempt to reorganize.

Chapter 13 Also called the "wage-earner plan," this form of personal *bankruptcy* allows you to keep most of your *assets* and discharge a large portion of your unsecured debt.

closed-end lease A lease for a car in which both the lease period and the monthly payments are fixed. You also have a fixed price for the car if you wish to purchase it at the end of the lease period.

With an *open-end lease*, both the lease period and the price you'd have to pay vary with the market value and the car's condition at the end of the lease period.

collar A maximum and minimum interest rate to be paid on an *adjustable rate* security. The interest rate can't fluctuate beyond the high and low (known as cap and floor) of the collar.

collateralized mortgage obligation (CMO) *Mortgage-backed security* offering a choice of maturity dates.

commercial paper Short-term *securities* sold by large corporations and other institutions. These unsecured notes, with maturities of 2 to 270 days, usually provide short-term working capital for the issuer.

commission Incentive-based pay scale directly related to the revenue a salesperson generates.

commodity The products underlying the contracts traded on the commodity exchanges. Examples include metals (like aluminum, copper, or gold), grains (like wheat), or foods (like corn).

common stock A *share* in a company's ownership.

conversion price The price at which conversion of a *security* can be exercised, usually expressed as a dollar value. For a convertible bond, for example, you might have a $1,000 *bond* that is convertible into common shares at $20 per share. Thus your conversion price would be $20.

conversion ratio Number of *common stock*

shares that an investor can get in return for a convertible security—usually a *convertible bond* or a share of *convertible preferred stock.*

convertible bond A *bond* that can be exchanged for a specified number of *shares* of *common stock*, usually at a predetermined price in the future.

convertible preferred stock A *security* that is similar to a *convertible bond*, except that it's a *preferred stock* (rather than a bond) that's convertible to *common stock*.

coupon rate The stated interest rate on a *security*, referred to as an annual percentage of face value.

current yield Percentage return on a *bond* arrived at by dividing the dollar amount of annual interest by the market price. See also *bond yield*.

debenture A *bond* that is backed by the issuer's "full faith and credit," but not by any hard *assets*.

debt security A *security* representing money borrowed that must be repaid, having a fixed amount, a specific maturity, and usually a specific rate of interest or an original purchase discount—such as a bill, *bond*, *commercial paper*, or note.

debt-to-capital ratio Measure of a company's debt load, intended to reflect creditworthiness.

EXAMPLE: The balance sheet for BUDDY'S BAKERY lists short-term debt of $30,000, long-term debt of $250,000, and total shareholders' equity of $500,000. So the debt-to-capital ratio is: ($30,000 + $250,000) ÷ ($30,000 + $250,000 + $500,000) = 0.359, or 35.9%

BUDDY'S has a debt-to-capital ratio of 35.9 percent. The idea is that—of Buddy's capitalization—about 36% of it comes from debt.

deduction An amount subtracted from your income for tax purposes, therefore lowering your tax bill.

deferred compensation Receiving pay or other compensation for a job after you've left.

defined benefit pension plan A kind of pension plan in which the money you receive is set (or defined) ahead of time. That's in contrast to the *defined contribution pension plan*, in which your payout depends on your own contributions, as well as on the plan's investment performance.

defined contribution pension plan See *defined benefit pension plan*.

derivatives A financial instrument that's based on an underlying *asset*, like a *stock* or index. Examples range from stock *options* (which are based on the underlying stock) to index options (which are based on a particular index, like the *S&P 500*) to *futures* (which can be based on currencies, indices, or *commodities*).

dilution Issuing more *shares* of *stock* so that the ownership of the company is divided among more shareholders.

discount rate See *internal rate of return*.

diversification Strategy for spreading risk by investing in a variety of markets, industries, or types of *securities*. For most investors, the primary categories of diversification will be cash, *bonds*, and *stocks*.

dividend Payment made to shareholders at the discretion of a company's management.

Dow Jones Industrial Average (DJIA) This is the oldest and most commonly followed U.S. stock market index. The DJIA is a price-weighted average of 30 widely traded stocks on the *New York Stock Exchange (NYSE)*; the companies change periodically, but usually represent between 15–20 percent of the market value of all actively traded stocks on the NYSE. See also *Standard & Poor's (S&P)*.

earnings before interest and taxes (EBIT) A company's net earnings before it pays income taxes and the interest on its loans.

earnings per share A company's net earnings divided by the number of *shares* outstanding. It's calculated simply enough:

Net Income	$12,000,000
Outstanding Shares	20,000,000
Earnings Per Share	$0.60 = ($12,000,000 ÷ 20,000,000)

EBIT See *earnings before interest and taxes*.

effective interest rate Actual percentage rate paid on borrowed money after taking into account the terms of the loan; it can differ from the stated interest rate.

emerging market stock A *stock* issued by countries with less developed or "emerging," economies, expected to show dramatic future growth (with greater risk).

enrolled agent A person who has passed

an IRS examination and is officially recognized as a tax preparer.

equity Ownership interest in a company. Owner's equity or *shareholders' equity* on a balance sheet is the company's *net worth*, or *assets* minus *liabilities*.

equity kicker Attaching an offer of stock ownership to a loan or debt instrument. Equity kickers attached to *bonds* may include *warrants*, *rights*, and *options*.

equity REITs Publicly traded companies that buy real estate. REIT stands for "Real Estate Invesment Trust." See also *mortgage REITs*.

equity-release A financing method where part of your monthly payment is credited toward your eventual purchase price.

escrow Something of value held by a neutral third party until conditions in a contract are met.

estate tax Tax on the value of your estate at death. This should be a key concern of anyone setting up an estate, will, or trust. The first $600,000 worth of property and valuables is tax-free, but the rest will be taxed at an estate tax rate.

Eurobonds Corporate *bonds* denominated in one country's currency but issued in another country. Also called "international bonds."

Eurocurrency Currency deposited in a financial institution outside its home country.

Eurodollars U.S. dollars deposited in banks outside the United States.

European currency unit (ECU) Common currency used by the 15 member countries of the European Community (EC) to help them simplify monetary transactions among themselves.

European option See *options*.

ex-dividend Term for a stock *dividend* which will no longer be paid to the buyer. When a *stock* has passed its "ex-dividend" date, the current owner of the stock is entitled to the dividend. A stock's price will often fall by the amount of the dividend on that date.

Fannie Mae Nickname for the Federal National Mortgage Association ("FNMA"). Fannie Mae is a quasi-government corporation that buys mortgages, combines them, and packages them into *securities* to sell to investors.

fixed rate mortgage A type of *mortgage* in which the interest rate does not fluctuate with general market conditions.

floating rate See *adjustable rate*.

FNMA See *Fannie Mae*.

fixed stock fund A stable fund without much movement. See *blue chip*.

fund manager The person or company in charge of investing money.

future value The amount that an investment will grow to if it earns a set rate of interest, compounded regularly, until a specific date. The basic formula for future value is:

$FV = PV [1 + I]^n$

Where FV=future value, PV=present value, I=interest rate and n=number of periods

futures A type of *derivative* that is based on the prices of various underlying *assets*. Futures may be based on (1) physical *commodities*, like corn and gold; (2) financial instruments, such as currencies and *Eurodollars*; (3) indices, such as the *S&P 500*.

general partners See *limited partnership*.

gift tax Tax paid when a person transfers *assets* to someone for free during their lifetime. As of 1996, the limit on tax-free gifts was $10,000 a year (in cash, *securities*, property, or other assets). Gifts that exceed that limit will need a gift tax return filed by the donor.

Ginnie Mae (Government National Mortgage Association) See *mortgage-backed security*.

government bond A *bond* issued by a municipal or state government, or by the federal government, as a means of acquiring capital.

graduated payment mortgage (GPM) Also nicknamed "jeeps," these are *mortgages* starting with low payments that increase over time. Young people who expect their income to increase over time often prefer GPMs.

green fund A nickname for a *mutual fund*

with an environmental focus.

growth stock A *stock* that has shown better-than-average earnings growth in recent years.

hedge A position that reduces the risk of a business transaction or investment, often through the use of a *derivative* product.

high-grade bonds Debt with a bond rating of Aaa through Baa3 by *Moody's Investment Service* and AAA through BBB– by *Standard & Poor's.* See also *investment-grade bonds.*

high-yield bonds Debt rated below *investment grade* by the major rating agencies. Also nicknamed *junk bonds.*

Although high-yield bonds have a risky reputation, they are typically the bonds issued by companies that are still growing. They usually pay higher interest rates to compensate investors for their lower rating.

home equity loan A loan based on the *equity* built up by a homeowner, which makes it a type of *secured debt.*

hybrid mortgage Also referred to as a multiyear mortgage. They offer an initial fixed rate for about 5 to 10 years (just like a traditional *fixed rate mortgage*), and then adjust like a traditional *adjustable rate mortgage.*

income bond A type of *bond* whose interest payments depend on the company's earnings.

increasing rate See *adjustable rate.*

indenture Written agreement detailing terms of a *bond* and the rights and responsibilities of the issuer and the bondholder.

index funds *Mutual funds* that invest in the same *securities* that make up market indexes, such as the *Dow Jones Industrial Average.*

indexing strategy A type of *passive portfolio management* that involves constructing a portfolio to match a popular index, like the *S&P 500.*

Individual Retirement Account (IRA) A retirement account through which savings may be accrued on a tax-free basis. In 1998, an individual was allowed to set aside up to $2,000 into a tax-free IRA. Any gains from underlying investments are also tax-free until they're withdrawn after age 59 ½. (Early withdrawals will accrue a 10 percent penalty.)

industrial development bond *Municipal bond* (issued by a state or local government) used to finance revenue-generating projects.

industrial revenue bond *Bond* issued by a state or local government to finance a facility that will generate revenue to make bond payments. The payments are guaranteed by the lease to a private company that will use the facilities.

initial public offering (IPO) The first public sale of *common stock*, usually by a privately owned company that wants to go public. After the IPO, the publicly held shares may be traded on a stock exchange or the *over-the-counter* (OTC) market.

institutional investor A large investing entity, such as a bank, *mutual fund*, or pension plan.

interest-rate swaps When two parties agree to exchange periodic interest payments. For example, two companies might swap loan payments because one company can get good terms on a fixed rate loan and another can do well on a *floating rate.*

internal rate of return (IRR) Measure of the return of an investment over time, expressed as an annual percentage rate; sometimes referred to as a *discount rate.*

IRA See *Individual Retirement Account.*

investment banker Middleman or agent between an organization issuing *securities* and the public. In most cases the investment banker buys the securities from the issuer at a discount and sells them to investors and other dealers. This arrangement is called *underwriting* and often is carried out by a syndicate of investment bankers.

investment-grade bonds Debt rated as Aaa through Baa3 by *Moody's Investment Service* and AAA through BBB– by *Standard & Poor's.* See also *high-grade bonds.*

investor relations The division of a company that serves the investment community—especially shareholders of the company's *stock.*

IRR See *internal rate of return.*

irrevocable trust Essentially, a trust that the benefactor can't take back. An irrevocable trust can only be changed or terminated with the permission of the beneficiary.

junk bond A *bond* with a rating lower than *investment-grade*. See also *high-yield bond.*

Keogh plan Retirement plan similar to a 401k, intended for the self-employed.

The self-employed have, since 1962, had the Keogh plan, named for Eugene Keogh, the congressman who sponsored the legislation. Anyone with self-employment income can set up one of these to put aside tax-deferred money for retirement.

kiddie tax Tax paid by children under the age of 14. The standard tax rate is 15 percent, but the limit they may earn is $1,300 (as of 1998). Any amount over that limit will be taxed at the parents' tax rate.

LBO See *leveraged buyout.*

LEAPS See *long-term equity anticipation securities.*

lease rate Also called the "money factor." The interest rate that applies to your leasing term.

leveraged buyout (LBO) Typically, when an investment group buys a company with money raised from debt. In this kind of buyout, the *assets* of the acquired company are used as collateral for the loans. The amount of borrowing, or leverage—sometimes more than 70 percent of total capitalization—allows the buyer to get control of the company with less *equity* capital.

liabilities This is the amount owed to another person or entity. Current liabilities are those expected to be paid within the year, while long-term liabilities are expected to be paid later.

LIBOR See *London Interbank Offered Rate.*

lien Creditor's claim against property. A mortgage is a lien against a house: if the *mortgage* is not paid on time, the house can be seized to satisfy the lien.

limited partners See *limited partnership.*

limited partnership Ownership structure with one or more *general partners* and a number of *limited partners.*

The general partners manage the business and are liable for its debts. The limited partners have no role in the business's day-to-day operations and no liability. In most cases, limited partners get a percentage of the business's income, some tax benefits, and *capital gains*. General partners may also receive fees.

liquid yield option note (LYON) A *zero-coupon bond* convertible into *common stock.*

Like other zero-coupons, LYONs don't make annual or semiannual interest payments and are sold at a deep discount. LYONs, however, can be converted into common stock at a future date—usually at a premium to the stock's price at issuance.

liquidity (1) In accounting, solvency, or the ability to pay obligations as they come due and still fund business operations. (2) In finance, whether the market for a *security* is big enough to sell holdings without depressing the price or incurring large transaction costs.

load fund A *mutual fund* bought through a brokerage firm, in which the cost includes a *commission.*

London Interbank Offered Rate (LIBOR) Interest rate international banks usually charge each other for large *Eurodollar* and *Eurocurrency* loans. Like the *prime rate* for dollar loans in the United States, LIBOR is also a base rate for Eurodollar and Eurocurrency loans to the international banks' customers.

long bond A *bond* with a maturity of 10 years or longer. See also *medium-term note.*

long-term equity anticipation securities (LEAPS) Long-term *option* contract that gives the owner the right to buy an *asset* (e.g., *stock*) at a specified price at a distant time in the future. Unlike conventional options that last a few months, LEAPS last up to 2 years.

LYON See *liquid yield option note.*

M&A See *merger/acquisition.*

margin Amount of money a customer may borrow in his or her brokerage account to buy more *securities*. If the balance in a margin account falls below the required minimum (usually because of a price drop in the security) the brokerage firm issues a *margin call*, meaning the customer must deposit more funds or face the liquidation of his or her securities.

margin call See *margin.*

market capitalization Current value of a company's *common stock*, determined by multiplying the *share* price by the total number of shares outstanding.

EXAMPLE: If the current price of a company's stock is $20 per share, and there are 2 million shares outstanding, then its market capitalization would be ($20 x 2 million) = $40 million.

market risk Sensitivity of a stock's price to the factors that affect all stocks—such as shifts in the economy, interest rates, inflation, and general investor confidence. This is also known as *systematic risk*. A stock's market risk is measured by its *beta (b)*.

medium-term note (MTN) *Bond* with a maturity between 2 and 10 years. As the terms are generally understood, an MTN falls between a *short-term note* (with a maturity of 2 years or shorter) and a *long bond* (with a maturity of 10 years or longer).

merger/acquisition (M&A) Two or more companies fusing into one. Usually, one company buys another, and the acquired company gives up its independent existence; the surviving company assumes all *assets* and *liabilities*.

money manager A person who is paid a fee to supervise the investment decisions of others. This term most often refers to managers of large financial institutions such as pension funds, insurance companies and *mutual funds*.

money market mutual fund account An open-ended *mutual fund* that invests in *commercial paper*, bankers' acceptances, repurchase agreements, government *securities*, *certificates of deposit*, and other highly liquid and safe *securities*, paying money market rates of interest. The fund's *net asset value* remains a constant $1 a share—only the interest rate goes up or down.

money markets Where you can buy and sell short-term notes (like *commercial paper*), or those with terms of less than one year.

Moody's Investment Service Company best known for its bond-rating service, along with *Standard & Poor's*, and Dun and Bradstreet. Moody's issues ratings on corporate bonds, *commercial paper*, *municipal bonds*, and *preferred* and *common stocks*.

mortgage A loan made to purchase a home, usually with the home used as collateral.

mortgage-backed bond See *mortage-backed security*.

mortgage-backed security *Security* made up of a pool of *mortgages*, whose monthly payments of interest and principal pass through to investors. "Mortgage-backs" were introduced in 1970 by the *Government National Mortgage Association (Ginnie Mae)*.

mortgage bond Debt *security* backed by a company's real estate and other fixed *assets*. A first-mortgage bond is secured by a *lien* on specific real property. A general-mortgage bond is backed by a claim on all of a company's fixed assets that aren't pledged as collateral for other debts.

mortgage REITs Type of *real estate investment trust (REIT)* that sells stock and bonds to the public, and invests the proceeds in *mortgages* or construction loans. See also *equity REITs*.

municipal bonds *Bonds* issued by a state or local government entity. The most attractive feature of "muni's" is that many have tax-exempt interest—usually from state and local taxes, and some from federal taxes too.

mutual fund A fund operated by an investment company that raises money from shareholders and invests it in *stocks*, *bonds*, *options*, *commodities*, or *money market securities*; offers the advantages of *diversification* and professional management.

NASDAQ National Association of Securities Dealers Automated Quotations, the world's first computerized stock market and second-largest in the United States, based in Washington, D.C. Lists more than 5,300 companies, many of which are eligible to be listed on the *New York Stock Exchange (NYSE)* or the *American Stock Exchange (AMEX)*.

negative amortization The *mortgage* feature that can allow principal balance to grow, instead of shrink, as prescribed monthly payments are made.

net asset value (NAV) An accounting term similar in meaning to *net worth*; most often used in reference to the value of a *mutual fund* and similar investment shares.

net earnings See *net income*.

net income Often referred to as *net earnings*, or *net profit*. For a company, it is the difference between *revenues* and expenses, and is basically the "bottom line" of profits. It is typically an "after-tax" number, although "net income before taxes" is also a popular measure. See also *EBIT*.

net present value (NPV) Current worth of future amounts of money. Also called "discounted cash flow" (DCF). See also *present value*.

net profit See *net income*.

net sales See *revenues*.

net working capital Your current *assets* minus your current *liabilities*. Net working capital is often used by lenders and analysts as a measure of a company's ability to pay its bills.

net worth The total value of one's possessions, property, and wealth; *assets* minus *liabilities*.

New York Stock Exchange (NYSE) Largest dollar-volume stock exchange in the world. Also called the *Big Board*.

no-load fund A *mutual fund* offered by an open-end investment company that imposes no sales charge (load) on its shareholders. Investors buy shares in no-load funds directly from the fund companies, rather than through a *broker*.

nonmarket risk Potential price swings in one company's *securities* for reasons specific to that company. Also called "diversifiable risk." These types of risk are in contrast to *market risk* factors, which affect all securities.

open-end lease See *closed-end lease*.

option A contract that gives you the right to buy an *asset* (like a *stock*) at a given price before an expiration date. A *call option* gives you the right to buy an asset at a particular price before a certain date, while a *put option* gives you the right to sell it before the expiration date.

With an *American option*, you may exercise your right to buy or sell any time before the expiration date. But with a *European option* you may only exercise on the expiration date. See also *derivatives*.

original issue discount bond (OID) A *bond* that is initially sold below its *par value*, or its redemption value at maturity. Also called "split coupon note."

over-the-counter (OTC) stocks *Shares* in companies traded outside of organized stock markets like the *New York Stock Exchange (NYSE)* and the *American Stock Exchange (AMEX)*.

par value Face value of a *security*. For *bonds*, the par value is the amount you will be repaid at the maturity date. (For most bonds, the par value is $1,000.)

passive portfolio management See *active portfolio management*.

pay-in-kind (PIK) securities *Bonds* or *preferred stock* that pay interest or *dividends* in the early years—either in cash or more *shares*.

payout ratio The relationship between the *dividend* and *earnings per share*. The idea is to measure the amount of earnings that a company "pays out" in dividends.

EXAMPLE: A company has earnings per share of $2.00 in the same year that it pays dividends of $0.50. Its payout ratio would be: .50 ÷ $2.00 = 0.25, or 25%

penny stocks High-risk *stocks* that generally sell for less than a dollar a *share*. Penny stocks are traded between *brokers* in *over-the-counter (OTC)* markets. Because these companies typically have erratic results and a small number of shares outstanding, their stock prices can be highly volatile.

P/E ratio See *price/earnings ratio*.

pension plans Investment plans that set aside money for future retirement income. See also *defined benefit* and *defined contribution* pension plans.

perpetuity An *annuity* that goes on indefinitely.

PIK See *pay-in-kind (PIK) securities*.

pink sheets Daily publication (pink, of course) that lists the "bid and asked" prices of thousands of *over-the-counter (OTC)* stocks.

points Another kind of fee that a bank gets for lending you money, generally included in closing costs. One point equals 1 percent of the loan amount, so one point on a $100,000 loan would be $1,000, 2 points (or 2 percent) would be $2,000, and so on.

preferred stock *Security* that, like *common stock*, shows ownership in a corporation. Preferred stock *dividends* are usually paid in fixed amounts, and preferred stockholders have priority in terms of dividend payments and in any liquidation of the company.

present value Current worth of money to be received in the future. The basic idea is that the $1,000 you'll get 10 years from now is worth a lot less than the $1,000 you can have today. If you had the money over those 10 years, you could invest it and make more, or you could cut your interest costs by reducing your debt. If you have to wait for your $1,000, you lose that benefit. That's the "time value" of money.

The basic formula for present value is:
$PV = FV \div [1 + I]^n$
Where FV=Future Value, PV=Present Value, I=interest rate, and n=the number of time periods.

price/earnings ratio (P/E) Company's *common stock* price divided by its *earnings per share* for the year. This ratio is often used by investors and investment analysts to decide whether a stock is a good buy.

prime rate The interest rate banks typically charge their most creditworthy commercial customers. The prime rate is often used as a benchmark in the financial markets, and for instruments such as *adjustable rate* securities.

private placement Sale of unregistered *securities*, including *stocks* and *bonds*, directly to an institutional investor.

privately held company A company that does not have publicly traded *stock*. It can be a corporation, partnership, *limited partnership*, joint venture, proprietorship, or limited liability corporation.

profit margin *Net earnings* divided by *revenues*. Also called "net profit margin" or "return on sales."

prospectus Formal written document giving the facts about a new offering of *securities*.

proxy statement A document sent to shareholders before a corporation's annual meeting.

publicly held company Corporation whose common shares are traded on a public exchange. Publicly held companies are subject to reporting requirements from regulatory agencies such as the Securities and Exchange Commission (SEC).

put option Contract that gives the holder the right to sell an *asset* at a particular price before a certain date. Buyers of these are betting that the value of the underlying asset will fall. See also *options* and *derivatives*.

repurchase agreement (repo) Transaction, usually with *Treasury* issues, where the seller agrees to buy the *security* back at a set price.

retained earnings Earnings accumulated on a company's balance sheet after *dividends* have been paid out.

return on shareholders' equity (ROE) Ratio of *net income* to average *shareholders' equity* for the accounting period.

ROE = Net Income ÷ Shareholders' Equity

reverse split Method of reducing the number of a company's *shares* outstanding. A company exchanges one share of *stock* for a larger number of shares outstanding. If a company with 100,000 shares performed a 1:2 reverse split, it would have 50,000 shares outstanding.

revenues Also referred to as *net sales* because they should be expressed net of all returns, allowances, and discounts.

Revenues are typically the "top line" on the income statement, and are all of the sales that a company made, as expressed in dollars.

right Short-term entitlement to buy *shares* of *stock*. Also called *subscription right*. Rights normally have a life of a few weeks and usually give the holder the opportunity to buy the shares at a price lower than the current market price.

S&P 500 See *Standard & Poor's (S&P)*

S-corporation Corporation taxed like a partnership or *sole proprietorship*. Thus, as with a partnership, the corporation pays no income tax; instead, shareholders include their proportionate share of the corporation's income or losses on their individual tax returns.

secondary market (1) Exchanges and *over-the-counter* stock markets where *securities* are bought and sold subsequent to original issuance, which first took place in the primary market. (2) Market in which money market instruments are traded among investors.

secondary offering Sale of a block of a company's previously issued *securities.* A secondary offering may be distinguished from an *initial public offering* (IPO) in which the company issues new *shares* to the public.

secured debt Debt that is backed up by some type of collateral. Examples of secured debt would be your *mortgage* or car loan.

security In investing, an instrument such as a *stock, bond,* or *option* that represents either ownership (stock), a creditor obligation (bond), or a right to ownership (option).

senior debt Owed money that is first in line in claims on the borrower's *assets.*

share A portion of something; interest in a corporation. See also *stock.*

shareholders' equity Item on a balance sheet showing the value of the corporation's assets after *liabilities* are deducted. Also called *stockholders' equity.* For an unincorporated business, it is called "owner's equity."

short-term note A *bond* with a maturity of two years or shorter. See also *commercial paper* and *medium-term note.*

simple interest Calculation of interest paid on a loan or a deposit without compounding.

sinking fund Money a company puts aside to redeem *bonds* or other obligations prior to maturity.

sole proprietorship Unincorporated business owned by one person. Sole proprietors are liable for their company's debts and pay taxes as though they and their business were one entity.

spot price Current cash price on the free market. The term is often used for *commodities* also traded under contract.

Standard & Poor's (S&P) The division of The McGraw-Hill Companies that publishes financial and statistical data and background information about companies. See also *bond ratings.*

stock (1) Ownership of a corporation represented by *shares* that are a claim on the corporation's earnings and *assets.* See also *common stock, preferred stock.*

stock dividend *Dividend* payout in the form of *stock* rather than cash.

stock options See *options.*

stock split Increasing the number of a company's outstanding *shares* without changing *shareholders' equity.* A company with 100,000 shares outstanding that performed a 2:1 stock split would end up with 200,000 shares outstanding. See also *reverse split.*

stockholders' equity See *shareholders' equity.*

street name Refers to *securities* registered to, or held by, a brokerage company or other outfit for an individual investor.

strike price Price at which an *option* can be exercised. See also *derivatives.*

subordinated debt Unsecured debt obligations that are junior to *senior debt* and *secured debt* in the event of a company's liquidation.

subscription right Authorization to buy newly issued *common stock* at a discount price. See also *right.*

subscription warrant *Security* that lets its holder buy a certain number of a company's *shares* at a set price. See also *warrant.*

swaps See *derivatives.*

synthetic convertible See *bond/warrant unit.*

systematic risk See *market risk.*

T-bill See *Treasuries.*

tax-exempt bonds *Bonds* whose interest is not taxed. The overwhelming majority of tax-exempt bonds are *municipal bonds.*

tender offer Public offer to buy a company's *shares.* Tender offers are sometimes made by a company for some of its own shares, but more often they are part of a takeover attempt.

Treasuries Marketable debt *securities* issued by the federal government to help finance the nation's debt.

Treasuries are backed by the full faith and credit of the U.S. government, so they're considered just about the safest securities you can buy. Their interest is exempt from state and local income taxes. Treasuries come in three basic forms:

	Maturities	Denominations
Treasury bills	Up to a year	At least $10,000
Treasury notes	One to ten years	$1,000 and up
Treasury bonds	Ten years or more	$1,000 and up

underwriting (1) In finance, an agreement by *investment bankers* to buy for resale a new issue of *securities* at a fixed price from the issuing company and/or existing securities from holders of unregistered *stock* also at a fixed price. (2) In insurance, underwriting refers to the assumption of risk in exchange for the premium.

universal life insurance Type of *whole life insurance* that unbundles the insurance, the investment portion, and the expense factors of your policy.

venture capital Funding for start-up companies and private research-and-development (R&D) projects. Also known as "risk capital." A number of private investors, investment companies, and *limited partnerships* provide venture capital.

warrant A *security* that gives you the right to buy *shares* in a company at a set price in the future. Also called a *subscription warrant.* Warrants are usually attached to another security, like a *bond* or *preferred stock.* Used in that way, warrants are a type of *equity kicker* that make the security more attractive.

whole life insurance Life insurance with a savings component that lasts for the lifetime of the insured; also known as "permanent," "straight," or "ordinary" life insurance.

variable annuity A life insurance *annuity* whose value flucuates with that of an underlying *securities* portfolio or other index of performance. The variable annuity contrasts with a conventional or fixed annuity, whose rate of return is constant.

variable universal life insurance Type of *whole life insurance* that combines the control of choosing your investments (variable life insurance) with the flexibility of structuring the type of policy you need (universal life insurance).

X-dividend See *ex-dividend.*

Yankee bond A *bond* issued in U.S. dollars in the United States by a foreign company. Yankee bonds are typically issued when market conditions are better in the United States than in the *Eurobond* market or in the issuer's home market.

yield curve For *bonds*, a graph showing the relationship between yield and time to maturity.

yield to maturity (YTM) The annual return on a *bond* that takes into account its current price, *par value*, *coupon rate*, and time to maturity. YTM can be approximated with a *bond yield* table, but it is usually done by using a calculator equipped for bond calculations.

zero-based budgeting (ZBB) A method of setting budgets for corporations and government agencies that requires a justification of all expenditures, not only those that exceed the prior year's allocations. Thus all budget lines are said to begin at a zero base, and are funded according to merit.

zero-coupon bonds *Bonds* that pay no interest until maturity—also known as "zeroes."

Zero-coupon bonds are sold at deep discounts to face value—investors receive the full face value when the bond matures. For example, you might buy a zero-coupon bond for $450 that matures in 10 years, when you'll receive the full $1000 face value. In this manner, the interest is "implied."

Index

Introducing
Spurge Ink!

Spurge Ink! is a business communications firm whose primary objectives are to empower consumers to take control of their own destiny—by helping them improve their careers, build their businesses, and invest their money. The company specializes in producing user-friendly information and delivers it through a wide variety of media including books, newsletters, seminars, videos, audio tapes, radio and television programming, as well as online. The company has won awards for its products, including the prestigious "50 Best Books of 1996" from the American Institute of Graphic Arts.

Our Services Include:

Publishing

•Books/Newsletters/Online

•Newspaper Columns/Magazine Articles

Media

•Radio/Television Programs

•Video/Audio/Interactive CD-ROMs

Training

•Investment/Career/Motivational

•Seminars/Presentations

•Educational/Business Products

Consulting

•Financial/Marketing/Management

Design

•Logo/Brand Image Development

•Informational/Marketing Materials

Spurge ink!

Making Business Accessible

Other Spurge Ink! Products

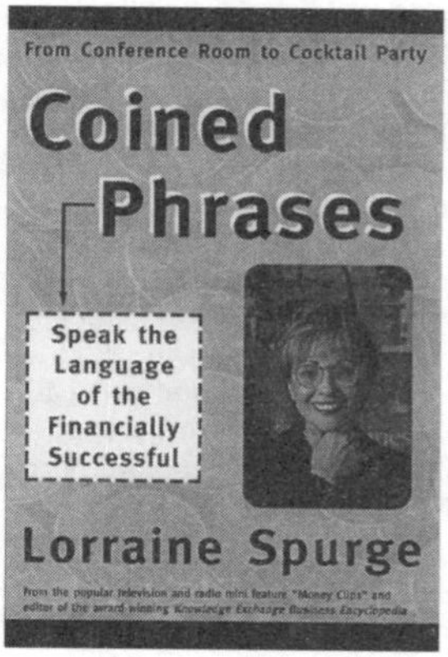

Coined Phrases

From Conference Room to Cocktail Party

By Lorraine Spurge

ISBN: 1-888232-47-1
250 pages 5.5" x 8.5"
Personal Finance/Reference
$12.95 U.S. paperback
($17.95 Canada)
Rights: World
50 b/w photos & illustrations

More than a dictionary, *Coined Phrases* unlocks the mystery behind the everyday expressions of Wall Street power brokers. With over 1000 alphabetized terms and phrases, this easy-to-use resource is your fundamental key to financial savvy.

The second volume in our Personal Finance Guides series, *Coined Phrases* includes examples of water-cooler chit-chat—real-life situations we can all relate to and learn from. Tips and traps, helpful quotes, retro pictures, and humorous anecdotes with an attitude will keep you on track.

If you're joining an investment club, a couple planning for the future, or retirees wanting to make the most from your pension, this book will shed light on the buzz words of the financial world. Instead of living paycheck to paycheck, adopt *Coined Phrases* into your vocabulary. You'll be learning the language of the rich—and on your way to money in the bank!

Reconnecting With Customers

Building Brands & Profits in the Relationship Age

By Jack Myers, creator of *The Myers Report*

ISBN: 1-888232-48-X
250 pages 5.5" x 8.5"
Business/Marketing
$27.95 U.S. hardcover
($38.95 Canada)
Rights: World
30 b/w photos & illustrations

Today, the more things change... the more they change. As the Information Age evolves, welcome to The Relationship Age—where relationships come first, "the deal" second. *Reconnecting with Customers* is a manual for all businesspeople, on how to reconnect advertising, promotion, marketing—and relationships—to sales, profits and brand equity.

In today's global marketplace, the irrevocable trend is away from commoditization, and towards marketing and brand-based relationships. Integration is an imperative. Success demands we apply the new "Three R's": Reconnecting, Relevance and Results. Myers, an accomplished media consultant, explains how.

For executives, marketing/sales professionals, small business entrepreneurs, and anyone seeking practical strategies for success in the new millennium.

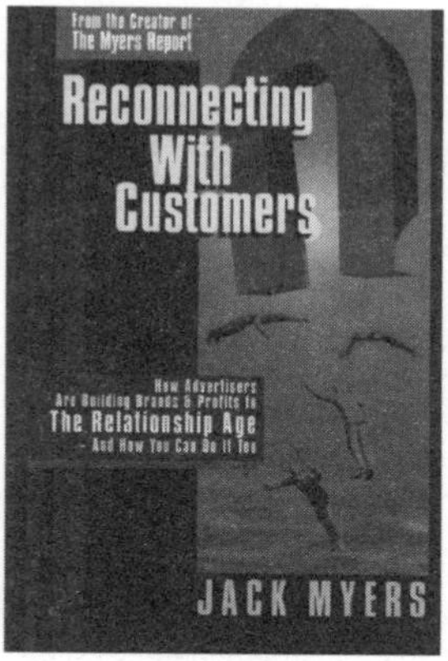

Financing the Future: An MCI Living Case Study

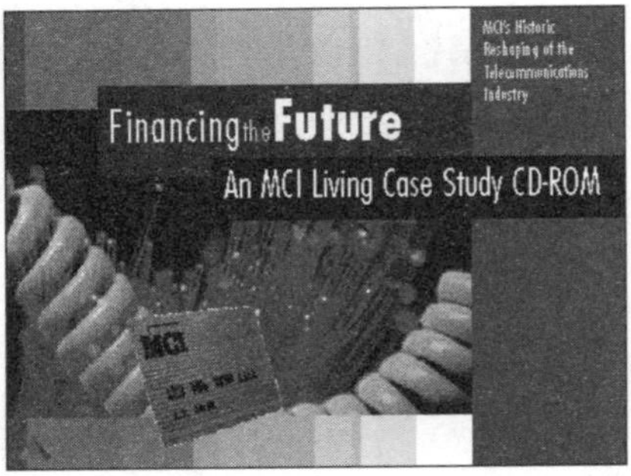

An interactive two-disk CD-ROM set featuring MCI Communications, Inc.

This program is currently being used at more than 20 business schools in 12 countries. Some of the participating colleges are University of Pennsylvania (Wharton), University of Chicago, University of Virginia (Darden), University of Michigan, Ohio State University, CUNY (City University of New York), Georgetown (Washington, D.C.), Southern Methodist University (Texas), London Business School (England), INSEAD (France), Tel Aviv University (Israel), University of Science and Technology (Hong Kong), and University of Western Ontario (Canada).

The case objective:

- To develop an understanding of the complex nature of corporate financial decisions.
- To gain insight into the highly regulated telecommunications industry.
- To explore financial alternatives facing a fast-growing company during volatile economic times.

Weaving a richly detailed database that covers more than 30 years of information on the economy, capital markets, the telecommunications industry, FCC regulations and worldwide events, with an in-depth analysis of telephony giant MCI, this two-disc CD-ROM set re-creates the circumstances surrounding MCI as it struggled for survival a decade ago.

This interactive, multimedia case study empowers each user to participate in the analysis and decision-making process to develop alternative courses of action.

Finally, an entertaining and informational multimedia program is available for business students, professionals and executive training programs. With hours of video and audio clips and well-designed graphics and slide presentations, this program brings to life one of America's greatest stories of business achievement, in order to enhance the research and learning process. The Living Case: It's 1983 and you've been hired by MCI's management to develop the right financial strategy. The company needs one billion dollars in order to build out its fiber optic network and go head to head with the world's largest corporate monopoly—AT&T. In order to make your decision, this two-disc CD-ROM set includes 30 years of general and MCI-specific background information you need on:

- Society (world events and popular culture)
- Economy (GDP, CPI, M2)
- Capital Markets (equity market valuations, S&P 500 Index, securities issuance and interest rates)
- Telecommunications Industry
- FCC Regulations
- MCI's Financial Data and Forecasts

These are some of the advantages of the CD-ROM learning medium:

- Large storage capacity of data on CD-ROMs allows depth and breadth of content coverage.

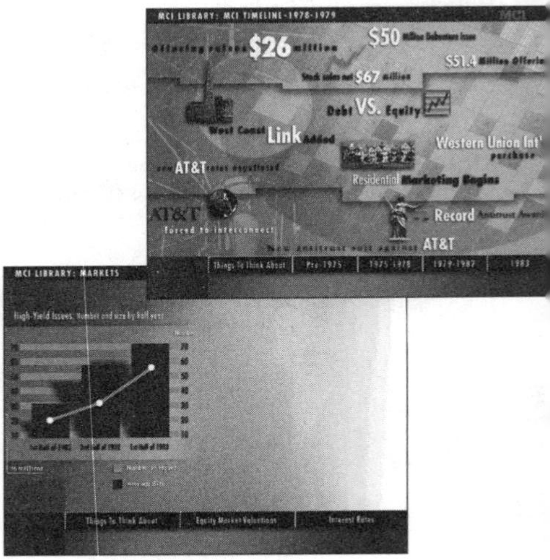

- Re-creation of the drama and realism of the events with the use of video, audio, photos, animation, graphs and charts, including extensive interviews with industry experts and MCI's founder and management.
- Easy-to-use interface captures the attention, with superior learning outcomes.
- Voice and pictures reinforce text as learning mechanisms.
- Professionals and academics can customize their learning/teaching approaches, inside and outside the classroom.
- A 500-word glossary provides clear definitions of the technical words used in the program.
- Financial information can be downloaded into Excel spreadsheets.
- Beta-tested at top business schools, including University of Pennsylvania (Wharton), University of Chicago, University of Virginia (Darden), Northwestern University (Kellogg) and University of Michigan. The CD-ROM program was beta-tested for more than three years and a formal marketing research firm was commissioned to perform educational testing services at UCLA with MBA students.

Other Supporting Materials Available:

Case Study

A written case study to complement the CD-ROM written by one of the most distinguished professors in finance, Professor J. Fred Weston of UCLA. The written case study is intended to parallel the multimedia version and can be employed where a school's technological constraints limit the ability to use the interactive version.

Teaching Note

Also available is a teaching note that analyzes and discusses possible solutions to the questions posed in the Weston case write-up.

Glossary

Plus, a glossary containing terms used in finance and the telecommunications industry. This is a useful guide that can be employed in conjunction with either version of the case or as a free-standing resource for users of the program.

Also available is *One-on-One*, video-taped interviews with senior management of MCI.

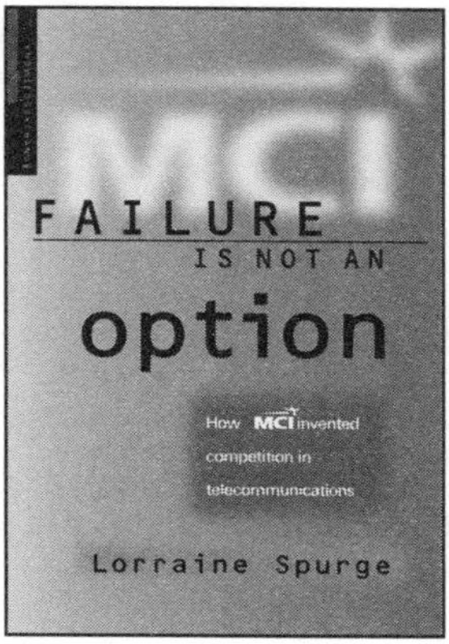

MCI: Failure Is Not an Option

How MCI Invented Competition in Telecommunications

By Lorraine Spurge

ISBN: 1-888232-08-0
384 pages 6.25" x 9.25"
Business/Finance
$27.95 U.S. hardcover
(In Canada: $38.95)
Rights: World
ISBN: 1-888232-41-2
$16.95 U.S. softcover
(In Canada: $23.95)

Educational and entertaining, *MCI: Failure Is Not an Option* profiles MCI's stirring history from its meager beginnings to its present success, offering an enlightening view of the financial, management, and marketing issues the company faced. Readers will experience the tension and suspense as MCI fights for survival, takes on AT&T (then the mightiest corporation in the world), shakes up federal regulatory agencies, races to raise desperately needed capital, and ultimately alters forever the American business landscape.

MCI: Failure Is Not an Option features a two-color layout sprinkled with charts, graphs, photos, and time lines illustrating the history of MCI and the telecommunications industry in general.

Case Study Videos and Audios

Wharton Real Estate Seminar

Wharton Real Estate CENTER

Running Time:
Tape 1 1 hour, 31 minutes
Tape 2 1 hour, 32 minutes
Tape 3 1 hour, 49 minutes
Includes a companion booklet

Dr. Peter Linneman, director of the Wharton Real Estate Center (ranked as the Number One real estate department according to *U.S. News & World Report*), hosts a three-part seminar with leading financial and business professionals. This seminar is an invaluable guide for any potential real estate investor or professional who wants to know how to survive—and even prosper—in the turbulent real estate market. Participants frankly share how to find and create value in the 1990s and beyond.

The three tapes encompass:

Session 1 The Future of Real Estate: Contrasting Perspectives
Session 2 Retail and Entertainment: Competing with the Home
Session 3 The Changing Demands of Real Estate Capital

The Merton Miller/Michael Milken Debate

Running Time: 1 hour, 10 minutes
Includes a companion booklet

Theory Meets Practice! Join Nobel laureate Merton Miller and financier Michael Milken for a stimulating debate about such important financial issues as:

- Does Capital Structure Matter?
- Are Markets Efficient?
- How Does Regulation Affect Business and Markets?

One-on-One

Michael Milken interviews the world's leading corporate entrepreneurs

MCI Communications: CEO Bert Roberts and past and present executives, William Conway, Jr., Laurence Harris and Wayne English, tell the story of how David took on Goliath in the telecommunications industry, and won!
Running Time: 1 hour
Includes a companion booklet

McCaw Cellular: Founder Craig McCaw and corporate executives Don Guthrie and John Stanton track the company's evolution from start-up to corporate giant, to its merger with AT&T.
Running Time: 1 hour
Includes a companion booklet

Introducing the Business Solutions System

As part of Knowledge Exchange's commitment to producing and disseminating the most useful and beneficial business knowledge available, we are proud to launch our new Business Solutions System. In order to provide a full range of products, this System will include practical, comprehensive, full-color, illustrated encyclopedias, dictionaries, and industry and trade books that cover all aspects of eight critical business disciplines.

Reference Essentials Series

Knowledge Exchange Business Encyclopedia

Your Complete Business Advisor

Lorraine Spurge, Editor-in-Chief

ISBN: 1-888232-05-6

750 pages 7.5" x 10.5"

Business/Reference

$45.00 U.S. hardcover

(In Canada: $54.00)

Rights: World

Knowledge Exchange Business Encyclopedia, an exciting new resource, provides hundreds of solutions to everyday business problems. Throughout its 750 information-packed pages you'll find authoritative definitions, detailed charts and graphs, illustrations, mini case studies and much more! The result of a collaboration among some of today's finest business minds, this reference contains valuable information from academics at such prestigious institutions as Carnegie Mellon, Harvard Business School, UCLA and The Wharton School.

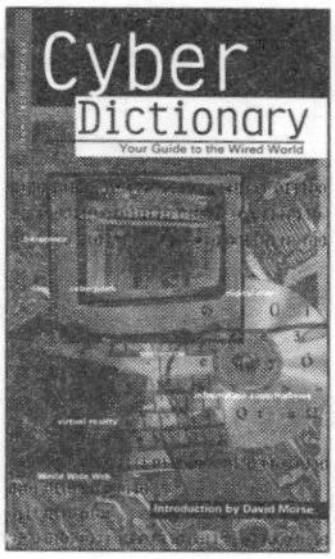

CyberDictionary

Your Guide to the Wired World

Edited and Introduced by David Morse

ISBN: 1-888232-04-8

336 pages 5.25" x 9.25"

Reference/Computer

$17.95 U.S. softcover

(In Canada: $21.95)

Rights: World

CyberDictionary is the book our 'Net-obsessed world has been waiting for—an indispensible guide to the wide-open frontier of cyberspace. Organized in an A-to-Z format, *CyberDictionary* is the book for the tens of millions of 'Net surfers and computer users. This reader-friendly, full-color reference book is packed with more than 900 easy-to-understand definitions of cyberwords, mini essays, and time-saving tips to make navigating the 'Net easy, exciting, and enlightening.

A Chronology of Business Poster

The full-color, exquisitely detailed poster (22" x 40") is based on the time line featured in the *Knowledge Exchange Business Encyclopedia*, which traces the history of business from its roots in 3000 B.C. to the present. $25.00 U.S.

KEX Canvas Tote Bag

Vibrantly colored, heavy-duty, natural canvas, oversized tote bag (14"h x 16"w x 9"d) displaying a sampling of terms and references from the *Knowledge Exchange Business Encyclopedia*. $50.00 U.S.

Management Consultant Series

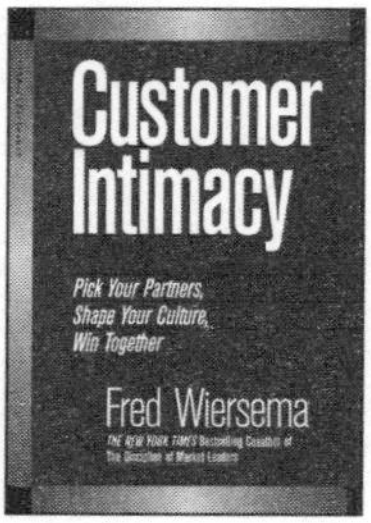

Customer Intimacy

Pick Your Partners, Shape Your Culture, Win Together

Fred Wiersema

ISBN: 1-888232-00-5
240 pages 6.25" x 9.25"
Business/Marketing
$22.95 U.S. hardcover
(In Canada: $27.95)
Rights: World
ISBN: 1-888232-42-0
$14.95 U.S. softcover
(In Canada: $19.95)
Audiobook
ISBN: 1-888232-01-3
$14.00 U.S. (In Canada: $17.00)
90 minutes/Read by the author

One in three market-leading companies attains prominence today by making the most of what author Fred Wiersema calls "customer intimacy." This engaging book reveals why the most successful businesses are those that build close win-win relationships with their customers.

Richly illustrated with examples of some of the best-known and most successful customer-intimate businesses, *Customer Intimacy* is for companies wondering what to do next after having exhausted the potential of quality thinking, lean management, and business reengineering.

Fad-Free Management

The Six Principles That Drive Successful Companies and Their Leaders

Richard Hamermesh

ISBN: 1-888232-20-X
208 pages 6.25" x 9.25"
Business/Management
$24.95 U.S. hardcover
(In Canada: $29.95)
Rights: World

The business place has become saturated with quick fixes that promise faster, better products and happier, more loyal employees. Unfortunately, however, these fads often waste time and energy. In this new book, Richard Hamermesh argues against this trend and stresses the necessity of getting back to basics.

Readers of *Fad-Free Management* will reap the benefits of the knowledge Hamermesh gained as a professor at the world-renowned Harvard Business School.

The Pursuit of Prime

Maximize Your Company's Success with the Adizes Program

Ichak Adizes, Ph.D.

ISBN: 1-888232-22-6
304 pages 6.25" x 9.25"
Business/Management
$24.95 U.S. hardcover
(In Canada: $29.95)
Rights: World

Companies, like people, follow definite growth stages—infancy, childhood, adolescence, and prime. It is in this last stage of development that both humans and companies are at their best. In *The Pursuit of Prime*, Ichak Adizes, Ph.D., provides a step-by-step guide for helping businesses reach this pinnacle of corporate life.

The Pursuit of Prime provides case studies of successful companies such as Bank of America and The Body Shop and enumerates the bad habits, philosophies, and myths that prevent companies from becoming attuned to their life cycles and thereby prosperous.

The Tao of Coaching

Boost Your Effectiveness by Inspiring Those Around You

Max Landsberg

ISBN: 1-888232-34-X
200 pages 6.25" x 9.25"
Business/Management
$22.95 U.S. hardcover
Rights: U.S.

Get the most out of your human capital—your employees—by transforming them into all-star managers and team players. Ideally, managers should be coaches who enhance the performance and learning abilities of others. They must provide feedback, motivation, and a master game plan.

In *The Tao of Coaching* Max Landsberg shares his belief that managers must possess a broad repertoire of management styles. The coaching skills managers can acquire from reading this book will allow them to diagnose different employee styles and use appropriate means to bring out the best in all individuals with whom they work.

Entrepreneurial Advisor Series

Staples for Success

From Business Plan to Billion-Dollar Business in Just a Decade

Thomas G. Stemberg

ISBN: 1-888232-24-2
192 pages 6.25" x 9.25"
Business
$22.95 U.S. hardcover
(In Canada: $27.95)
Rights: World
Audiobook
ISBN: 1-888232-25-0
$12.00 U.S. (In Canada: $15.00)
60 minutes/Read by Campbell Scott

This engaging story details Staples' birth and subsequent transformation into office-superstore giant. Stemberg's hard work and commitment to excellence turned a radically simple idea into the $11-billion office-superstore industry we know today. The Staples story stands as a guide to forward thinking and successful management from genesis to innovation, to large-scale, almost limitless growth.

Staples for Success is a must-read for every entrepreneur and anyone who believes in a great idea.

The World On Time

The 11 Management Principles That Made FedEx an Overnight Sensation

James C. Wetherbe

ISBN: 1-888232-06-4
200 pages 6.25" x 9.25"
Business/Management
$22.95 U.S. hardcover
(In Canada: $27.95)
Rights: World
Audiobook
ISBN: 1-888232-07-2
$12.00 U.S. (In Canada: $15.00)
90 minutes/Read by the author

The World On Time is the inspirational story of how Federal Express became a leader in the overnight-delivery industry.

James C. Wetherbe, a preeminent business consultant and academic, provides a richly detailed, intimate portrait of Federal Express. Readers will learn how eleven innovative management strategies employed by Federal Express have set the standard for the way companies manage time and information, plan logistics, and serve customers.

Industry Expert Series: Health Care

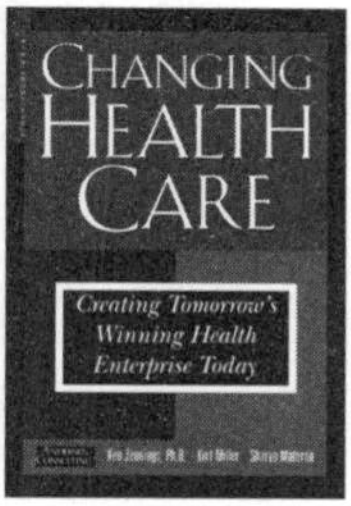

Changing Health Care

Creating Tomorrow's Winning Health Enterprise Today

Ken Jennings, Ph.D., Kurt Miller, and Sharyn Materna of Andersen Consulting

ISBN: 1-888232-18-8
336 pages 6.25" x 9.25"
Business/Health Care
$24.95 U.S. hardcover
(In Canada: $29.95)
Rights: World

One of the major health care tasks is to deliver more value to consumers through better and expanded products and services. *Changing Health Care* outlines the strategies that all health care organizations must adopt if they want to regain their competitive edge.

The authors propose eight winning strategies designed to keep health care providers on the cutting edge—Keep Ahead of Consumers; Keep the Promise; Cut to the Moment of Value; Mind the Cycle of Life; Capitalize on Knowledge; Ride the Technology Wave; Give Your Best, Virtualize the Rest; and Mine the Riches of Outcomes.

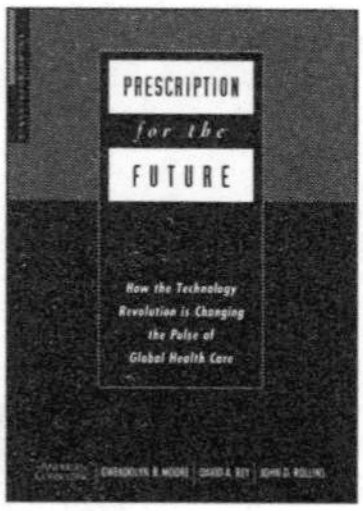

Prescription for the Future

How the Technology Revolution Is Changing the Pulse of Global Health Care

Gwendolyn B. Moore, David A. Rey, and John D. Rollins of Andersen Consulting

ISBN: 1-888232-10-2
200 pages 6.25" x 9.25"
Business/Health Care
$24.95 U.S. hardcover
(In Canada: $29.95)
Rights: World
Audiobook
ISBN: 1-888232-11-0
$12.00 U.S. (In Canada: $15.00)
60 minutes/Read by the authors

Prescription for the Future profiles an industry undergoing transformation and offers insights into the challenges facing the health care industry as it employs new technologies. This book directly addresses the concerns of managers and professionals regarding rapidly advancing information technology, which creates both new freedoms and new problems.

Spurge Ink! and Knowledge Exchange
Price List

Spurge Ink! Titles	Book	Order #	Audio	Order #
Coined Phrases	$12.95	471	na	
MCI: Failure Is Not an Option (hardcover)	$27.95	080	na	
MCI: Failure Is Not an Option (softcover)	$16.95	412	na	
Money Clips (softcover)	$14.95	447	na	
Reconnecting With Customers	$27.95	48X	na	
Reference Essentials Series				
KEX Business Encyclopedia (hardcover)	$45.00	056	na	
CyberDictionary (softcover)	$17.95	048	na	
Management Consultant Series				
Customer Intimacy (hardcover)	$22.95	005	$14.00	013
Customer Intimacy (softcover)	$14.95	420	na	
Fad-Free Management (hardcover)	$24.95	20X	na	
The Pursuit of Prime (hardcover)	$24.95	226	na	
The Tao of Coaching (hardcover)	$22.95	34X	na	
Entrepreneurial Advisor Series				
Staples for Success (hardcover)	$22.95	242	$12.00	250
The World On Time (hardcover)	$22.95	064	$12.00	072
Industry Expert Series: Health Care				
Changing Health Care (hardcover)	$24.95	188	na	
Prescription for the Future (hardcover)	$24.95	102	$12.00	110
CD-ROM				
Financing the Future: An MCI Living Case Study (two-disk set)	$150.00	027	na	
Video/Audio Tapes	**Video**	**Order #**	**Audio**	**Order #**
Wharton Real Estate Seminar				
Video/audiotapes (3) and booklet set	$150.00	003	$60.00	176
Volumes 1, 2 and 3	$60.00 ea.	178, 180, 182	$25.00 ea	177, 179, 181
The Merton Miller/Michael Milken Debate				
Videotape or audiotape and booklet	$195.00	164	$80.00	172
One-on-One Interview Series				
Video/audiotapes (2) and booklet set	$150.00	171	$60.00	184
McCaw Cellular	$100.00	156	$40.00	168
MCI Communications	$100.00	170	$40.00	169

Spurge Ink! and Knowledge Exchange products are available wherever books are sold.
Spurge Ink! is the exclusive representative of Knowledge Exchange books, audiobooks and multimedia products.
For bulk orders, call for purchase order information and corporate price discounts.
All direct orders are non-returnable.

For more information contact:

Spurge Ink!
16350 Ventura Boulevard, Suite 362
Encino, California 91436
Tel: 800-854-6239 or 818-705-3740
Fax: 818-708-8764 or 818-705-0692
E-mail: info@spurgeink.com
Visit us on the Internet at www.spurgeink.com

Spurge ink!
Making Business Accessible